Brahm
in Kṛṣṇa Consciousness

by Bhakti Vikāsa Swami

with extensive quotes from
His Divine Grace
A.C. Bhaktivedanta Swami Prabhupāda
Founder–*Ācārya* of the International Society for Krishna Consciousness

and

A Brahmacārī Reader

Quotes from Śrīla Prabhupāda and others
especially relevant to *brahmacārīs*

ISBN 978-81-902332-3-1

www.bvks.com
books@bvks.com

Previous printings of the first and second editions: 18,250 copies
Fifth printing of the second edition, 2015: 3,000 copies

Available also in Bengali, Croatian, Gujarati, Hindi, Indonesian, Italian, Mandarin, Portuguese, Russian, and Tamil

---

Published by Bhakti Vikāsa Trust, Surat, India

Printed in India.

Dedicated to

my lord and master, His Divine Grace A.C. Bhaktivedanta Swami Prabhupāda, the Founder-*Ācārya* of this wonderful International Society for Kṛṣṇa Consciousness. He informed us (all ignorant fools) of the absolute necessity of *brahmacarya*, trained us as *brahmacārīs*, and taught us to go beyond *brahmacarya* to achieve pure love of Kṛṣṇa. The greatest benediction of my life will be to be counted among the atoms in the dust of his lotus feet.

Books Authored by Bhakti Vikāsa Swami

A Beginner's Guide to Kṛṣṇa Consciousness
A Message to the Youth of India
Brahmacarya in Kṛṣṇa Consciousness
Glimpses of Traditional Indian Life
Jaya Śrīla Prabhupāda!
My Memories of Śrīla Prabhupāda
On Pilgrimage in Holy India
On Speaking Strongly in Śrīla Prabhupāda's Service
Patropadeśa
Śrī Bhaktisiddhānta Vaibhava (three volumes)
Śrī Caitanya Mahāprabhu
Śrī Vaṁśīdāsa Bābājī
Vaiṣṇava Śikhā o Sādhana (Bengali)

Books Edited or Compiled by Bhakti Vikāsa Swami

Rāmāyaṇa
The Story of Rasikānanda
Gauḍīya Vaiṣṇava Padyāvalī (Bengali)

PRAYERS

oṁ namo bhagavate narasiṁhāya namas tejas-tejase āvir-āvirbhava vajra-nakha vajra-daṁṣṭra karmāśayān randhaya randhaya tamo grasa grasa oṁ svāhā; abhayam abhayam ātmani bhūyiṣṭhā oṁ kṣraum.

"I offer my respectful obeisances unto Lord Nṛsiṁhadeva, the source of all power. O my Lord who possesses nails and teeth just like thunderbolts, kindly vanquish our demon-like desires for fruitive activity in this material world. Please appear in our hearts and drive away our ignorance so that by Your mercy we may become fearless in the struggle for existence in this material world."

Unless one is completely freed of all material desires, which are caused by the dense darkness of ignorance, one cannot fully engage in the devotional service of the Lord. Therefore we should always offer our prayers to Lord Nṛsiṁhadeva, who killed Hiraṇyakaśipu, the personification of material desire. *Hiraṇya* means "gold," and *kaśipu* means "a soft cushion or bed." Materialistic persons always desire to make the body comfortable, and for this they require huge amounts of gold. Thus Hiraṇyakaśipu was the perfect representative of materialistic life. He was therefore the cause of great disturbance to the topmost devotee, Prahlāda Mahārāja, until Lord Nṛsiṁhadeva killed him. Any devotee aspiring to be free of material desires should offer his respectful prayers to Nṛsiṁhadeva as Prahlāda Mahārāja did in this verse. (*S.B.* 5.18.8. Text and Purport. See also 5.18.10 and 14)

yadi dāsyasi me kāmān
varāṁs tvaṁ varadarṣabha
kāmānāṁ hṛdy asaṁrohaṁ
bhavatas tu vṛṇe varam

"O my Lord, best of the givers of benediction, if You at all want to bestow a desirable benediction upon me, then I pray from Your Lordship that within the core of my heart there be no material desires." (*S.B.*7.10.7 Text)

ABBREVIATIONS USED IN THIS BOOK

(in reference to books by and about Śrīla Prabhupāda)

Bg.	*Bhagavad-gītā As It Is*
S.B.	*Śrīmad-Bhāgavatam*
Cc.	*Caitanya-caritāmṛta*
DS	*Dialectic Spiritualism*
LOB	*Light of the Bhāgavata*
NOI	*The Nectar of Instruction*
SPL	*Śrīla Prabhupāda-līlāmṛta*

This book features many quotations from Śrīla Prabhupāda's purports, letters, lectures, and conversations. These are all copyrighted by Bhaktivedanta Book Trust International. Unless otherwise stated, referenced quotations from Śrīla Prabhupāda's books or from the portion of *Śrīmad-Bhāgavatam* completed by his disciples are from the purports therein. To peruse the complete context in which these statements were made, readers may consult the books, letters, and recorded lectures and conversations of Śrīla Prabhupāda. Dates have been numerically represented according to British usage (i.e., day/month/year; 03/05/72 represents "3rd May, 1972").

Table of Contents

PREFACE TO THE FIRST EDITION

During the late 60's and 70's, upon the order of his spiritual master, the illustrious empowered preacher His Divine Grace A.C. Bhaktivedanta Swami Prabhupāda brought the science of Kṛṣṇa consciousness to the Western world. At that time most of the world was experiencing an increasing degradation and departure from religious and moral principles. However, Śrīla Prabhupāda gradually introduced a lifestyle hitherto unknown but to a few devoted souls in India: the Vedic culture of austerity for the goal of self-realization. The principles of *brahmacarya* formed an important part of this culture.

Purified and enlivened by following the teachings and practice of *bhakti-yoga* as authoritatively presented by Śrīla Prabhupāda, hundreds of bright-faced young men and women appeared on the streets of towns and villages throughout the world, taking up Śrīla Prabhupāda's mission to fulfill the prediction of Lord Caitanya to spread the holy name of Kṛṣṇa to every corner of the globe. During those years of the expansion of the Kṛṣṇa consciousness movement under the banner of ISKCON, the reasoning, principles and practice of *brahmacarya* were often taught and heard in and around the increasing number of temples and *āśramas* of the Society. The devotees became stronger in following the principles of *brahmacarya* under the exemplary guidance of the Founder-*Ācārya* of ISKCON, Śrīla Prabhupāda.

There are numerous instructions about *brahmacarya* contained in the large body of literature, lectures, and letters left by Śrīla Prabhupāda, for those diligent enough to study them. However, until now much of the principles and practice of *brahmacarya* has remained an oral tradition within ISKCON. But human lives and memories are short, and many of Śrīla Prabhupāda's young students have now entered other *āśramas,* or left for other spheres of activity. In order that the purity and momentum of the Kṛṣṇa consciousness movement not be diminished with the passing of time, many devotees feel that this important aspect of the philosophy and application of Kṛṣṇa consciousness should remain easily and frequently accessible to the present and future generations of devotees—in all *āśramas* and statuses.

Therefore it is timely that His Holiness Bhakti Vikāsa Swami has, with the good wishes of many of his godbrother comrades in active preaching, diligently prepared this compendium of the principles and practice of *brahmacārī* life. Bhakti Vikāsa Mahārāja is respected as a staunch practitioner of these spiritual principles. He is dear to the devotees, especially in Eastern India, Bangladesh, and South East Asia, where he has dedicated so many years of his life to traveling and preaching on behalf of Śrīla Prabhupāda. He is certainly qualified to present this book, and has done a great service by doing so.

This book may accurately be called a "user's guide" to *brahmacārī* life. The first part consists of elaborate discussion of and down-to-earth practical guidance on the many aspects of *brahmacarya.* The second part is a compilation of quotes from Śrīla Prabhupāda's books, tapes, and letters about this subject matter.

The importance of this matter should not be underestimated. *Brahmacarya* is the basis of all four *āśramas,* and must be practiced by any man or woman serious and sincere about making tangible progress on the path back to Godhead. *Tapasā brahmacaryeṇa śamena ca damena ca:* "There is no possibility of controlling the mind and senses without following the principles of *brahmacarya.* "Śrīla Prabhupāda lamented the dearth of educational institutions teaching the principles of *brahmacarya* (celibacy), and cited this as one reason for the lack of qualified members of the other three *āśramas.*[1]

We pray that by Śrīla Prabhupāda's mercy this book may help to educate and train the members of the Kṛṣṇa consciousness movement to seriously understand and follow the principles of *brahmacarya,* and thus be pleasing to Śrīla Prabhupāda and beneficial to the devotees and the Society.

We feel fortunate to have met our dear godbrother Bhakti Vikāsa Swami (then Ilāpati Prabhu) just as he was finishing the manuscript of this book and requesting the blessings of the ISKCON Publications Board for its publication, and thus be given the chance to assist in its production. Historically, books which present heavy blows to Māyā in her work of keeping the fallen souls in illusion have often had to pass through many impediments before finally becoming manifest. We are glad that after passing through a long series of obstacles this book could finally go to press. We beg the forgiveness of the readers for any unintentional errors or lack of quality in the present volume. We pray that the readers may nonetheless reap the full benefit of understanding and determined practice of the principles contained in this book, which may in turn help them to rapidly advance on the path straight back to home, back to Godhead.

Butterworth-Bangkok International Express
27th August, 1988, Appearance Day of Lord Balarāma
The Publisher (Gauḍa-maṇḍala-bhūmi dāsa)

PREFACE TO THE SECOND EDITION

It has been about twelve years since the first edition of this book came out. Subsequently, it has been re-printed three times in English, and also in Russian, Croatian, Mandarin, Italian, Indonesian, and Portuguese, with a total of about 10,000 copies in print. Although there are not 10,000 *brahmacārīs* in our movement, devotees from all *āśramas* have expressed appreciation of this book, and it continues to be in demand.

Since the first edition was first published, I have collected more snippets of information suitable for *brahmacārīs*. This edition is not in essence different from the first, but gives more of the same substance. I pray that devotees may find it helpful in their ongoing journey toward the lotus feet of Kṛṣṇa.

Dāsānudāsa,
Bhakti Vikāsa Swami

INTRODUCTION

Human life, especially the male form, is meant for self-realization: to understand our eternal relationship with God, Kṛṣṇa. This book is meant for men who have seriously taken to Kṛṣṇa consciousness, and especially for those devotees who have joined the *brahmacārī-āśrama* with no training or background in spiritual life.

Brahmacarya means "the life of celibacy." Unfortunately, the very concept of such a lifestyle is still incomprehensible to the vast majority of human society, especially in the Western countries. Indeed, even though the rudiments of Kṛṣṇa conscious philosophy—service to God, simple living, high thinking, and so on—may be explained to open-minded persons, the principles of celibacy and austerity remain an anathema to most. Some even consider celibacy to be dangerous fanaticism or, at best, something unnatural and strange. This book will definitely not be understandable to or appreciated by, nor is it meant for, the common man.

In Kṛṣṇa consciousness we stand apart from the general masses. For all their liberality and free sex, their society is a mess, a hell. We have taken the decision to walk on a different path. We cannot compromise our principles to satisfy misguided persons who have no idea that there is a goal of life, let alone how to attain it. Our goal is Kṛṣṇa, and we are prepared to do whatever is necessary to attain to Him. Why should we descend into the stool pit of material enjoyment? *Brahmacarya* is that training whereby, developing knowledge and detachment *(vairāgya-vidyā),* one becomes immune from the pushing of the senses. Enjoying life in Kṛṣṇa consciousness and renunciation, one prepares himself to enter the kingdom of God.

It is not expected that all *brahmacārīs* will remain so without ever marrying. The *brahmacārī* period is traditionally a preparation for what will follow. For most, that means *gṛhastha* life and beyond. Certainly, if a *brahmacārī* is determined and strong then there is no reason why he cannot remain unmarried throughout his life; indeed, some fortunate few will succeed in remaining celibate throughout their entire lives. But the Vedic system prescribes four *āśramas,* and it is understood that most *brahmacārīs* will eventually marry. Yet one's initial training in Kṛṣṇa consciousness is most important. And we must give newly recruited devotees a vision of lifelong commitment to Kṛṣṇa consciousness, whatever their external situation may be.

So *brahmacarya* in Kṛṣṇa consciousness shouldn't just mean wearing saffron cloth for a while before getting married ("the waiting room"). It is a serious training program for both the attached, those who intend to marry, and the detached, those who want to remain single throughout their lives. The more strictly we follow, the more benefit we derive.

Of course, *brahmacarya* is not the goal of life—Kṛṣṇa consciousness is. Not simply by accepting *brahmacarya* will one become a pure devotee of Kṛṣṇa. Indeed, many already married couples take to Kṛṣṇa consciousness and make steady advancement without ever having had *brahmacārī* training.

However, if one is afforded the opportunity for *brahmacārī* training he should eagerly accept it, as it is the best possible start on the long ascent to Vaikuṇṭha. Training and personal guidance are essential, especially for new and inexperienced devotees. Hence this book is not intended as, nor could it possibly be, a substitute for personal supervision. It can only be auxiliary to such tutelage.

Many classes of devotees may benefit from this book. *Gurukula* students and teachers will find value herein. For despite a boy's *gurukula* education, the present social atmosphere is such that upon attaining puberty, sex desire may well hit him like the in-rushing waves of the sea. How then will he cope? This book will help him.

Herein there is also much valuable information for gurus, *sannyāsīs,* temple leaders, and other senior devotees for whom preaching to and caring for *brahmacārīs* is an important aspect of their service. Certainly every temple president wants to have a team of enthusiastic *brahmacārīs,* for when inspired, *brahmacārīs* render tremendous service.

Gṛhastha men may also derive strength from this book, in preparation for the renunciation that they must ultimately accept as *vānaprasthas* if they actually intend to perfect their lives.

And herein devotee women can learn more about how and why to act cautiously around men. For while the scriptures repeatedly warn men not to be captivated by the charms of women, for women *māyā* appears in the form of man. As long as man and woman are attached to each other for material enjoyment, they remain dangerous to each other.

Gṛhastha couples should be especially aware of their tremendous responsibility to send their sons to be trained as *brahmacārīs,* to be molded as great personalities and thus be saved from a bestial life of sense gratification.

Therefore this book should be read by all classes of devotees, for every genuine devotee must be a *brahmacārī*, i.e., a self-controlled celibate. Indeed, in many instances within this book the word *devotee* could substitute for the word *brahmacārī.*

Of course, simply to read this book and say *Jaya!* will not be good enough, for it is a call to practical action. Although many of the precepts discussed herein are already part of daily life in our ISKCON centers throughout the world, nevertheless to enliven our *brahmacārīs* and to create a strong, healthy mood of *brahmacarya,* constant and sustained input from older devotees is required. Therefore I am hopeful that this book will inspire many senior devotees to start taking a more personal interest in the junior men, thus replenishing their own spiritual lives and those of the entire movement.

I don't claim to be a perfect *brahmacārī.* Writing about high standards is often easier than strictly following them. But Śrī Caitanya Mahāprabhu wanted to maintain the highest standard,[2] so we should know what that standard is and seriously endeavor to follow it. If we keep the highest standards, sincere people will be impressed by our seriousness. And if we do not keep high standards, then what is the meaning to our being devotees?

This book is therefore meant to give an indication of the ideal standard. Obviously, there will be discrepancies in various circumstances and individuals, and it will not always be possible for everyone to attain to the highest level. Those who are *sāra-grahi* Vaiṣṇavas (realists)[3] will accept the essence of the instructions herein and intelligently apply it in their lives, whatever situation they are in.

In this book I have avoided the complex discussion of *varṇāśrama-dharma,* which is now a focus of attention and concern for the intellectuals in our Society. I have simply tried to present practical advice that *brahmacārīs* may apply in their lives. No doubt some will dismiss it as fanaticism. But without one-pointed determination, has anyone ever achieved anything great? To conquer sex desire is no small achievement. Indeed, it is the greatest accomplishment attainable in the material world. A wishy-washy, half-hearted attempt will only lead to frustration. Without being fully dedicated, no one will be successful.

This book is especially meant to help the many sincere young men who join ISKCON, but it should also be relevant and of interest to all devotees serious about improving their spiritual lives. It will hopefully also be appreciated by those *brahmacārīs* who have been in Kṛṣṇa consciousness for some time, who have a basic understanding of this movement and the philosophy yet would appreciate guidance on how best to make further spiritual advancement. And some sections of this book are directed more toward *bhakta* leaders, temple presidents, and other senior devotees. There is ample practical advice herein, plus several sections which philosophically analyze the farce of so-called sexual happiness.

I am known for giving strong advice, and although some devotees reject it as impractical, others appreciate it, apply it in their lives, and thus benefit. My guidance is especially meant for devotees who are serious about advancing in Kṛṣṇa consciousness and are willing to make the sacrifices required to do so. Persons desiring instruction for a compromised style of Kṛṣṇa consciousness may find it elsewhere. My books are not meant for them.

I have taken up this task also for my much-needed self-purification. Those who know me know that I am still trying to come to the level of a real devotee. Despite lacking full realization, I have made many forceful statements. I hope this will not be considered hypocritical.

Desiring the mercy of all the Vaiṣṇavas,
Yours in the service of Śrīla Prabhupāda,

Bhakti Vikāsa Swami

THE MEANING OF BRAHMACARYA

Basically, *brahmacarya* means celibacy.

karmaṇā manasā vācā
sarvāvasthāsu sarvadā
sarvatra maithuna-tyāgo
brahmacaryaṁ pracakṣate

"The vow of *brahmacarya* is meant to help one completely abstain from sex indulgence in work, words, and mind—at all times, under all circumstances and in all places."[4]

There are eight aspects of *brahmacarya*, as described in Śrīdhara Svāmī's commentary on *Śrīmad-Bhāgavatam* 6.1.12:

smaraṇaṁ kīrtanaṁ keliḥ
prekṣaṇaṁ guhyabhāṣaṇam
saṅkalpo 'dhyavasāyaś ca
kriyā-nirvṛttir eva ca

One should not:

1. Think about women.
2. Speak about sex life.
3. Dally with women.
4. Look lustfully at women.
5. Talk intimately with women.
6. Decide to engage in sexual intercourse.
7. Endeavor for sex life.
8. Engage in sex life.[5]

One who practices *brahmacarya* is called a *brahmacārī*. In the *varṇāśrama* system, the *brahmacārī-āśrama* is the first of four, namely, *brahmacārī*, *gṛhastha*, *vānaprastha,* and *sannyāsa*.

"According to Vedic principles, the first part of life should be utilized in *brahmacarya* for the development of character and spiritual qualities."[6]

Brahmacarya is thus student life. It was traditionally rigorous, disciplined, and austere. It is a life of cultivation, of preparing for the future. In all *āśramas* devotees are cultivating Kṛṣṇa consciousness, preparing for the examination of death. But the *brahmacārī* period is specifically meant for training: training in how to control the senses and subdue the mind; training to be a *gṛhastha, vānaprastha,* and *sannyāsī*. This training is by submission to, service to, and friendship to the guru.[7]

In terms of *varṇāśrama* principles, the highest standard of *brahmacarya* means the vow not to marry but to observe strict celibacy throughout life.[8] This is called the *bṛhad-vrata* ("great vow"), or *naiṣṭhika-brahmacarya*. "*Naiṣṭhika-brahmacārī* refers to one who never wastes his semen at any time."[9] "The word *mahā-vrata-dharaḥ* indicates a *brahmacārī* who has never fallen down."[10]

In Indian society, *brahmacarya* has often been considered as a set of restrictions aimed at upholding good health and moral principles, with the ultimate purpose of enjoying civilized sense gratification. *Brahmacarya* in Kṛṣṇa consciousness, however, operates on the dynamic principle of knowledge and renunciation fully engaged in the service of God. Śrīla Prabhupāda: "One practicing *brahmacarya* should be completely engaged in the service of the Lord and should not in any way associate with women."[11] According to the definition of *brahmacarya* given in *Śrīmad-Bhāgavatam* (7.12.1), an unmarried person who does not live in the guru's *āśrama,* who has not submitted himself to the rigid life of surrender, and is not directly and exclusively engaged in the service of his guru, cannot properly claim to be a *brahmacārī.*

The broader meaning of *brahmacarya* is, as Śrīla Prabhupāda would cite, *brāhme carati iti brahmacarya:* "To act on the spiritual platform."

THE BENEFITS OF BRAHMACARYA

āyus tejo balaṁ vīryaṁ
prajñā śrīś ca yaśas tathā
puṇyatā satpriyatvaṁ ca
vardhate brahmacaryayā

"By the practice of brahmacarya, longevity, luster, strength, vigor, knowledge, beauty, fame, piety, and devotion to truth increase."[12]

Practice of *brahmacarya* gives good health, inner strength, peace of mind, fortitude, and long life. It helps to conserve physical and mental energy. It augments memory, will-power, clear thinking, power of concentration, and ability to grasp philosophical subjects. It bestows physical strength, vigor, vitality, courage, boldness, and strength of character. To one who practices *brahmacarya,* divine knowledge comes as if naturally. His words convey meaning and authority, and leave an impression on the hearers.

Conversely, those who do not practice *brahmacarya* must always remain in illusion. Śrīla Prabhupāda: *"Brahmacarya* is very, very essential. When one becomes detestful to sex life, that is the beginning of spiritual life."[13] "Without becoming *brahmacārī,* nobody can understand spiritual life."[14]

"BRAHMACĀRĪ" IS ALSO A DESIGNATION

Śrī Caitanya Mahāprabhu declared: "I am not a *brāhmaṇa,* a *kṣatriya,* a *vaiśya,* or a *śūdra.* I am not a *brahmacārī,* a *gṛhastha,* a *vānaprastha,* or a *sannyāsī.* I identify myself only as the servant of the servant of Kṛṣṇa, the maintainer of the *gopīs."*[15] The goal of life is not to be a *brahmacārī,* nor a *gṛhastha,* nor even a *sannyāsī.* It is to be a pure devotee of Kṛṣṇa. Śrīla Prabhupāda often quoted from the *Nārada-pañcarātra:*

sarvopādhi-vinirmuktaṁ
tat-paratvena nirmalam
hṛṣīkeṇa hṛṣīkeśa-
sevanaṁ bhaktir ucyate

"Pure devotional service means being freed from all material designations."

"*Brahmacārī*" is also a designation. If we put too much emphasis on making distinctions between *varṇas* and *āśramas,* especially amongst devotees, we are in the bodily concept of life. For, "One cannot realize the Absolute Truth simply by observing celibacy."[16] In India there are Māyāvādī *sannyāsīs* who follow difficult rules and regulations far more strictly than most devotees could even dream of. But they are not dear to Kṛṣṇa.

Caitanya Mahāprabhu would give respect even to Māyāvādī *sannyāsīs,* as was the social etiquette, but He associated only with devotees. When He visited Vārāṇasī, Mahāprabhu avoided the numerous Māyāvādī *sannyāsīs* and chose to live amongst His *gṛhastha* devotees instead—Tapana Miśra, Candraśekhara (a *śūdra* by caste), and the Maharashtrian *brāhmaṇa*. The Māyāvādī *sannyāsīs* were astonished at this and criticized the Lord. Only after He had converted them to Vaiṣṇavism was the Lord pleased to sit amongst them and take *prasāda*.[17]

In considering a devotee's spiritual advancement, Caitanya Mahāprabhu never considered his external situation. Of His "three and a half" intimate associates, two (Rāmānanda Rāya and Śikhi Māhiti) were householders, "half" (Mādhavī-devī) was an old woman, and one (Svarūpa Dāmodara) was a renunciate who had not even bothered to accept all the external formalities of *sannyāsa*. Many of Lord Caitanya's leading devotees were householders and some were rejects from society. Indeed, Lord Caitanya blessed Haridāsa Ṭhākura (who was born in a Muslim family) to be the *ācārya* of the holy name, just to demonstrate that spiritual advancement is not dependent on being respectable according to *varṇa* and *āśrama* considerations.

So we should not be overly concerned with externals: "I am a *brahmacārī*," "I am a *sannyāsī.*" We are all servants of Kṛṣṇa. *Jīvera 'svarūpa' haya—kṛṣṇera 'nitya-dāsa':* "The constitutional position of the living entity is as the eternal servant of Kṛṣṇa."[18] The relative advancement of a Vaiṣṇava is understood only by the quality of his devotion to Kṛṣṇa. *Varṇa* and *āśrama* don't matter.[19]

Still, in our present position, *brahmacarya* must be emphasized as an essential part of the means to our end of attaining love of Kṛṣṇa. In our present neophyte position, unless we make a rigid program to control our senses, there will never be any possibility of advancement to higher levels.

"A human being is meant to be trained according to certain principles to revive his original knowledge. Such a methodical life is described as *tapasya*. One can gradually be elevated to the standard of real knowledge, or Kṛṣṇa consciousness, by practicing austerity and celibacy *(brahmacarya),* by controlling the mind, by controlling the senses, by giving up one's possessions in charity, by being avowedly truthful, by keeping clean, and by practicing *yoga-āsanas*... Unless one is master of his senses, he should not be called *gosvāmī,* but *go-dāsa*, servant of the senses. Following in the footsteps of the six Gosvāmīs of Vṛndāvana, all *svāmīs* and *gosvāmīs* should fully engage in the transcendental loving service of the Lord. As opposed to this, the *go-dāsas* engage in the service of the senses or in the service of the material world. They have no other engagement. Prahlāda Mahārāja has further described the *go-dāsa* as *adānta-go*, which refers to one whose senses are not controlled. An *adānta-go* cannot become a servant of Kṛṣṇa."[20]

ĀDI-RASA

Sex is so overwhelmingly present in the material world that the question must arise, "Where has this sex desire come from?" The answer is that sex originates from God. In the spiritual world, Kṛṣṇa and His consorts are spontaneously attracted to each other and engage in pastimes of love together. This is called *ādi-rasa*, the original and real sex desire, the supermost platform of spiritual exchange. This *ādi-rasa* is free from all material contamination, and is as different to mundane sex attraction as gold is to iron.[21]

Devotees who are without a trace of any mundane desire and who are situated on the highest platform of spiritual understanding, such as Śukadeva Gosvāmī, Rūpa Gosvāmī, and Rāmānanda Rāya, have appreciated and glorified this *ādi-rasa*. Indeed, Kṛṣṇa Himself accepts the form of Lord Caitanya, adopting the mood of Śrīmatī Rādhārāṇī, just to taste the full sweetness of this *ādi-rasa*. When this incomprehensibly elevated service mood is perverted and twisted by souls envious of Kṛṣṇa's enjoyment, it comes out as nasty mundane sex desire, which enthralls the conditioned souls and poses an ever-present menace for the aspiring transcendentalist.

Why is it that the *jñānīs* and yogis undergo great austerities, strenuously endeavoring to overcome material desires, but still can only make slow advancement over many lifetimes? Why is it that neophyte devotees, despite chanting and praying to God, are still prone to fall down at any time? It is because of sex desire. The perverted expression of *ādi-rasa* known as mundane sex desire is the main obstacle to spiritual progress.

MUNDANE SEX DESIRES

The conditioned soul in the material world is in a state of madness. *Nūnaṁ pramattaḥ kurute vikarma.*[22] Forgetting his eternal, blissful relationship with Kṛṣṇa, he is suffering life after life, being kicked and spat upon by *māyā*. But he is smiling, taking it as enjoyment. Why? Because he is charmed by the glitter of false happiness, beginning with sex pleasure. Sex desire is the main symptom of insanity exhibited by the conditioned soul.

Such foolish beings are always intrigued and charmed by the opposite sex. With the onset of puberty, male youths, especially those who have not been trained otherwise, become overwhelmed by sexual desires. They take every opportunity to mingle with and enter into relationships with the opposite sex. Although they get limited opportunities to do so, their consciousness is always saturated with thoughts of touching the bodies of the opposite sex, seeing their naked forms, and engaging in sexual intercourse. They say "love," but they have only lust.

Even the more sober members of society who are not cultivating gross sexual lust as their main business in life may be captivated by fantasies of enjoying the body of a sexual partner, for the thought of sex is never far away from the mind of a conditioned soul.

But there is nothing intrinsically beautiful about any material body. Even the bodies of beauty queens are simply bags of skin filled with foul-smelling, revolting substances. Blood, mucous, bile, stool, and urine combined as muscles, bones, fat, liver, heart, and intestines—that is what they are having sex with! Sexual happiness is the happiness of uniting the two urine-producing parts. Yet by the mighty power of illusion, an arrangement of skin and flesh overrides all logic and sanity and brings even a person of intelligence down to the level of a dog. As a pig is attracted to a sow, or a male cockroach to a female, so is the sexual desire of a man for a woman. It is not even slightly more elevated than that of the pigs.

There is really nothing special about sex. It is not wonderful, it is not noble, it is not romantic—it is just a bodily function, a response to raw gut feeling. If you think about it soberly, the whole prospect of sex seems rather silly. Still, everybody is doing it. The president of America is doing it, the bums on the street are doing it, the cats and dogs are doing it. Only a few great souls are attempting to conquer over it.

In human society sex desire is expanded into many forms, under the headings of profit, adoration, and distinction. All the trappings of so-called civilization—society, friendship, love, house, cars, clothes, position, power, prestige, money, and so on—are simply for facilitating and expanding this animal instinct called sex desire. But despite its external glamour, unless human society seeks out real beauty, which is Kṛṣṇa, then it has not advanced any more than the pigs or any other animals.

And despite all their emphasis on it, still, as surveys show, many *karmīs* are actually bored at the time of sex. Then why don't they give it up and take to Kṛṣṇa consciousness, the real nectar of life? Because they know nothing better, don't want to change, and are hoping against hope that sex will make them happy.

Those who are fortunate will take to Kṛṣṇa consciousness for real advancement of life. Kṛṣṇa consciousness is far above the perversions of the gross materialists and the fruitless efforts of the *jñānīs* and yogis. Even a neophyte devotee can be confident of gradually conquering over lust, because he has got the right method; that is, to revive his natural, real love—his love for Kṛṣṇa. If he sticks to the path, then he will in due course of time achieve full Kṛṣṇa consciousness. Then he will be completely satisfied forever. *Brahmacarya* is meant for developing clear, unsentimental, uncompromising understanding of these points as the basis for making rapid, determined progress in spiritual life.

All the advice given in this book is based on this understanding: sex cannot make us happy; only Kṛṣṇa can make us happy. Devotees who regularly study Śrīla Prabhupāda's books can keep this understanding active in their hearts. Then following all the rules and regulations of spiritual life will come naturally.

SEX—THE CAUSE OF UNLIMITED SUFFERING

"Of all kinds of suffering and bondage arising from various attachments, none is greater than the suffering and bondage arising from attachment to women and intimate contact with those attached to women."[23]

Because the experience and urges of sex are so intense, and the syndrome of man/woman relationships surrounding it is so complex, it diverts the conditioned soul's attention away from Kṛṣṇa and deludes him more than any other trick of *māyā.* Sometimes the foolish conditioned soul experiences great delight in enjoying sex; at other times he is frustrated and burns in the fire of lust. Or, when spurned by a lover, he suffers mental agony, sometimes so severe that he is driven to kill the loved one, or himself, or both. The loss of a partner to whom one is intimately emotionally attached, by death or other means, leaves the remaining partner with a broken heart. And especially in our most abominably degraded modern society, thousands of people's lives become shattered by having their bodies exploited, either forcefully or tactfully, by others.

The greatest myth in human society is that sex is the cause of happiness and that by adjusting or increasing one's sex life one can find happiness. Factually, the opposite is true: the more one becomes involved in sex, the more he becomes entangled by the complexities of the actions and reactions of material life. This ultimately leads the unrestricted enjoyer to take birth in the animal kingdom, where he is awarded improved facilities to carry on with his sexual activities, and with minimal restrictions. Birth after birth he can enjoy 8,400,000 varieties of sex to his heart's content. He will also experience varieties of birth, death, old age, and disease. And he will never be happy.

The much advertised pleasure of sex is more fantasized about than real. People assume that sex will bring them pleasure, but the actual act is over in a few minutes and gives far less sensual gratification than was imagined in the mind. In the long run it brings much more trouble than enjoyment.

On the physical platform also, sex is debilitating and can be dangerous. Sensual enjoyers forget that "the body, which is the vehicle of sexual pleasure, is also the vehicle of pain, disease, and death."[24] It takes the essence of sixty drops of blood to make one drop of semen; furthermore, much subtle life energy *(prāṇa)* is lost in sex life. Rapid breathing during sex also shortens one's life, for the number of breaths a person will have in his lifetime is fixed at birth (therefore yogis practice breath restraint to prolong their lives). Then there is the danger of sexually transmitted diseases, which are extremely painful and nasty.

Furthermore, to the extent that a person becomes interested in sex, that much he loses all good qualities. For from lust develop all other bad qualities such as greed, personal ambition, hatred, and cruelty. Śrīla Prabhupāda: "Sex life is the background of material existence. Demons are very fond of sex life. The more one is freed from the desire for sex, the more he is promoted to the level of the demigods; the more one is inclined to enjoy sex, the more he is degraded to the level of demonic life."[25]

A lusty person becomes not only keenly interested in sexual enjoyment, but in all other forms of sense gratification also. Although such people may generally appear to act fairly reasonably, actually they are all self-centered and selfish—they are after what they can get for themselves. The *Śrīmad-Bhāgavatam* (5.18.12) therefore analyzes that nondevotees have no good qualities, even though they may appear to. They are simply suffering and causing others to suffer in a mesh of greed, envy, and mutual exploitation, with just a veneer of social civility. This is especially evident in today's "me first" generation—a whole society raised on consumeristic greed and lust, with no higher moral than "get what you can grab."

SEX FASCINATION—THE DISEASE OF THE MODERN AGE

Sex is the overwhelming obsession of modern society. Sexual promiscuity is so unrelentingly stressed that anyone who does not appear to be highly interested in it is generally considered to be a crank. Social pressure induces people to try to maintain juvenile lustiness long after the sensual high of youth has subsided. Thus millions of people remain emotionally immature all their lives. It is a sick world.

Ignorant of their relationship with Kṛṣṇa, and unsure of their status in rapidly changing societies with no fixed values, people desperately desire an identity—an image of themselves which they feel good with and which others respect. The essence of image, as inculcated by the mass media, is sexual attractiveness. The power of the media to mold people's attitudes and behavior is a pathetic but documented fact. Even if the average person's mind would not have been always absorbed in sexual thoughts, the media makes sure it is.

The advertising industry in particular churns out unending pictures of dressed-up or undressed women—in magazines, on billboards, on television—always and everywhere. Despite grossly exploiting the bodies of women and the basest impulses of men, solely for the sake of making some already over-rich people even richer, their activities continue for the most part unquestioned. The general public absorb their propaganda and remain ever steeped in lust, having no knowledge of the necessity to resist. Thus advertisements oozing with sexual overtones allure the willingly gullible public to mindlessly purchase everything from back-scrubbers to brandy. And the consumer society rolls on, its members forever sexually jacked-up.

Constant titillation of the senses, however, increasingly dulls the spirit. Thus despite all the celluloid promises, people find themselves cheated of real happiness. In adolescence, when the senses appear to have unlimited power to invoke euphoric delights, happiness through sense enjoyment seems not only to be a distinct possibility, but the very meaning of life. But the pleasures of youth, as the poets lament, is but a fleeting frolic. The ability of the body to enjoy is like a water-laden sponge. At first, if you just pinch it, water gushes out. But as it is squeezed more and more, it gradually becomes difficult to get even a few drops from it.

Similarly, attempts for sexual enjoyment increasingly result in emptiness and frustration. Still, most people fail to recognize the limits of sexual enjoyment. Due to misdirected education, they think that their lack of satisfaction with sex means there is something wrong in their approach to it. They may end up on a psychologist's couch or reading some of the hundreds of books on "improved" sex life (*Yoga for Sex, Tao for Sex, The Modern Woman's Guide to Sex, A Doctor's Sex Secrets, Diet for Better Sex,* etc.). However, the harder they grope for pleasure, the more surely it eludes them. As they furiously try to force their bodies into giving them the happiness which they regard as a natural birthright, they may turn to frequent masturbation, increased promiscuity, pornography, varieties of perversity, and ultimately violence.

Actual civilization teaches its members to sublimate their sexual desires for higher, spiritual purposes. Modern civilization exploits people's sexual cravings, makes a business out of it, and sends people to hell by the millions.

Seeing all this, the Vaiṣṇavas are sorry. They know that every living being is an eternal servant of Kṛṣṇa, and that sexual desire is simply a perverted reflection of the heart's deepest longings to love Kṛṣṇa. Just by understanding this simple principle the whole world could be happy. But in the darkness of the modern age it is very difficult to convince anyone that there is anything wrong with sex at all. The members of the Kṛṣṇa consciousness movement have a great responsibility to somehow or other give this real knowledge to the people of the world. Śrīla Prabhupāda: "The Kṛṣṇa consciousness movement will go down in history as having saved mankind in its darkest hour."

SENSE GRATIFICATION

"The idea that we can achieve happiness through the enjoyment of our senses, especially through that prototype of all pleasure, sex and sexual love, is an illusion which is perhaps the most deeply rooted and pervasive of all human convictions. With the disintegration of traditional religions and the official establishment of secular philosophies this illusion has gained the force of an obsession."[26]

Sex desire is based on the touch sensation. It is the topmost pleasure in, and therefore the main binding force of, the material world. But there are five other senses also: the senses of seeing, smelling, tasting, hearing, and the mind. Any one of them can carry away the mind even of a man of discrimination who is endeavoring to control them.[27] Furthermore, "each sense has many desires to be fulfilled."[28] The pull of the senses is very strong and dangerous.

However, there is no real enjoyment in sense gratification. On the contrary, there is built-in pain in material pleasure. "Happiness derived from a combination of the senses and the sense objects is always a cause of distress."[29] And, "as one's body engages in sense gratification, it becomes weaker and weaker daily."[30]

Real pleasure means Kṛṣṇa consciousness, the happiness of the soul. The so-called pleasure of material life is simply an illusory construction of the mind.

"As for the agitations of the flickering mind, they are divided into two divisions. The first is called *avirodha-prīti*, or unrestricted attachment, and the other is called *virodha-yukta-krodha*, anger arising from frustration. Adherence to the philosophy of the Māyāvādīs, belief in the fruitive results of the *karma-vādīs*, and belief in plans based on materialistic desires are called *avirodha-prīti*. *Jñānīs*, *karmīs,* and materialistic planmakers generally attract the attention of conditioned souls, but when the materialists cannot fulfill their plans and when their devices are frustrated, they become angry. Frustration of material desires produces anger."[31]

"Satisfaction of the mind can be obtained only by taking the mind away from thoughts of sense enjoyment. The more the mind dwells on sense gratification, the more it is dissatisfied."[32]

Understanding this, the transcendentalist undergoes *tapasya* (austerity), giving up sense gratification. But even giving up sense gratification by practicing the rules and regulations of spiritual life is not enough—we also have to give up meditating on sense gratification. Unless and until we completely give up all hope of trying to enjoy this material world, we will not be able to firmly fix our intelligence; we will have ups and downs and will not taste the true bliss of Kṛṣṇa consciousness.

Śrīla Prabhupāda: "If our mind is filled with sense gratification, even though we want Kṛṣṇa consciousness, by continuous practice we cannot forget the subject of sense gratification."[33] And, "in the *Caitanya-caritāmṛta* it is stated that if someone sincerely wants to see the Lord and at the same time wants to enjoy this material world, he is considered to be a fool only."[34] Therefore, "it is the duty of the transcendentalist to try strenuously to control desire."[35]

RESTRICTING ASSOCIATION WITH WOMEN

Since the dawn of history, materialists have written thousands of books about dealing with women, and it is still a mystery to them. Especially if women are accepted as sense objects, relationships with them remain inextricably complex: nectar in the beginning, poison in the end. The *brahmacārī* has no real business associating with women—whatever must be there, he keeps as brief as possible. He knows that the male human form is meant for self-realization, and that attraction to the female form blocks such spiritual advancement.

Therefore the Vedic culture has always carefully restricted the mixing of men and women. Most of the time traditional *brahmacārīs* wouldn't see women at all, as they would be busy with their studies. Addressing all women as *mātā* (mother), the only relationship they might have was with their guru's wife, who in the absence of their real mother would look after the boys. Even then there were restrictions, especially after the boys reached puberty and if the wife was young. *Brahmacārīs* would not even see any young woman for the first twenty-five years of their lives.[36] *Vānaprasthas* kept the company of their aging wives, under strict vows, but for *sannyāsīs,* association with women was meant to be zero. Even *gṛhasthas* were only allowed limited association. Free mixing with women was only for *śūdras* and outcastes (i.e., those with no higher values of life).

For those interested in spiritual advancement, association with women must be restricted to the minimum. In the presence of a woman, the consciousness of a man changes. Even if several serious *brahmacārīs* are present in a room, and a chaste devotee woman enters for some reason, the mentality of the men consciously or unconsciously will change. They will become self-conscious in their words and actions. So, even having philosophically accepted that we are all spirit souls, and even if we want to be liberal and forget the formalities and relate to women on a person-to-person basis, the *śāstra* forbids us to do so.

"As long as a living entity is not completely self-realized—as long as he is not independent of the misconception of identifying with his body, which is nothing but a reflection of the original body and senses—he cannot be relieved of the conception of duality, which is epitomized by the duality between man and woman. Thus there is every chance that he will fall down because his intelligence is bewildered."[37]

In the purport to this verse, Śrīla Prabhupāda elaborates: "One must realize perfectly that the living being is a spirit soul and is tasting various types of material bodies. One may theoretically understand this, but when one has practical realization, then he becomes a *paṇḍita,* one who knows. Until that time, the duality continues, and the conception of man and woman also continues. In this stage, one should be very careful in mixing with women. No one should think himself perfect and forget the *śāstric* injunction that one should be careful about associating even with his daughter, mother, or sister, not to speak of other women."

In Kṛṣṇa consciousness, man is good and woman is good; but, in the conditional stage, the combination is always dangerous.[38] Better to be careful than sorry. Even in the short history of ISKCON, we have seen many stalwart, sincere devotees (including *sannyāsīs*) fall down because of carelessness and complacency in dealing with women. "In our Kṛṣṇa consciousness movement it is advised that the *sannyāsīs* and *brahmacārīs* keep strictly aloof from the association of women so that there will be no chance of their falling down again as victims of lusty desires."[39]

The material world is so designed that unless one goes to the jungles or mountains, he must have some dealings with the opposite sex. In the modern world there is no protection for *brahmacārīs;* man-woman relationships are quite free (which is the beginning of all hellish life, and quite unsuitable for spiritual progress).

ISKCON *brahmacārīs* have to deal with women (both devotees and nondevotees) a lot more than traditional *brahmacārīs* did, and in less favorable circumstances. Dealings with women should he formal, polite—and as little as possible. If some talk must be there, keep your distance (stand well apart), avoid eye contact, and finish the business as soon as possible. Never get into an argument with a woman. Strict *brahmacārīs* do not attend marriage ceremonies,[40] watch dramas with parts played by women,[41] or see women dancing or hear their singing.[42] The general principle to avoid intimate association must be strictly maintained. It is foolish to think that one can freely mix with the opposite sex and remain unagitated. Even the great *brahmacārī* Bhīṣmadeva expressed that he could not save himself if he were to associate with young girls.[43]

Nor should *brahmacārīs* accept service from women (even *prasāda* service should be separate). It is especially dangerous for a *brahmacārī* to see and talk to the same woman repeatedly. Once a friendly relationship is established, the downfall of the *brahmacārī* has begun.

Remember, women are powerful. Caesar controlled a mighty empire, but Cleopatra controlled Caesar. Of course, having to speak with women or sometimes discuss something with them is unavoidable. If at all possible mold your life in such a way that you don't normally have to have any dealings with women—the tendency should be toward zero dealings.

Brahmacārīs should avoid physically touching women, for to do so even accidentally will agitate the mind. Keep at least far enough away so that there is not even a possibility of brushing against a woman's clothing; and preferably further still. Lord Caitanya, even in His householder life, would stand well to the side if He saw a woman approaching on the path. Nor did He joke with women. *Brahmacārīs* should follow the Lord's example.

The eyes have a tendency to stray toward women, but this should be given up. When a man looks at a woman, then Cupid (Kāmadeva), standing nearby with his flower-bow, immediately shoots an arrow called Mohana (meaning infatuation, delusion, or folly) which causes the man to be fascinated by the female form. After this preliminary bewilderment, Cupid sends a further four arrows, namely: Stambhana, which stuns the man and causes him to forget all else; Unmādana, which causes him to be as if intoxicated; Śoṣaṇa, which causes intense attraction; and Tāpana, which deeply pierces the heart and causes it to burn.

Hardly anyone in the three worlds has the power to resist the influence of these arrows. *Māyā* is so strong that even in the midst of an enlivening *kīrtana,* a devotee engaged in chanting the pure names of the Supreme Lord may become attracted upon seeing the form of the opposite sex (especially a dancing form). Therefore a *brahmacārī* should practice not looking at women, and should especially never see a woman dressing, combing her hair, running, playing sports, sleeping, bathing, undressed or partially dressed.

Never trust the mind. The mind will tell us, "I can speak to this woman, I won't get agitated," "She is only a child," or, "She is much older than me, so no problem," or "She is the chaste wife of so and so," or, "Anyway, I know the philosophy, I'm not going to speak to her for long, it's important, and I'm not going to fall down." But *śāstra* states that, what to speak of lusty rascals brought up in the modern sex-centered so-called civilization, even learned scholars of the Vedic age were totally forbidden from sitting close to their mother, sister, or daughter![44]

Such chaste behavior helps to control the mind. The natural tendency to be lusty is checked by deliberate restraint in dealings with the opposite sex. As soon as one even slightly indulges in looking at, unnecessarily talking with, or in any way behaving loosely with women, then the guard is let down and lusty desires begin to enter. Soon the intelligence becomes bewildered and, being impelled by the senses, one cannot distinguish between activities that are beneficial and those that should be avoided. One who loses control of his mind loses control of his life, and becomes controlled by *māyā* in the form of a woman.

Therefore a *brahmacārī* must be careful to control his mind and senses and not indulge them in the illusory pleasure derived from seeing, thinking about, or talking with women. The mind and senses are so strong that they can never, never, never be trusted. The only thing they can be trusted to do is to sell us off to *māyā* if given even a shadow of an opportunity. One slip into illicit sex will cause havoc in the life of a devotee.

Such strong strictures may seem odd in the context of modern social relationships, but the fact is that unless this discrimination between the sexes is reestablished, there is no hope for human society. "A civilization that allows men to mix unrestrictedly with women is an animal civilization. In Kali-yuga, people are extremely liberal, but mixing with women and talking with them as equals actually constitutes an uncivilized way of life."[45]

The scriptures enjoin that we see all women as our mother. That's a healthy approach for a *brahmacārī*—even if most women, due to lack of training, don't act like mothers.

Don't try to impress women. We may not even be fully conscious of it, but when women are present, the tendency is to try to impress them by our good behavior, eloquent speaking, athletic dancing, or whatever. Be careful.

However, fanatical anti-womanism is also unhealthy. How many woman-hating "staunch *brahmacārīs*" have succumbed and become big enjoyer householders? The roughness of so-called "super-*brahmacārīs*"—as if unkindness and rudeness to women were proof of their freedom from sex desire—is actually indicative of their agitation. Indeed, undesirable traits such as the desire to dominate or impress others, unnecessary anger, and voracious eating are all symptoms of sex desire manifest in different ways. Attachment and rejection are two sides of the coin of the mode of passion. Neutrality and detachment born of *sattva-guṇa* are required of a steady devotee. One must come to the mode of goodness to maintain *brahmacarya.* In goodness, knowledge and renunciation develop.

Our philosophy begins with *ātma-jñāna*—we are not these bodies, male or female. So we shouldn't develop a superiority complex: "I'm a big renounced *brahmacārī.* Who are these less intelligent women?" Who knows, possibly in our last lives we were in women's bodies and the women were in men's bodies! Still, we must keep the distinction. "Danger—keep your distance." Don't be rough, don't be rude, but don't worry about being considered odd or anti-social by being distant. Better be safe than sorry.

ATTITUDES IN DEVOTIONAL SERVICE

One of the most important statements about Kṛṣṇa consciousness is in Śrīla Prabhupāda's Preface to *the Nectar of Instruction:* "Advancement in Kṛṣṇa consciousness depends on the attitude of the follower." Śrīla Prabhupāda has stated that anyone can become a pure devotee of Kṛṣṇa immediately, if he simply desires to. Advancement in devotional service means to purify our desires, and pure devotional service means to be fully absorbed in serving Kṛṣṇa without even the subtlest desire for any personal sense gratification.

Only the most fortunate people can come to Kṛṣṇa consciousness. People come to devotional service for a variety of reasons. Some are seeking shelter from intense distress, others are looking for a simple, alternative lifestyle, some come out of curiosity, to see what it is all about, some because they want a cleaner, better life for themselves and their families. Some are directly searching for God and the meaning of life.

Of course, real devotional service is completely unmotivated, even by desires for peace and holistic well-being. Only such a surrendered attitude can bring complete satisfaction to the self. Those who are most intelligent will, from the beginning of their practice of Kṛṣṇa consciousness, sincerely endeavor to be pure devotees of Kṛṣṇa. Such an attitude is always to be encouraged, for it is the essence of our movement.

Others, however, may consider such an outlook to be utopian. How is it possible, they will postulate, for those coming from such sinful backgrounds to consider seriously the prospect of becoming pure devotees, completely free from all material desires? "Better be realistic," they say, "Make some compromise with *māyā,* and continue at some level of Kṛṣṇa consciousness." Of course, everyone is encouraged to begin devotional service at whatever level he finds convenient, and it is not expected that all will take to it fully from the very beginning. Indeed, the whole system of *varṇāśrama-dharma* (which forms the basis of Vedic culture) is meant for the gradual elevation of materially contaminated persons who are willing to adopt some measure of Kṛṣṇa consciousness into their lives but are not yet prepared for full surrender to Kṛṣṇa.

However, Śrīla Prabhupāda's whole mood (and that of Lord Caitanya and of our entire *sampradāya*) is that Kṛṣṇa consciousness is so easily available in this Kali-yuga by the easy process of chanting Hare Kṛṣṇa, so why not take full advantage of it, perfect our lives, and go back home, back to Godhead? Śrīla Prabhupāda: "Don't think that this chanting and dancing will not lead to the desired goal. It will. It is the assurance of Lord Caitanya Mahāprabhu that one will get all perfection by this process."[46]

It is with this faith that *brahmacārīs* engage in devotional activities. True *brahmacārīs* strive for the mood of *ahaituky-apratihatā-bhakti*—constant engagement in devotional service without any personal motive.[47] They are always eager for service and do not expect any special facilities or respect in return. Such pure devotional service is the ideal and essence of *brahmacārī* life.

Devotees who are not thus striving for perfection, who are executing mixed devotional service, may consider the prospect of becoming a pure devotee in this life to be impossible. Especially those who were once thus endeavoring, but who have fallen away from the strict standard of devotional service, may even be cynical about the efforts of those devotees who continue to perform devotional service with enthusiasm. But we should know this for what it is: *māyā.*

Just because someone has fallen away doesn't mean that everybody will fall away. The process of Kṛṣṇa consciousness is perfect. If anybody follows it with sincerity and vigor and refuses to leave the path under any circumstances, his success is guaranteed. If anybody leaves this movement it is not the fault of the process. It is the failure of the individual to surrender to it.

We should be careful to avoid developing negative attitudes in our devotional life. After all, whatever difficulties the material energy throws at us (as she undoubtedly will, to test our sincerity and fortitude), we always have cause for optimism because we are on the path back to Godhead. Śrīla Prabhupāda: "As long as a person is fully in cooperation with the wishes of the Lord, guided by the bona fide *brāhmaṇas* and Vaiṣṇavas and strictly following regulative principles, one has no cause for despondency, however trying the circumstances of life."[48] So it is better to avoid the company of doubters and groaners and make our lifetime plans for serving Kṛṣṇa within this movement. Why not?

We have already come so far. We have turned our backs on materialistic values, shaved our heads, donned dhotis and *tilaka*—so why not go the whole way and surrender fully to Kṛṣṇa? At least we should try for that. Śrīla Prabhupāda gave the example that if a student makes the effort to pass an exam in the top grade he will at least get a passing grade; but if he simply aims for a pass, he is likely to fail.[49] So we should think, "In this life I will end all association with this material world forever. I will attain Kṛṣṇa consciousness."

Often young *brahmacārīs,* fresh from the grind of material life, are bursting with enthusiasm; but after some time they may lose that freshness. Śrīla Prabhupāda noted that, "Beginners in Kṛṣṇa consciousness have a tendency to relax their efforts in a short time, but to advance spiritually you must resist this temptation and continually increase your efforts and devotion."[50]

Young *brahmacārīs* are usually trained strictly in the beginning. But after being in the movement a few years, when they become a little mature in devotional service, the pressure is often relaxed. It may be that no one is pushing them to surrender or to follow the temple programs diligently. At that time the devotee's spiritual advancement will depend to a much greater extent on his own determination to apply himself to the process of Kṛṣṇa consciousness. It is required that devotees become spiritually grown-up. Make a commitment to stay in this movement and go on practicing Kṛṣṇa consciousness no matter what. And always endeavor to become an advanced devotee. "Without sincere endeavor in devotional service one cannot obtain love of Godhead."[51] "An easygoing life and attainment of perfection in transcendental realization cannot go together."[52]

TRAINING

To become free from material desires and fixed in Kṛṣṇa consciousness, training under the guidance of an expert devotee is absolutely required. Traditionally, therefore, *brahmacārīs* lived under the direct tutelage of their spiritual master, being surrendered to him and serving him as a menial servant under strict regulation. *Brahmacārīs* would perform all kinds of menial services, would beg for the guru, and would not even eat unless called by the guru. They accepted any chastisements, with no question of arguing. This was complete training for smashing the false ego.

Although such rigid discipline is hardly possible nowadays, our movement is nevertheless primarily educational and is meant to provide training. Kṛṣṇa conscious training is so powerful that it quickly raises even the most fallen to the position of *mahātmas,* great souls.

It is the duty of those who are able to help others to do so. One who has spiritual knowledge, but out of miserliness fails to impart it to others, is never blessed with realization of it, and gradually he loses that knowledge altogether. Therefore, for our own good as well as for the good of others, we have to preach, teach, and train. Devotees are joining this wonderful Kṛṣṇa consciousness movement, eagerly hopeful of attaining Kṛṣṇa's lotus feet. If senior devotees don't help them get fixed on the path, who will?

However, training new men is not easy. It requires great tolerance, dedication, and humility. But whether or not a temple has a formal Bhakta Program, that atmosphere of training and instruction must be there. Junior devotees should, as soon as possible, become qualified as competent preachers, able to give classes and present Kṛṣṇa consciousness anywhere, anytime. This movement needs hundreds and thousands of convinced devotees to dedicate their lives for spreading the glories of Caitanya Mahāprabhu, so when new recruits come they will certainly need training.

Śrīla Prabhupāda was always training his disciples. Everything we know about Kṛṣṇa consciousness and about how to live as human beings we know because Śrīla Prabhupāda took the trouble to instruct us, day after day, minute after minute. He trained his disciples so that they could train others. This is *guru-paramparā.* Śrīla Prabhupāda: "What is the use of a lecture unless you train them?"[53]

If Kṛṣṇa sees that we are serious to look after the devotees that we have, he will send us many more new recruits to expand His movement more and more. All our temples should be dynamic centers where new people are coming all the time to discover the transcendental experience being imparted there.

WHY SO MANY RULES AND REGULATIONS?

All devotees, especially *brahmacārīs* and *sannyāsīs,* have to follow a set of rules and regulations that would surprise a materialist: rising before 4:00 a.m., attending services, bowing down before the Deities, and so on throughout the day. "It's brainwashing," the anti-cultists scream, "for weak-minded morons only." It's a fact—our minds are weak before Māyā, and following the rules and regulations of Kṛṣṇa consciousness protects us from her onslaught. The *Bhagavad-gītā* (2.64) describes that by following the regulative principles of freedom, one can control his senses and obtain the complete mercy of the Lord.

Beginners in Kṛṣṇa consciousness may have apprehensions about so many restrictions. Such neophytes need not be forced to follow all the subsidiary rules, but may be requested to simply chant, dance, take *prasāda,* and hear about Kṛṣṇa. Rūpa Gosvāmī advised that if somehow or other nondevotees can be brought to Kṛṣṇa consciousness, then all the rules and regulations can be introduced later.

To become successful in Kṛṣṇa consciousness, we must accept the devotional syllabus given by the previous *ācāryas.* Śrīla Prabhupāda: "No one can be situated in an exalted position without having undertaken a regulative life of rules and regulations."[54] When an aspiring devotee comes to realize this, he will happily take up the practice of Kṛṣṇa consciousness strictly. Forcing austerity on new and unwilling candidates is not a good policy. But those who have submitted themselves for initiation must be serious, otherwise their initiation is meaningless.

Śrīla Prabhupāda: "Kṛṣṇa consciousness is not difficult but determination is difficult. That determination comes by *tapasya* and therefore we have rules and regulations. If you follow the rules and regulations then you'll be determined, otherwise you will be a victim of *māyā,* The rules and regulations are there just to keep you fixed up in your determination. But if you don't follow then you fall down."[55]

SUBMISSION AND THE GURU-DISCIPLE RELATIONSHIP

"A student should practice completely controlling his senses. He should be submissive and should have an attitude of firm friendship for the spiritual master. With a great vow, the *brahmacārī* should live at the *gurukula,* only for the benefit of the guru."[56]

Traditionally, *brahmacārī* life begins when a young boy is sent to a *gurukula*. Dependence upon the guru is so intrinsic to *brahmacārī* life that one cannot properly be considered a *brahmacārī* unless he has accepted the shelter of a guru. Simply being celibate does not constitute *brahmacarya*.

In all the four *āśramas,* one must be submissive to the guru. But submission is especially practiced by *brahmacārīs.* In the Vedic tradition, *brahmacārīs* live with the guru and are subject to constant discipline. This is training in surrender—by serving the guru one learns the selfless service mood needed to approach Kṛṣṇa. The business of a *brahmacārī* is to work hard to please his spiritual master. Such service should be single-minded, without any thought of personal comfort or gain. A *brahmacārī* is meant for one-pointedly executing the order of his spiritual master, not doing whatever he likes, however he likes, whenever he likes.

"*Brahmacārī's* life means to serve the spiritual master as a menial servant. Whatever he asks, the *brahmacārī* will do."[57]

The *brahmacārī* is expected to be strongly attached to his guru. Before resting and on rising he offers his obeisances and prays to him. The guru is reciprocally conscientious in the discharge of his duties. Although not personally inclined to, the guru accepts the services of disciples so as to train and uplift them. Thus the guru has every right to ask any service of his disciples, particularly *brahmacārī* disciples (that he does not misuse this power is his qualification as guru). He asks his disciples, especially *brahmacārī* disciples, to sacrifice and be austere, but he himself is most prepared to sacrifice. And reciprocally he delivers Kṛṣṇa consciousness.

DETACHMENT, AUSTERITY, AND RENUNCIATION

"Of all the living entities who have accepted material bodies in this world, one who has been awarded this human form should not work hard day and night simply for sense gratification, which is available for the dogs and hogs that eat stool. One should engage in penance and austerity to attain the divine position of devotional service. By such activity, one's heart is purified, and when one attains this position, he attains eternal, blissful life, which is transcendental to material happiness and which continues forever."[58]

Human life is meant for self-realization. Self-realization can be developed only from the platform of detachment from everything material. Śrīla Prabhupāda describes detachment as one of the characteristics of ecstatic love:

"The senses are always desiring sense enjoyment, but when a devotee develops transcendental love for Kṛṣṇa, his senses are no longer attracted by material desires. This state of mind is called detachment. There is a nice example of this detachment in connection with the character of King Bharata. In the Fifth Canto, Fourteenth Chapter, Verse 43, of *Śrīmad-Bhāgavatam* it is stated, 'Emperor Bharata was so attracted by the beauty of the lotus feet of Kṛṣṇa that even in his youthful life he gave up all kinds of attachments to family, children, friends, kingdom, etc., as though they were untouchable stools.'

"Emperor Bharata provides a typical example of detachment. He had everything enjoyable in the world, but he left it. This means that detachment does not mean artificially keeping oneself aloof and apart from the allurements of attachment. Even in the presence of such allurements, if one can remain unattracted by material attachments, he is called detached. In the beginning, of course, a neophyte devotee must try to keep himself apart from all kinds of alluring attachments, but the real position of a mature devotee is that even in the presence of all allurements, he is not at all attracted. This is the actual criterion of detachment."[59]

To develop detachment, *tapasya* (austerity) and knowledge are necessary. "*Tapasya* (denial of material activities) is the first principle of spiritual life."[60] "If we purify our existence by *tapasya,* we can also do wonderful things by the grace of the Lord. Indeed, nothing is possible without *tapasya.* The more we engage in austerity the more we become powerful by the grace of the Lord."[61] "*Tapasya* means voluntary austerities performed for spiritual perfection."[62] "No one can become an advanced devotee without developing detachment, and to develop detachment, training in austerity is required. Voluntarily we have to accept things which may not be very comfortable for the body, but are conducive for self-realization. The *smṛti-śāstra* defines *tapasya* as 'complete control of the mind and senses for their complete concentration on one kind of activity.'"[63]

In civilized human life, three *āśramas* are meant purely for *tapasya.* Only in the *gṛhastha-āśrama* is a little sense enjoyment allowed. However, in Kali-yuga people cannot perform severe austerities as were practiced in bygone ages. Therefore Lord Caitanya has mercifully introduced His *saṅkīrtana* movement, which is transcendentally pleasing from the very beginning. Indeed, in Kali-yuga, if one overly stresses austerity without taking to *saṅkīrtana,* his heart simply becomes hard and dry, like that of a Māyāvādī. On the other hand, sense gratification must be given up. If one tries to enjoy transcendental bliss without a service mood, without discipline, and without giving up sense gratification, he becomes a *prākṛta sahajiyā*—an impostor.

Detachment is automatically acquired by performing devotional service.[64] So why are discipline and austerity necessary? The reason is that in the neophyte stage we are not fixed. Sometimes we feel like performing our devotional duties and sometimes we don't. But *sādhana-bhakti* means that we *must* follow. For instance, we may not feel like rising for *maṅgala-ārati.* But the stricture is there: we must get up. In this way the irrational mind is conquered. By submitting to the disciplinary process we are forced to do what is good for us, even if we don't feel like doing it.

Advanced devotees are spontaneously fixed in pure devotional service and don't need to accept austerity or discipline—although they usually do so anyway. But the vast majority of us are far below that level and should not foolishly think that we are free from *māyā's* attack. As soon as we think that we are safe, *māyā* will smash us. So better to be as strict as possible in performing devotional service.

After all, austerity cannot be avoided. The *karmīs* also have to undertake so many difficulties to maintain their standard of sense gratification. And the little austerity we do accept is insignificant compared to that of transcendentalists in previous ages, or even compared to many *sādhus* in India today. So if we find the austerities in devotional service difficult, we need not become disturbed. After all, the very meaning of austerity is "difficult."

Śrīla Prabhupāda: "There is undoubtedly trouble in executing penance. But the trouble accepted in executing *bhakti-yoga* is transcendental happiness from the very beginning, whereas the trouble of penance in other processes of self-realization (*jñāna-yoga, dhyāna-yoga,* etc.) without any Vaikuṇṭha realization, ends in trouble only and nothing more."[65]

Basic austerities for *brahmacārīs* are: following all the rules and regulations of devotional life (rising early, taking only *kṛṣṇa-prasāda,* etc.); dedicating all our time and energy to work hard in Kṛṣṇa's service;[66] living simply, accepting whatever living conditions are available without making elaborate arrangements for our comfort; living without sex and family life; and submitting to the order of the guru in all respects. Our whole life is austere: hard work, long hours, no pay, no privacy, no prestige, no sense gratification, and no holidays—pure bliss.

On top of this, we should try to minimize eating and sleeping. However, it is not our process to mortify the body as the yogis do. Artificial penances and austerities will not help. Sometimes devotees become enthusiastic to follow rigid observances for radically reducing eating and sleeping, but Śrīla Prabhupāda was more interested that his disciples accept the austerities involved in preaching than those of full Ekādaśī fasting, rigid Cāturmāsya observance, or concocted austerities. Sometimes devotees embark on a program of drastic reduction of eating and sleeping, but such endeavors usually end in a massive meal and a long sleep. Better to be regulated, steady, sensible, and patient. Attainment of perfection in Kṛṣṇa consciousness requires a sustained haul, not a passionate fling.

Austerities that do not help us to develop an attraction for Kṛṣṇa are simply a waste of time, no matter how painstakingly performed. *Śrama eva hi kevalam.*[67] Although the observance of certain austerities are required for those desiring success in devotional life, our movement is not puritanical. We stress the positive bliss of Kṛṣṇa consciousness more than the apparently negative aspect of having to undertake many difficulties.

"We are trying to give as much happiness to our students as possible. Otherwise, unless one is happy, it is a little difficult, unless one is very advanced in Kṛṣṇa consciousness. Therefore our policy is *'yogo bhavati siddhi.' 'Yuktāhāra-vihārasya yogo bhavati siddhi.'* We are yogis, but we are not that kind of yogi, unnecessarily giving trouble to the body. No. *Yuktāhāra.* You require to eat, and you eat. Don't starve. Don't unnecessarily fast. But don't eat voraciously. That is bad. That is not *yukta.* You eat, but don't eat voraciously. 'Because there is something very palatable, let me eat voraciously.' And then fall sick. And if you cannot digest, then you will sleep. You will sleep only. Therefore don't eat more, but eat whatever is necessary."[68]

Devotional service under the direction of a bona fide spiritual master is the only method of satisfying Kṛṣṇa; there is no mechanical means of attaining Kṛṣṇa consciousness. Although great advanced devotees like the six Gosvāmīs almost completely gave up eating and sleeping, we should not attempt to imitate them. After all, they were experiencing the highest transcendental bliss and were almost oblivious of their bodily condition. Śrīla Prabhupāda: "If we immediately try to become like Raghunātha dāsa Gosvāmī by imitating him, we are sure to fail, and whatever progress we have made will be defeated."[69]

DISCIPLINE

One should mold his life so as to always think of Kṛṣṇa. "Always think of Kṛṣṇa and never forget Him." Our whole life is dedicated to understanding Kṛṣṇa. Why then, can't we think of Kṛṣṇa? Because our consciousness is polluted. Our heads are full of all kinds of nonsense which blocks remembrance of Kṛṣṇa. These contaminations begin with sex desire. Śrīla Prabhupāda stated that if one can just get free from sex desire, he is 50% liberated.[70] As much as we are afflicted by sex desire, that much we cannot remember Kṛṣṇa. Until we completely reject sense gratification, physical and mental, once and for all, we will not be able to fix the intelligence.

Acts of sense gratification are preceded by desires and contemplation. Since these are functions of the mind, a *brahmacārī* is trained to control the mind by the intelligence. One whose intelligence remains controlled by his mind is no better than an animal or a child; nothing auspicious is possible for him. However, the mind is as difficult to control as the raging wind. Therefore, Śrīla Bhaktisiddhānta Sarasvatī Ṭhākura has advised us to discipline the rascal mind by beating it a hundred times in the morning with shoes, and a hundred times at night with a broom![71] As long as our intelligence is not completely fixed at the lotus feet of Kṛṣṇa, such stringent discipline is necessary.

The *brahmacārī* voluntarily agrees to be disciplined by the expert spiritual master. By his mercy, the impossible—controlling the mind and senses—becomes possible.

DETERMINATION

Without being fully determined, no one can hope to get free from sexual bondage. "*Māyā* is so strong that unless one is determined not to fall victim, even the Supreme Personality of Godhead cannot give protection."[72]

Especially for one who has not been trained from childhood, to follow the eight aspects of celibacy may seem almost impossible. But it is possible, as stated by the greatest *brahmacārī,* Nārada Muni, in the *Śrīmad-Bhāgavatam* (7.15.22): "By making plans with determination, one should give up lusty desires for sense gratification." In the purport Śrīla Prabhupāda writes: "Śrīla Viśvanātha Cakravartī has suggested how one can conquer lusty desires for sense gratification. One cannot give up thinking of women, for thinking in this way is natural; even while walking on the streets one will see so many women. However, if one is determined not to live with a woman, even while seeing a woman he will not become lusty. If one is determined not to have sex, he can automatically conquer lusty desires. An example given in this regard is that even if one is hungry, if on that particular day he has decided to observe fasting, he can naturally conquer the disturbances of hunger and thirst."

HIGHER TASTE

We have to be determined to maintain our celibacy, but how do we maintain our determination? A philosophical understanding of the miseries of material life will certainly help us, but is not in itself a guarantee of safety from fall down. We have seen even philosophically competent devotees slip away. Especially in Kali-yuga, unless one develops a sense of *bhakti,* satisfaction within celibacy is almost impossible. As parts and parcels of Kṛṣṇa, the Supreme Enjoyer, we have the pleasure-seeking propensity *(ānandamayo 'bhyāsāt).*[73] Unless we get some real taste from our devotional service, we will be attracted to material enjoyment.

Often, newly surrendered devotees get a rush of Kṛṣṇa conscious bliss. Kṛṣṇa gives them a strong dose of nectar to make their commitment solid. But after some time the bliss doesn't come automatically; you have to work for it. Even advanced devotees must constantly re-apply themselves to the surrendering process. Then Kṛṣṇa will bless them, and they will never think of going away.

However, if we perform devotional service with our own pleasure in mind, we will never be able to achieve it. As parts and parcels of Kṛṣṇa, we can only be satisfied by satisfying Him, as much as the limbs of the body become satisfied by satisfying the stomach. We simply have to hear and chant the names of Kṛṣṇa, and surrender to Him, willingly undertaking all difficulties in His service. Then, when He is satisfied with us, He will make us happy.

Kṛṣṇa consciousness is a happy movement. Enthusiastic devotees taste bliss at every moment. And for exalted devotees who are actually experiencing the unlimited transcendental happiness of advanced Kṛṣṇa consciousness, the so-called pleasure of mundane sex enjoyment seems no more significant than straw in the street. Most of us are unfortunately not so elevated, but at least we have all at some time tasted some drops of bliss and had a tiny insight into what it would be like if we were actually Kṛṣṇa conscious.

So if we are suffering from an attack from *māyā,* are feeling down and out, and are not very enthusiastic to serve, we can reflect back on better times in Kṛṣṇa consciousness, when Kṛṣṇa revealed a little of His mercy to us and we were moved to tears or to jump up and down in ecstasy. We have to go on searching for that nectar. If we go back to the process—chant Hare Kṛṣṇa, dance for Kṛṣṇa, take Kṛṣṇa *prasāda,* hear about Kṛṣṇa, do some service—we will become happy. Devotional service is non-different from Kṛṣṇa, and Kṛṣṇa is the reservoir of all pleasure. *Uttiṣṭha jāgrata prāpya varān nibodhata:* "Wake up from the sleep of *māyā* and attain the boon of eternal nectarean life."[74]

ASSOCIATION

Good association is essential to help maintain the determination necessary for making strong progress in spiritual life. On the other hand, bad association can easily and quickly destroy whatever spiritual development we have made. Throughout his books Śrīla Prabhupāda again and again stresses the need for proper association. A few quotes:

"Without the association (of persons who are Kṛṣṇa conscious and engaged in devotional service) one cannot make advancement. Simply by theoretical knowledge or study one cannot make any appreciable advancement. One must give up the association of materialistic persons and seek the association of devotees because without the association of devotees one cannot understand the activities of the Lord... Association with devotees means association with the Lord. The devotee who takes this association develops the consciousness of rendering service to the

Lord and then, being situated in the transcendental position of devotional service, he gradually becomes perfect."[75]

"One should not associate with a coarse fool who is bereft of all knowledge of self-realization and who is no more than a dancing dog in the hands of a woman. The restriction of association with such foolish persons is especially meant for those who are in the line of advancement in Kṛṣṇa consciousness.

"If one associates with a *śūdra,* a foolish person who is like a dancing dog in the hands of a woman, then he cannot make any progress. Lord Caitanya has advised that any person who is engaged in Kṛṣṇa consciousness and who desires to pass beyond material nescience must not associate himself with women or with persons interested in material enjoyment. For a person seeking advancement in Kṛṣṇa consciousness, such association is more dangerous than suicide."[76]

"Realization of the Lord is possible only in the association of devotees."[77]

"Dhruva Mahārāja said: 'O unlimited Lord, kindly bless me so that I may associate with great devotees who engage in your transcendental service constantly, as the waves of the river constantly flow.' The significant point in Dhruva Mahārāja's statement is that he wanted the association of pure devotees. Transcendental devotional service cannot be complete and cannot be relishable without the association of devotees. We have therefore established the International Society for Krishna Consciousness. Anyone who is trying to be aloof from this Kṛṣṇa Consciousness Society and yet engage in Kṛṣṇa consciousness is living in a great hallucination, for this is not possible. From this statement by Dhruva Mahārāja it is clear that unless one is associated with devotees, his devotional service does not mature; it does not become distinct from material activities. Only in the association of pure devotees can the words of Lord Kṛṣṇa be fully potent and relishable to the heart and ear. Devotional service in the association of devotees is the cause of the development of further devotional service. It is possible to mature in devotional service only in the association of devotees."[78]

A single twig can easily be broken, but many twigs bundled together become impossible to break. We want to become Kṛṣṇa conscious, but in our heart there are still many mundane desires. We all need help to make advancement. By associating with enthusiastic devotees we can help each other nourish our desires for Kṛṣṇa consciousness. Strong association creates a strong atmosphere.

Therefore even in associating with devotees, strict *brahmacārīs* must be selective. Those who want to remain strong *brahmacārīs* must associate with those who are very serious about spiritual life, whose association encourages and inspires remaining purely on the spiritual platform. The best association for *brahmacārīs* is with *sannyāsīs* or senior *brahmacārīs,* with those who are convinced of the necessity of living separately from women. If a *gṛhastha* or even a so-called *brahmacārī* is loose ("loose" means not committed to Kṛṣṇa consciousness, not following strict *sādhana,* not following the regulative principles, or often talking *prajalpa* or mixing freely with women), his association should be avoided by serious *brahmacārīs*.

Serious *brahmacārīs* should also be careful of associating with devotees whose philosophical understanding of Kṛṣṇa consciousness is different from that taught by Śrīla Prabhupāda, or who have a tendency to be "political." It is best for *brahmacārīs* to remain simple, pure, and aloof from politics and chronic complainers. Remaining respectful and polite, they should rather seek the association of well-situated devotees, whatever *āśrama* they may be in.

Everyone is looking for *rasa* ("juice") in their relationships. A real *brahmacārī* does not identify himself materially as a man, but as an eternal servant of Lord Kṛṣṇa. A man needs a woman, but a servant of the Lord needs the Lord. Therefore a committed *brahmacārī* stays in the association of devotees and experiences taste in spiritual relationships. He does not try to enjoy material relationships. By serving together, encouraging and checking each other, and providing help in times of spiritual crisis, devotees build solid friendships based on Kṛṣṇa consciousness—unlike materialistic friendships that are based on sense gratification. This is real friendship, perhaps for the first time in many lifetimes. If a *brahmacārī* does not get such *rasa* in his relationships with devotees, he will tend to look for it amongst women and *karmīs*.

However, devotees are often intense, and living with them can be austere and hard on the false ego. This is especially so for *brahmacārīs,* who have less independence, and are expected to surrender more than, the members of any other *āśrama*. New devotees in particular may find it hard to adjust to a new lifestyle. And because of their lack of training, they may sometimes act or speak improperly, and need to be corrected. But despite all difficulties, *brahmacārīs* should resolve to stick to the path. Better take the knocks of the *brahmacārī-āśrama* than the much harder knocks of life outside of Kṛṣṇa consciousness or of married life within Kṛṣṇa consciousness. If you a need a break, take shelter of the holy name, Śrīla Prabhupāda's books, and Kṛṣṇa *prasāda*. Don't go outside.

The best association is to be found within the International Society for Krishna Consciousness. There are many Vaiṣṇava societies in the world, but ISKCON is Śrīla Prabhupāda's movement. Śrīla Prabhupāda was especially benedicted by Lord Caitanya to fulfill His preaching mission, and ISKCON is the special movement meant for receiving and distributing Lord Caitanya's mercy.

In this preaching movement, by the pressure of practical necessity, devotees are forced to work hard, cooperate, and surrender. Sometimes devotees make mistakes or may not seem very sophisticated, but we should know that they are being purified in the fire of *saṅkīrtana* and that we will be too, if we remain sincere and stick with the devotees.

Sometimes junior devotees may be living in the same temple with senior devotees and would like to take their association (which they so much need to help them in their spiritual development) but are hesitant to do so, thinking that such senior devotees will not like to be disturbed by them. But actually the opposite is true. If approached in a proper and respectful way, any senior Vaiṣṇava will happily give direction and advice. Indeed, it is the duty of senior devotees to help junior devotees advance. Bhaktivinoda Ṭhākura advises that one become the dog of a Vaiṣṇava. Just as a puppy dog eagerly tries to take shelter of a master, so we should not be shy in approaching Vaiṣṇavas to take their association. We should not be overly familiar with Vaiṣṇavas senior to us, but should approach them with submissive inquiry and should offer to render some service to such Vaiṣṇavas. This is the process for receiving spiritual knowledge given by Lord Kṛṣṇa in *Bhagavad-gītā* (4.34).

A practical point regarding association is that, as far as possible, a *brahmacārī* should never be alone, but should always be in the association of other devotees (preferably also *brahmacārīs).* In the Madhva-*sampradāya, brahmacārīs* going outside the *āśrama* are supposed to do so in groups of at least four, to give each other association and protection. It is especially dangerous and improper for *brahmacārīs* to go anywhere alone without taking permission from (or if they be more senior *brahmacārīs*, without at least informing) their authorities. For a *brahmacārī* to go anywhere alone in *karmī* dress is particularly jeopardous and should not be encouraged or allowed except in extraordinary circumstances.

SIMPLICITY

"Our life is simple. We do not want luxury."[79] Simplicity, mental and external, is the hallmark of a *brahmacārī.* He does not accumulate possessions, but keeps only what he needs. He certainly does not have a personal bank account. Whatever he has, he considers to be his guru's property, not his own. Śrīla Bhaktisiddhānta Sarasvatī Ṭhākura said that *saralatā* (simplicity) is the first qualification of a Vaiṣṇava.[80] If a *brahmacārī* feels attracted to accumulating possessions and opulent life, it is not a good sign for his spiritual advancement. Nevertheless, if he wants such things, he can marry, earn money, and buy whatever his wife allows him to. But as long as he is in the *brahmacārī-āśrama* he should live and dress simply.

Śrīla Prabhupāda: "For a devotee to be satisfied with the bare necessities is the best advice for spiritual advancement."[81] "A *brahmacārī* factually has no needs."[82]

Brahmacārīs should be satisfied with whatever comes to them of its own accord and should not make arrangements for comfortable living. They should be wary of material opulence, even if it comes to them without endeavor.

Brahmacārīs are supposed to be simple and renounced, so it is not proper for them to accumulate money beyond their immediate needs. Even if a *brahmacārī* is collecting much *lakṣmī,* he shouldn't want to, or feel that he has a right to, spend it on unnecessary purchases for himself. For a *brahmacārī* to have a large sum of money without a specific Kṛṣṇa conscious purpose, or to keep savings, is antithetical to the *brahmacārī* ethic. It is also dangerous, for to keep money without using it for Kṛṣṇa is Rāvaṇa's policy and leads to fall down. The proper standard for *brahmacārīs* is to give all money that comes their way to the temple.

In this way a *brahmacārī's* mind can remain uncluttered. He has only one interest in life: service to guru and Kṛṣṇa. He does not have family responsibilities to worry about, nor is he involved in cliques or political factions. His clear mind is a potent breeding ground for Kṛṣṇa consciousness. Referring to *gurukula,* Śrīla Prabhupāda once said, "Simple, honest, *brahmacārī brāhmaṇas;* that is what I want."[83]

SĀDHANA

"My dear Arjuna, O winner of wealth, if you cannot fix your mind upon Me without deviation, then follow the regulative principles of *bhakti-yoga.* In this way develop a desire to attain Me."[84]

Good *sādhana* is the basis of steady advancement in Kṛṣṇa consciousness. *Brahmacārī* life is traditionally centered around *sādhana:* chanting mantras, studying the scriptures, and worship.

Śrīla Prabhupāda gave us a standard morning program of *maṅgala-ārati, tulasī-ārati,* Deity greeting, *guru-pūjā,* and *Śrīmad-*

Bhāgavatam class; and an evening program of *tulasī-ārati, sandhyā-ārati,* and *Bhagavad-gītā* class—plus of course chanting at least sixteen rounds of the Hare Kṛṣṇa *mahā-mantra.* If we strictly follow this schedule with faith and enthusiasm, we will always remain enlivened in Kṛṣṇa consciousness.

So devotees should get off the mental platform and get right into the program. Don't just stand around in *kīrtana*—dance nicely for the pleasure of the Lord. Don't slur sixteen rounds—pray to the Holy Name. Tune into class with mind and ears open. There is so much nectar in hearing and chanting about Kṛṣṇa that Kṛṣṇa Himself comes as Lord Caitanya to relish that *rasa.* But we have to apply ourselves to become eligible to get that taste. We have to actually take that one step, and then Kṛṣṇa will take His hundred toward us.

Good *sādhana* means to attend the whole morning program every single day without fail, rising by 4:00 a.m. at the latest, being present at every function (*guru-pūjā*, class, etc.) from the beginning to the end (not wandering in late or wandering out early), to chant all or most of one's prescribed rounds during the morning program, and to be enthusiastic and attentive throughout. A good morning program gives us spiritual strength to carry out our Kṛṣṇa conscious duties throughout the day.

Devotees who are conscientious about the morning program gradually develop strength and depth in Kṛṣṇa consciousness; but those who, for whatever reason, decrease their inclination toward early morning hearing and chanting, gradually become weakened and susceptible to *māyā's* attack. Certainly, those not committed to rising early and strong *sādhana* cannot remain as *brahmacārīs,* nor should such persons be allowed to live in the *brahmacārī-āśrama.*

Śrīla Prabhupāda also wanted devotees to attend the evening program, or to utilize the evening hours for preaching engagements.

Some adjustments may be necessary for *pūjārīs,* cooks, and traveling preachers, but we must be careful not to become lax in, or get insufficient, hearing and chanting. If we are obliged to miss a part of the morning or evening *sādhana* programs, we must set some time aside at another time of the day to make up. Best for cooks and *pūjārīs* is to rise very early and chant *japa* before *maṅgala-ārati.*

If devotees feel weak in Kṛṣṇa consciousness, with decreased enthusiasm for devotional service and an increase in material desires, the root cause is usually poor hearing and chanting. How to get the enthusiasm back? Just by acting enthusiastically, enthusiasm comes. Just try jumping in *kīrtana,* even mechanically, and see if you can stay morose. Śrīla Prabhupāda: "Dance. Even if there is no ecstasy, dance and it will come."[85]

Reading and attentive *japa* are extremely important. *Japa* should be chanted clearly and properly heard. And *brahmacārīs* must find time to read. *Bhagavad-gītā* (16.1) states that *svādhyāya,* study of the scriptures, is especially meant for *brahmacārīs.* Therefore *brahmacārīs* should assiduously study Śrīla Prabhupāda's books and other authorized Kṛṣṇa conscious literature, and avoid reading useless *karmī* or Māyāvādī rubbish. Reading Śrīla Prabhupāda's books helps attach us to Kṛṣṇa and free us from *māyā.*

Māyā is always trying to take away our enthusiasm, and often attacks devotees in the form of doubt. Doubt is a disease which can culminate in spiritual death.[86] Many devotees, especially new devotees, despite going on with the Kṛṣṇa conscious process, are not fully convinced of what they are doing. For them Kṛṣṇa recommends: "The doubts which have arisen in your heart out of ignorance should be slashed with the weapon of knowledge."[87] Hearing *kṛṣṇa-kathā* is *bhavauṣadhi,* the medicine for the disease of material life.[88]

Without reading Śrīla Prabhupāda's books, how will we maintain the firm conviction needed to voluntarily undertake the austerities necessary for self-realization? "All the devotees connected with the Kṛṣṇa consciousness movement must read all the books that have been translated; otherwise they will simply eat, sleep, and fall down from their position. Thus they will miss the opportunity to attain an eternal blissful life of transcendental pleasure."[89]

Śrīla Prabhupāda recommended that those who want to be *gosvāmīs* (masters of the senses) should carefully study *The Nectar of Instruction;* therefore *brahmacārīs* can obviously benefit from the advice given therein.

About *japa* Śrīla Prabhupāda has written: "Of all the regulative principles, the spiritual master's order to chant at least sixteen rounds is most essential."[90] Satsvarūpa dāsa Gosvāmī has compiled a *Japa Reform Notebook* and *Reading Reform Notebook* to help devotees develop good *japa* and reading habits.

REGULATION

Regulation means to do the same thing at the same time every day, or if not at exactly the same time, at least in a fixed sequence based around an approximate schedule. For instance, a devotee may be regulated to rise by 3.30 a.m., bathe, and chant a few rounds before *maṅgala-ārati*, to eat his main meal at midday, and so on. Such regulation helps to fix the determination and to get off the mental platform. A devotee with a fixed time to rise does not think, "I'm too tired," or "It's too cold." He just gets up. He does not have to think what to do next; he just sticks to his schedule.

Regulation helps to keep the mind peaceful and makes for the most efficient use of time. Without regulation, life tends to become chaotic. Most importantly, regulation is the basis of steady *sādhana.* Without regulation, proper *sādhana* is impossible. For physical health also, it is good to sleep and rise, eat, evacuate, and shower at fixed times every day.

In our temples, devotional programs and *prasāda* timings are fixed; so if we simply follow the temple programs and take *prasāda* with the devotees, that much we will automatically be regulated.

It is more difficult to be regulated when traveling, but it is possible. Śrīla Prabhupāda followed a regulated schedule, despite constant travel.

ENGAGEMENT

A pure devotee of Kṛṣṇa is satisfied to do any service for Kṛṣṇa, however menial it may appear to be. The *brahmacārī* is trained like that—to do whatever is asked of him. Even if he is highly qualified, a *brahmacārī* is always ready and willing to do the needful in Kṛṣṇa's service, including all kinds of humble services. The ideal *brahmacārī* performs all kinds of services quickly, efficiently, and cheerfully.

In the traditional *gurukula* system, young children are strictly disciplined. As they grow older, the guru engages them according to the propensities he has observed in them. Similarly, when a young man joins ISKCON, ideally he will take up any service he is asked to do. (Śrīla Bhaktisiddhānta Sarasvatī Ṭhākura would have new men wash pots, even if they were highly educated, just to test their sincerity.) But after some time, if he is not suitably engaged according to his psychophysical propensities, he may become dissatisfied. Indeed, if a *brahmacārī* is not absorbed in a devotional engagement, he will soon end up with another engagement that will keep him fully busy for many years—namely, a marriage engagement.

Begging for the guru is a traditional duty of *brahmacārīs*. "A *brahmacārī* is trained up from the very beginning how to become a *sannyāsī* at the end of life. He is trained up by collecting alms for the guru."[91]

Fund raising for temple projects and maintenance is not the same as traditional *brahmacārī* begging, and some devotees opine that *brahmacārīs* should not be engaged thus. However, Śrīla Prabhupāda personally engaged *brahmacārīs* in collecting large sums of money. By begging alms, a *brahmacārī* learns humility. By offering all he collects to the guru, he fortifies the mood of slavery to the spiritual master. He practices sacrifice and detachment, and practically applies the maxim that "nothing belongs to me."

Although traditional-style begging is not always practical in the modern world, the ISKCON *brahmacārī's* alms collecting has been dovetailed with preaching through the most ingenious transcendental plan ever devised: book distribution.

By book distribution, the spiritual master, Lord Caitanya, Kṛṣṇa, and the whole *paramparā* are satisfied. The *karmīs* are benedicted, the book distributor is blessed, the Kṛṣṇa consciousness movement expands, and *lakṣmī* is liberated for Kṛṣṇa's service. Book distribution is the ideal service for a *brahmacārī.* Once when it was suggested that a leading *brahmacārī* book distributor be awarded *sannyāsa,* Śrīla Prabhupāda replied that it was not necessary because "He is doing more than any *sannyāsī* by personally distributing hundreds of books day after day and inspiring others to follow."[92]

"Book distribution is definitely excellent training. One remains detached from material life by constantly seeing the temporary, miserable nature of the material world, while at the same time developing his faith in Kṛṣṇa consciousness by daily witnessing the extraordinary mercy of Lord Caitanya upon the fallen conditioned souls. And by having to defeat opposing arguments and convince others to take up spiritual life, one becomes a capable preacher." (Indradyumna Swami)

To go on a *saṅkīrtana* party is a great fortune for a *brahmacārī.* It is an intense, one-pointed mission—to pass out as many of Śrīla Prabhupāda's books as possible to the conditioned souls, day after day, week after week, month after month, year after year. Such highly surrendered *saṅkīrtana* soldiers become powerful in austerity and concentration, and develop a solid, fixed-up foundation in Kṛṣṇa consciousness. It is recommended that new devotees in Kṛṣṇa consciousness spend at least their first two to four years in the movement engaged in *saṅkīrtana,* especially traveling *saṅkīrtana.* Whatever they may do after that, their standing in Kṛṣṇa consciousness will have been fixed, and it will help them to go on remembering Kṛṣṇa throughout their lives.

However, not every *brahmacārī* will go daily for book distribution. Some devotees just won't be able to adjust to it. But that is not a disqualification; there are plenty of other services that devotees can be happily engaged in. For instance, Śrīla Prabhupāda wrote, "*Brahmaṇa brahmacārīs* are very nice for Deity worship."[93]

But if *brahmacārīs* can preach, that is best. Preaching gives a taste and realization in Kṛṣṇa consciousness which *brahmacārīs* especially need to maintain the high level of renunciation which their *āśrama* requires. Ultimately, every service is preaching, because the whole Kṛṣṇa consciousness movement is meant for preaching. But book distribution, *harināma saṅkīrtana*, college programs, and so on bring us directly into contact with nondevotees, giving them Kṛṣṇa consciousness. This enables us to directly experience the shower of Lord Caitanya's mercy.

No one should get a superiority complex, however, for pride comes before a fall. It is not necessarily true that a *brahmacārī* out distributing books is more advanced than another staying back cleaning the floor. In the absolute sense, all services are equal. Kṛṣṇa accepts the service attitude of the devotee, not exactly the service externally performed.

Brahmacārīs are engaged in service by the guru or his representative. A sensitive guru or temple president will deal personally with the *brahmacārī* under his command, understanding that all are on different levels of advancement and surrender. Junior devotees especially need encouragement and guidance. Ours is a pushing movement, so pressure must be there. But the best leaders inspire enthusiasm in their followers. Force will not always stand. It is better to command respect rather than demand it.

As much as possible, *brahmacārīs* should be engaged so as to have as little dealings with women as possible. Outside of India, service in temple management brings *brahmacārīs* in contact with women in such a way that their *brahmacārī* principles are almost always compromised. Similarly, business is not at all a suitable engagement for *brahmacārīs.* Wheeling and dealing breeds the profit/loss mentality and makes for materialistic dealings with nondevotees and women. Devotees who get into moneymaking too often end up selling their souls. If anyone has to do business, let the *gṛhasthas* do it.

Ultimately, whatever engagement we are awarded, we can be happy to get the chance to do something for Kṛṣṇa. Devotional service is, after all, a privilege—it's not that we have anything wonderful to offer to Kṛṣṇa. But one way or another we have to keep busy in Kṛṣṇa's service, for an idle mind is the devil's workshop. There is always something to do. If not, a devotee should find something to do. He can help another devotee, read, chant, learn a *śloka,* or whatever. Devotees: do not be dull. Keep busy! Be alert! Be alive! Be Kṛṣṇa conscious! Keeping busy with mind, body, and words in Kṛṣṇa's service is the sure way to keep out of *māyā.*

PREACHING

Attack is the best means of defense, and the most effective weapon against *māyā* is the preaching of Kṛṣṇa consciousness. By preaching, we not only strike against the *māyā* all around but also cleanse our hearts of the *māyā* within. "If one is not interested in preaching, talking constantly to nondevotees, the influence of the modes of nature is very difficult to surpass."[94] Śrīla Prabhupāda: "For those who engage in the preaching of these two Vedic literatures (*Bhagavad-gītā* and *Śrīmad-Bhāgavatam*) it is very easy to get out of the illusory conditioned life imposed on us by *māyā.*"[95]

So, *brahmacārīs,* get into the preaching mood. Preach to the *karmīs,* preach to the devotees, preach to yourself, preach to the walls. If we always think of how to spread this Kṛṣṇa consciousness movement, Lord Caitanya will surely protect us.

Śrīla Prabhupāda: "This Kṛṣṇa consciousness movement means preaching. Without preaching, one can have no taste. And without taste, you won't be able to go on with this Hari Hari Bol. If you don't preach, in a few years after I leave, there will be no more Hare Kṛṣṇa movement. Because no one is preaching in the churches, they are all closing up. So why don't you get serious about this preaching work? Practically speaking, my Guru Mahārāja has invented this movement for that purpose. My ambition is that you make a revolution against this godless society. That is my mission. That is why I continue on, even at this advanced age. We want to guide everyone. So you have to know my books. Read and preach—both things must be there—then you will have potency. Preaching means fighting."[96]

TRAVELING

Traveling and preaching in the association of *brahmacārīs* and *sannyāsīs* is a wonderful life. Detachment, dependence on Kṛṣṇa, simple living and high thinking, self-reliance, transcendental adventure, variety, gaining of experience, fun—it's all included in the package. A rolling stone gathers no moss—there is no question of developing relationships with women for a man on the move. A traveling *saṅkīrtana brahmacārī* will not even know the names of the *brahmacāriṇīs* in the temple, let alone what they look like. He won't be accumulating possessions either—how much can you keep in a nylon kit bag?

Śrīla Prabhupāda: "*Brahmacārīs* and *sannyāsīs* are meant for moving."[97] "For spiritually inclined persons, traveling is very good. You'll be more popular and there will be no difficulty; the mind will be steady."[98]

HEALTH

"The highest goal of life can be achieved as long as one's body is stout and strong. We should therefore live in such a way that we keep ourselves always healthy and strong in mind and intelligence so that we can distinguish the goal of life from a life full of problems."[99]

Brahmacarya is itself the best tonic for health. As Dhanvantari told his disciples, "*Brahmacarya* is truly a precious gem. It is the most effective medicine. It is nectar that destroys diseases, decay, and death. For attaining peace, luster, memory, knowledge, health, and self-realization, one should observe *brahmacarya*. *Brahmacarya* is the highest dharma, the highest knowledge, the greatest strength." Therefore, "A *brahmacārī* should not have any complaint of bodily disease."[100]

Health has become a special problem for the present generation, however, brought up as we were in junk-food ignorance and self-destructive indulgence. Some devotees respond to their health problems by neglect, hardly caring for the condition of their bodies. But this is akin to the Māyāvādī attitude that "I am not this body, and I have nothing to do with it." The Vaiṣṇava thinks, "This body is not mine. It belongs to Kṛṣṇa, and I have to serve Kṛṣṇa with it. It must be kept fit enough to serve Kṛṣṇa."

Śrīla Prabhupāda was concerned that his disciples maintain good health, and would often give detailed advice on diet and medication. He would sign off his letters, "Hoping this meets you in good health," because this body is meant for serving Kṛṣṇa. Therefore, "For the Vaiṣṇava, the protection of the body for the service of the Lord is a part of devotional service."[101] As servants of Kṛṣṇa, we must see to our health without falling into the trap of becoming overly preoccupied with the physical at the expense of proper spiritual culture and development.

A balanced approach is needed. Devotees should have a basic knowledge of practical health care, should live and eat sensibly (taking regular temple *prasāda* at scheduled times), and should go on with devotional service, making whatever adjustments are necessary to maintain proper health. They should avoid being influenced by health food fads, unnecessary special diets, or speculative *karmī* infatuations with health.

Śrīla Prabhupāda: "A devotee should accept only those things that are favorable to keep his body and soul together and should reject those things that increase the demands of the body. Only the bare necessities for bodily maintenance should be accepted. By minimizing bodily necessities, one can primarily devote his time to the cultivation of Kṛṣṇa consciousness through the chanting of the holy names of God."[102] "There is no possibility of one's becoming a yogi if one eats too much or eats too little, sleeps too much or does not sleep enough. He who is temperate in his habits of eating, sleeping, recreation and work can mitigate all material pains by practicing the yoga system."[103]

Eating

According to Śrīla Prabhupāda, sickness is usually caused by overeating, uncleanness, and/or anxiety. Excess eating is the root cause of dozens of diseases. It also leads to excess sleeping, which is another obstacle to progressive devotional life. Overeating can refer to quality as well as quantity, for to regularly ingest rich foods is not good for health, what to speak of being unsuitable for *brahmacārīs.* "Disturbances from various diseases can be avoided by regulated diets."[104]

Śrīla Prabhupāda discusses the importance of controlling the tongue in *brahmacarya* as follows.

"In the *bhakti-mārga*, the path of devotional service, one must strictly follow the regulative principles by first controlling the tongue *(sevonmukhe hi jihvādau svayam eva sphuraty adaḥ).* The tongue *(jihvā)* can be controlled if one chants the Hare Kṛṣṇa *mahā-mantra*, does not speak of any subjects other than those concerning Kṛṣṇa and does not taste anything not offered to Kṛṣṇa. If one can control the tongue in this way, *brahmacarya* and other purifying processes will automatically follow."[105]

Traditionally, *brahmacārīs* are meant to be austere, especially in eating. Eating too much, or eating rich or heavy foods (i.e., foods with a high percentage of protein, butterfat, oil, or sugar, including honey, dried fruits and nuts), and very spicy food, make the senses strong and difficult to control. Everyone can practically experience this. Therefore such foods should be taken in small quantities only. Śrīla Prabhupāda: "Devotees should eat as simply as possible. Otherwise, attachment for material things will gradually increase, and the senses, being very strong, will soon require more and more material enjoyment. Then the real business of life—to advance in Kṛṣṇa consciousness—will stop."[106] "Especially for a devotee, too much eating is very, very bad."[107]

Milk is an important food for devotees. ("Milk means cow's milk."[108]) Milk nourishes the brain tissues which help one to understand spiritual knowledge. "One should take ample milk, and thus one can prolong one's life, develop his brain, execute devotional service, and ultimately gain the favor of the Supreme Personality of Godhead."[109] "We have to make our brain very clean and for that we require to drink, not very much, one pound or half a pound of milk daily. That is essential."[110] Milk should be drunk very hot and slightly sweetened so as to be easily digested and beneficial to the brain. Taking too much milk is not good, though. When Śrīla Prabhupāda was told that some devotees drank lots of milk with the intention of increasing their brain power, Śrīla Prabhupāda said that drinking excess milk is *rājasika*.[111]

"The eating program should be nutritious and simple, not luxurious. That means *chapātīs*, *dāl*, vegetables, some butter, some fruits, and milk. This is necessary for keeping good health. But we should not indulge in sweetballs or *halava* or like that daily. Too much first-class eating may stimulate our sex desires, especially sweet preparations. Anyway, eat Kṛṣṇa *prasāda,* but be careful that we may not indulge in luxury. For Kṛṣṇa we can offer the most beautiful preparations, but for us *prasāda* should be very simple."[112]

"Eating should be minimized. Too much eating leads to too much sleeping, and then sex desire."[113]

Some devotees lament their inability to control the tongue while taking *prasāda.* But there is no reason for disappointment. By following the vow of taking only Kṛṣṇa *prasāda,* the tongue is already controlled inasmuch as it is restrained from all nonsense foods. And if we simply continue patiently with our devotional service, the tendency to overeat will automatically be overcome in course of time. Kṛṣṇa will help us.

Overeating of *prasāda* is not always a great vice, anyway. After all, Kṛṣṇa consciousness is "the kitchen religion." As *brahmacārīs,* we must try to control, but as devotees we know that it's better to take ten times too much *prasāda* rather than eat just the right amount of *bhoga*. Sometimes, in a festive mood, devotees even encourage each other to eat more and more. Even Lord Caitanya was doing that. In devotional service there is both austerity and festivity, and knowing when and how to apply them without being caught in *niyamāgrahaḥ*[114] is an art to be learned by devotees.

(Once in South India Śrīla Prabhupāda was going to take *prasāda* in a Life Member's home. But Pradyumna, Śrīla Prabhupāda's Sanskrit assistant, refused to eat on the plea of fasting. Śrīla Prabhupāda said that his fasting was whimsical.[115])

Our gurus, the six Gosvāmīs of Vṛndāvana, ate next to nothing. They were so absorbed in serving Rādhā-Kṛṣṇa that they practically forgot to eat or sleep. There is no question of our imitating these great *ācāryas*. We simply have to follow in their footsteps by faithfully executing devotional service according to their instructions. (For more on eating and diet see the section on "Retention of Semen.")

Sleeping

Sleeping is a condition of the mode of ignorance; therefore devotees try to minimize it as far as possible. "One should not sleep more than six hours daily. One who sleeps more than six hours out of twenty-four is certainly influenced by the mode of ignorance."[116] "A Kṛṣṇa conscious person is always alert in the discharge of his duties in Kṛṣṇa consciousness, and therefore any unnecessary time spent sleeping is considered a great loss. A Kṛṣṇa conscious person cannot bear to pass a minute of his life without being engaged in the service of the Lord. Therefore his sleeping is kept to a minimum."[117] "By spiritual culture one is able to conquer sleep."[118]

Some devotees may be able to get by on five hours of sleep a day or less; some need six hours or more. Regulation—rising and resting at fixed times—helps to control sleep. Generally, one should sleep no more than six hours at a stretch. Day-time sleeping is traditionally not allowed for *brahmacārīs*, and should be minimized as much as possible. Rising before 4:00 a.m. is a must (Śrīla Prabhupāda insisted). Napping during the morning program should be avoided as much as possible, for that is when we need to be widest awake, to absorb transcendental sound. Splashing the face with cold water is advised for devotees who feel sleepy during the morning program.

To want to work hard, putting in long hours in Kṛṣṇa's service, is good. But remember, eighteen wide-awake hours are better than twenty hours half awake. (Drivers especially note: don't drive if tired!) Those who find themselves regularly struggling through the morning program should probably arrange to take rest earlier at night, or if that is not possible, to take a little rest in the day.

Sleeping in a secluded place is not good, especially for neophyte devotees. Like eating alone, the tendency is to take it as sense gratification and overdo it. Before and after sleeping, offer obeisances to your spiritual master, remembering that the purpose of rest is only to recuperate energy for serving him. And on rising, remember to roll up your bedding and put it away tidily.

It is best for *brahmacārīs* to sleep on a thin mat, not a mattress. In India, grass sleeping mats are available, and in the West, synthetic rubber or foam. The latter also help to keep out the cold from the floor. In India in winter, a mattress may be required to serve the same purpose. Those who suffer from bodily pain may also require a mattress. Mattresses should be thin. Thick, luxury mattresses are not meant for *brahmacārīs*.

(More on sleeping in the section "Retention of Semen.")

Exercise

Śrīla Prabhupāda was not much in favor of exercise, but he was not wholly against it either. He said that swimming, wrestling, and pushups are suitable forms of exercise for *brahmacārīs*. So if devotees feel the need for a few minutes of exercise daily, there should be no objection. One's need for exercise varies greatly in terms of age, health, and proclivity. But in general, if devotees are physically active, they should not need an elaborate exercise program. Dancing in *kīrtana* and walking while chanting *japa* automatically exercise the body, even without thinking about it. Devotees are advised to exercise moderately; otherwise bodily consciousness will increase. Listening to a Śrīla Prabhupāda *bhajana* or lecture cassette while exercising will help keep us on the Kṛṣṇa conscious platform, as opposed to the bodily platform. Heavy exercise at night is not recommended, as it increases the heat and activity of the body at a time when it should be winding down.

Physique

Śrīla Prabhupāda once remarked that a devotee named Ṛṣi Kumāra had the ideal physique for a *brahmacārī.* He was of medium build, with a little soft fat—not pudgy, not skinny, and not muscular.[119] Of course, we can't change our basic bodily structure, but to become fat is especially bad for devotees.[120] Yet also, to become thin and starved like the yogis is not our process. Śrīla Prabhupāda would become concerned if he saw that any of his disciples were underweight and would insist that they eat sufficiently.[121] And *brahmacārīs* definitely shouldn't endeavor to develop a muscular torso. Anyone who wants to imitate Mr. Universe is obviously highly illusioned by the bodily concept of life and is a long way from even beginning to understand the first instruction of *Bhagavad-gītā:* "You're not that body." Similarly, sunbathing to get a nice tan, or any such activity for making the body attractive, is simply *māyā*.

Cleanliness

Cleanliness is an elaborate part of Vedic culture. External purity is a prerequisite for developing internal purity. If we can't even keep our bodies and surroundings clean, then how can we hope to remove the dirt encrusted on our hearts since time immemorial? "Cleanliness is next to Godliness." Śrīla Prabhupāda: "If you are not clean, Kṛṣṇa will remain a thousand miles away." Śrīla Prabhupāda wanted "revolutionary cleanliness."[122] Cleanliness is *sāttvika* and healthy; uncleanness is *tāmasika* and intolerable. Vedic culture requires that *brahmacārīs* be clean. Indeed, one of the symptoms of degradation in Kali-yuga predicted in *Śrīmad-Bhāgavatam* is that "*Brahmacārīs* will be unclean."[123] Let's not be that kind of *brahmacārī.*

External cleanliness necessitates taking full bath three times daily (morning, noon, and evening) or at least twice a day, or absolute minimum once on rising. It is not necessary to use soap every time, as water alone is purifying. Bathing is compulsory after passing stool. While bathing, quickly clean under the skin flap on the penis so that scum cannot accumulate there.

Once used, a towel or *gāmcha* (a light bathing cloth commonly used in India) is contaminated and should be washed. To dry off with an unclean towel is like the elephant's bathing—one simply becomes contaminated again. *Gāmchas* dry quicker than towels and are therefore practical for devotees. To wash a *gāmcha* with soap after each shower is not necessary—a thorough rinse in clean water will do. But do wash it with soap regularly, and certainly don't let it get to the point of smelling bad.

After urinating, wash traces of urine off the penis with water from a *loṭā* (as Śrīla Prabhupāda always did), then wash the hands (with soap, Śrīla Prabhupāda said), and rinse the feet. Wash the hands after touching anything impure (such as the mouth, nostrils, feet, or any dirty thing).

Teeth, ears, and nails need to be kept clean, the tongue scraped daily, nails trimmed, and face and head regularly shaved. Hair is produced from the body's waste matter and thus resembles stool. Regular shaving not only helps us look clean but also helps us to feel clean and clear-headed. Clothes, bead-bags (Śrīla Prabhupāda said to keep two), sacred thread, shoes, the *brahmacārī-āśrama,* vehicles—everything must be kept neat and clean. A lot can be understood about a person by observing how clean and tidy he is. Śrīla Prabhupāda was always clean—a spotless transcendental aristocrat.

Of course, external cleanliness without internal cleanliness is useless. For internal cleanliness, chant Hare Kṛṣṇa and don't think of sex.

RETENTION OF SEMEN

Retention of semen is so essential in progressive human life that it is simply astounding how the whole endeavor of modern civilization is based on discharging it as much as possible. Semen retained in the body goes upwards to nourish the brain, rendering the body robust and the memory and intellect sharp. Determination, optimism, confidence, will-power, fixed intelligence, noble character, photographic memory, and shining good health are all fruits of conserved semen. It is said that the four Kumāras were unwilling to adopt materialistic activities because they were highly elevated due to their semens' flowing upwards *(ūrdhva-retasaḥ)*.[124]

Scientists have analyzed semen to be amazingly rich in hormones, proteins, vitamins, minerals, ions, enzymes, trace elements, and other vital substances. By nature's arrangement, this substance, when mixed with the ovum, is sufficient for the procreation of a new body. By nature's arrangement also, if it is not used for procreation but is kept within, it nourishes the body and brain in a way impossible for any tonic or dietary aid to emulate. The current craze for vitamin and mineral supplements is an attempt to make up for self-imposed deficiencies. Most people don't know that they are passing out their very life energy with that essential bodily fluid. If semen is lost, all bodily and sensory functions are weakened. Repeated loss of semen spoils the determination and clear, *sāttvika* intelligence necessary for spiritual understanding. However, if semen is retained in the body, there develops what Āyurveda refers to as *ojas,* a vital fluid that gives strength, luster, enhanced mental abilities and immunity to diseases, and slows the aging process.

Scientists cannot prove or disprove this, but it is observable in the brightness of yogis and the dullness of those who regularly "spill their brains out." Retention of semen, then, is ultimately meant for the evolution of the human being to higher levels of spiritual consciousness. Simply by retaining semen in the body, one develops a tendency toward greatness.

On the other hand, those who are addicted to discharging semen become petty and bestially lusty. The disastrous fruits of their promiscuity await them. They will be forced to devolve into lower species of life. Even in this life, excessive seminal loss can lead to physical and mental weakness. As the body ages, vitality and the will to get things done ebb away, and perpetual tiredness sets in. The pills and intoxicants people take to artificially keep them bright and active further add to their physical and mental degeneration. As premature old age sets in, their exhausted bodies cannot resist the dozens of diseases which proceed to ravage every cell in their organism. For such persons, the all-too-common senility comes as a relief. Śrīla Prabhupāda: "The more one enjoys in youth, the more he suffers in old age."[125]

Śrīla Prabhupāda: "Wasting semen is also illicit sex."[126] "The faculty to discharge semen is the cause of death. Therefore, yogis and transcendentalists who want to live for greater spans of life voluntarily restrain themselves from discharging semen. The more one can restrain the discharge of semen, the more one can be aloof from the problem of death. There are many yogis living up to three hundred or seven hundred years by this process, and in the *Bhāgavatam* it is clearly stated that discharging semen is the cause of horrible death. The more one is addicted to sexual enjoyment, the more susceptible he is to a quick death."[127]

Therefore, *brahmacārīs* are trained not to squander their semen. They must resist the temporary feeling of gratification that is bought at the cost of their own life energy.

Unfortunately, almost all devotees coming to Kṛṣṇa consciousness never had such training—rather, the opposite. And for those who regularly discharged semen, it will be difficult to stop the downward flow. But we have to try. Śrīla Prabhupāda: "Everyone should be taught to be very careful not to discharge semen unnecessarily. This is very important for all human beings."[128] Here are a few hints that will help.

First and foremost: don't think of women. Lustful thoughts provoke activity in the sexual glands. If we think of sex, we shouldn't be surprised if we suffer a nocturnal discharge.

But even a devotee seriously striving for *brahmacarya* may nevertheless be tormented by sex dreams. In the waking state he can control his mind with good intelligence, but in dreams low desires deeply ingrained in his subconsciousness may become manifest. The real cure for this is complete purification of consciousness by devotional service, but as this may take some time, the several physical factors that affect the retention of semen may be taken into consideration.

It is important not to excessively raise the internal heat of the body. Āyurveda describes high internal heat as a condition of excess *pitta* (bile) that is associated with the mode of passion, experienced as heat in the body generated by a passionate mood or by eating hot *rājasika* food such as that with much chili powder. Āyurveda also cautions putting downward pressure on the genitals by packing the stomach with food.

Diet and eating habits, therefore, are very important. Transcendentalists should eat simply (See section on "Eating" under "Health") and moderately. By overeating, more energy is taken into the body than it can use, which tends to make it come out in the form of seminal discharge. And an overly filled belly exerts pressure on the genitals, causing a tendency toward seminal discharge.

Avoid sleeping with a full belly—a yogi practices not eating at night. The last meal should be taken at least 2-3 hours before sleeping. The food should be light and easily digestible. Even hot milk should not be taken immediately before retiring, but about half an hour before. Rich, heavy, fried, spicy, and sweet foods heat the body, so be cautious with them, especially at night. Sour foods (such as sour or acidic fruit and yogurt) and bitter foods should be avoided at night, as should sweets, cheese, and thick milk preparations. Milk that has gone even slightly sour should not be taken at night.

Some vegetables contain a substance that thins the semen, making it prone to discharge. Worst among them is eggplant. The skin of eggplant is especially bad. Next worst is green chilies. Traditional Śrī Vaiṣṇavas exclude chilies, tamarind, and drumsticks (a type of vegetable) from their diet because of their sexually stimulating effect. Carrots, drumsticks, and to a lesser extent beetroot, heat the semen and therefore make it prone to discharge. However, this effect is not very pronounced, and *brahmacārīs* can take these vegetables in moderate quantities.

It is best to sleep no more than six hours at night and minimally or not at all during the day. If one cannot rise early, his so-called practice of *brahmacarya* is simply a farce. And late nights are bad for overall health as well as for seminal retention. So best is early to bed and early to rise. Sleeping during the *brahma-muhūrta,* at dawn or dusk, or when not really tired, are also dangerous—there's a high seminal loss risk. When a person is actually tired, his sleep will be deep, and disturbance from dreams will be less likely—another good reason for devotees to minimize sleep.

Āyurvedic authorities recommend sleeping on the side as best for *brahmacarya*. Not so good is on the back, and absolutely bad for health and dangerous for seminal discharge is sleeping on the stomach. Sleep with the back more or less straight (not curled up) and with the hands away from the genital area. If you are a light sleeper, try to rest in such a place that you won't be disturbed. Before resting, pass all water out of the bladder, wash hands and feet with cool water, and dry them.

Constipation is a major factor behind nocturnal emission. If the bowels are not cleared daily, stool and associated toxins accumulate in the rectum or colon. This increases the *pitta* (heat) in the area and also exerts pressure on the seminal sac, facilitating the excretion of semen. However, straining when passing stool should be avoided, as this also exerts pressure on the seminal sac.

Other points: Bathing with cool (not very cold) water is better than with hot. Or use warm water first to get clean then finish with cold. For cooling the body, bucket bath is more effective than showering. Pouring plenty of cool water over the whole genital area may be done as a daily practice. Rinsing the penis after urination removes uric acid that can agitate the sexual gland. Fasting as completely as possible on *Ekādaśī* is supposed to help. There are several Āyurvedic medicines and *yogāsanas* which are specifically meant to enhance *brahmacarya,* and although Śrīla Prabhupāda never recommended them, that does not necessarily mean that we cannot use them—although they may not work wonders. *Triphalā* (usually taken as *Triphalā Churna*) is a well-known, inexpensive Āyurvedic medicine that is helpful for many conditions and is good for *brahmacarya*. Licorice (Sanskrit: *Yaṣṭi-madhu*), taken regularly, can help prevent seminal discharge. However, it is best you take raw licorice rather than in the form of commercially prepared sweets. Āyurvedic treatment may help if one can find a good doctor and follow his instructions strictly over an extended period of time; but this should not be necessary for most devotees.

At least once, when Śrīla Prabhupāda saw a devotee shaking his legs while sitting cross-legged, he stopped him. Such leg-shaking is a sign of mental agitation and further agitates the genitals.

In a *Bhāgavatam* class in Melbourne, Śrīla Prabhupāda said, "If one can just retain his semen up to age twenty-five, the brain becomes *so* fertile for spiritual realization." Then, looking around and seeing all the depressed faces, he continued, "But if you just chant Hare Kṛṣṇa, everything will be alright anyway."[129]

It's Kali-yuga; we're all fallen. Many devotees have lost semen so many times in their pre-devotional lives that even though they want to, they can't stop their bodies involuntarily discharging it now. Even serious devotees who are averse to losing semen may nevertheless inadvertently do so, due to external influences on the body and mind, such as residual contamination from pre-devotional life, physical disorders that render the body weak, bodily heat, and subtle contaminations through eating the food of sinful people.

There is no cause for excessive lamentation if loss of semen is not a result of a conscientious endeavor for or meditation on sex. Inadvertent discharge of semen may be as accidental (and undesirable) as, for instance, the loss of a tooth. Considering that the body is always producing semen, occasional spillage may be taken as natural overflow. *Śāstra* gives rituals for physical and mental purification for such accidental emissions, although for ISKCON *brahmacārīs,* bathing and chanting Hare Kṛṣṇa is sufficient. In such cases, *brahmacārīs* need not be blamed for breaking the principles or not practicing them properly.

Still, the less it happens the better, and *brahmacārīs,* besides engaging in directly devotional practices, must try to control seminal loss by whatever methods they can easily adopt. They should be mindful about what, when, how much and where they eat, their sleeping habits, who they talk with and listen to, their posture while sleeping and sitting, and their overall physical health. They may also take to physical exercises or yoga if it genuinely helps their *brahmacārī* life.

Despite all endeavors, if a *brahmacārī* still loses semen, he may feel disgusted, but should know that it is not a disqualification for devotional service. The real qualification of a *brahmacārī* is that he wants to surrender his life to Kṛṣṇa and thus be free of sex life forever. Such determination transcends any material conditions, for Kṛṣṇa helps those who are sincere. *Brahmacārīs* suffering from nocturnal emissions may take comfort in knowing that they are by no means alone with this problem. Let us all chant Hare Kṛṣṇa and pray for the mercy of Lord Caitanya, the savior of the fallen.

The following quote from Śrīla Prabhupāda may be applied to unwanted seminal discharges. "(A devotee) is callous toward incidental occurrences, but he is always alert to execute his duties in Kṛṣṇa consciousness, or *bhakti-yoga.* Accidents never deviate him from his duty. As stated in the *Bhagavad-gītā* (2.14), *āgamāpāyino 'nityās tāṁs titikṣasva bhārata*. He endures all such incidental occurrences because he knows that they come and go and do not affect his duties. In this way he achieves the highest perfection in yoga practice."[130]

THE APPEARANCE AND DRESS OF A BRAHMACĀRĪ

"Carrying pure *kuśa* grass in his hand, the *brahmacārī* should dress regularly with a belt of straw and with deerskin garments. He should wear matted hair, carry a rod and waterpot and be decorated with a sacred thread, as recommended in the *śāstras*."[131]

This is Nārada Muni's description of a *brahmacārī's* apparel. Śrīla Prabhupāda, the *ācārya* for the modern age in the line of Nārada Muni, dressed his *brahmacārīs* in saffron and had them shave their heads.

ISKCON *brahmacārīs* should have a shaved head with *śikhā*, and *tilaka* markings on twelve places of the body; wear saffron cloth; wear a *kaupīna*; be simple, neat, and clean; and look blissful.

Shaved head, *śikhā*, *tilaka*, and saffron robes are, after all, the very signs of a devotee *brahmacārī*. We're famous for it. Never mind what people think (and often it's not nearly as bad as some devotees imagine), if they see a devotee in Vaiṣṇava dress, they think, "That's a Hare Kṛṣṇa" and thus make a little spiritual advancement.

If we're bold enough to always present ourselves as devotees, eventually we'll be accepted on our own terms. Sometimes it may be necessary for a devotee to wear *karmī* clothes. But if we make a habit of disguising ourselves, people will think we have something to hide. Therefore, as much as possible devotees should present themselves straightforwardly as devotees.

Dressing as a Vaiṣṇava is good for us, too. It helps us to feel like we are devotees—we are different from materialistic people, and that's the way we want to be. When we go out into the material world, we'll have to remember that we are representing Śrīla Prabhupāda and ISKCON, and behave accordingly. Dressed as Vaiṣṇavas, we often provoke questions which get us preaching to people who might otherwise never speak to a devotee.

Dressing as devotees also acts as a shield against indulgence in sense gratification. *Karmī* dress is dangerous—a subtle license to do things we could not in dhoti and *kurtā.* For instance, *brahmacārīs* are usually young, healthy, and bright, and therefore attractive to women; but a lot less so if they're shaven-headed, with *tilaka* and saffron robes. The ultimate argument for wearing devotee clothes and *tilaka,* with shaved head and *śikhā,* is simply that Śrīla Prabhupāda wanted us to do so.

Devotees who are obliged to wear *karmī* clothes in the course of performing devotional service should not become habituated to them. The best thing is, on returning to the *āśrama,* to immediately shower, apply *tilaka,* and don devotee clothes. For attendance in temple programs, there should be no question of wearing *karmī* clothes. For male and female devotees to regularly and unnecessarily be around each other in *karmī* clothes tends to create an unchaste atmosphere and should be avoided.

Hair means attachment, so unless it is really necessary to keep some hair, *brahmacārīs* should shave their heads once a week, once a fortnight, or absolute minimum once a month.* Saffron cloth with long hair looks incongruous—the color of renunciation with the symptoms of attachment.

The face should also be kept clean-shaved, with no stubble, sideburns, or mustaches. It is good to keep the armpits shaved also, especially in hot climates where shirts are not always worn, and for devotees who go on the altar.

The *śikhā* should be small (Śrīla Prabhupāda: "Gaudiya Vaiṣṇava *śikhā* is an inch and a half across—no bigger. Bigger *śikhā* means another *sampradāya.*"[132]) and knotted. It should not be braided or allowed to become matted.

Just keep as many clothes as you need—say three sets of devotee clothes and, if necessary, some *karmī* clothes. Don't build up a wardrobe—that is *atyāhāraḥ,* over-collecting, and is detrimental to devotional advancement.[133]

Householders wear white, and *brahmacārīs* and *sannyāsīs* saffron. So the two should not be mixed up. Devotees should wear one or the other, and make it clear which *āśrama* they are in. Traditionally, saffron is the color of *sannyāsa,* renunciation. It should not be worn as a fashion, but by those responsible enough to uphold the seriousness it implies.

Clothes should not be dyed too red. Dark red cloth is worn by Māyāvādīs and worshipers of Śiva and Kālī. And devotees wearing saffron look better if all their clothes are of the same shade—not that their dhoti is pale pink and their *kurtā* bright orange.

Some *brahmacārīs* opt to wear white, considering the saffron dress and the responsibility that goes with it unsuitable for them in their present state of consciousness. They may have decided to get married, or are tending toward marriage, but have no immediate plan to actually enter into marriage. Or they may consider their consciousness too contaminated or their approach to devotional service insufficiently strict to merit their wearing of saffron. On the

* According to Āyurveda, it is harmful for the health of growing boys to shave their heads very often. It is better they be shaved not more than once in two weeks.

whole, it is better that those who are neither married nor strictly practicing renunciation wear white and not misrepresent themselves as renunciates. Certainly no one who accepts payment for services rendered should dare to don saffron.

When buying socks, *cādaras*, jackets, scarves, or hats, if pink or orange are not available, beige, brown, gray, or maroon are also acceptable. Red, white, yellow, and even black are also possible colors for auxiliary clothing for *brahmacārīs;* green, blue, and multicolored are best avoided.

Brahmacārīs wear a full-length dhoti with a *kacha* (the piece tucked in at the back). To go without a *kaccha* is for *sannyāsīs* only. Similarly, the saffron knotted top-piece, whether worn to the front or to the side, is only for *sannyāsīs*. However, there is no restriction on householders, especially those engaged in *pūjārī* service, sometimes wearing a white knotted top-piece.

Kaupīnas aid in sense control by regulating certain nerves that can otherwise cause agitation. They should be worn firmly, but not so tight as to hurt. *Kaupīnas* are practical for *brāhmaṇas* taking bath three times daily, because they dry quickly. They are also cheap. It is unfortunate that many of our devotees prefer to wear *karmī* underpants. The *kaupīna* should be tucked in at the back, not sticking out like a monkey's tail. *Kaupīnas* should be made of two pieces of cloth. The width should be equal to the distance between the two nipples, and the length should be equal to the girth of the waist plus two fists. According to *śāstra,* the part that goes around the waist should be knotted on the right side.

T-shirts with nondevotional themes are useless and unnecessary for devotees. When wearing a T-shirt with the holy names or a devotional motif printed on it, or a *harināma cādara,* be careful when paying obeisances not to touch them to the ground. And better not wash them (or your bead-bag) in a toilet-cum-bathroom, or along with socks, *kaupīnas* or other contaminated articles.

A *brahmacārī* dresses simply and neatly and keeps himself and his cloth clean. In certain preaching circumstances there may be justification for "fancy dress," but generally simple cotton dhoti and *kurtā* are most suitable for *brahmacārīs.* But we should not look like poverty-stricken beggars. Badly torn or soiled cloth should be replaced. And we must have some kind of footwear. If we go barefoot people will take us for hippies. And, for preaching in formal situations, it is best that clothes be ironed.

Dress sensibly. If it's cold, wear warm clothes. Especially the feet should be kept warm. Wear socks while standing or walking on cold floors.

Rings, bracelets, expensive watches, designer sunglasses, embroidered *kurtās*, and dhotis with fancy borders are generally signs of someone who is promoting his body, or in other words, trying to attract women. *Gṛhasthas* may or may not use them, and no one is likely to say anything, but they are not suitable for *brahmacārīs.* The same goes for strongly scented after-shave, deodorants, and soaps.

Sometimes it is postulated that people may be attracted by a show of opulence. That is especially true in poor countries, and therefore Śrīla Prabhupāda built gorgeous temples in India. Our preachers in India often wear expensive cloth, just to create a good impression. But sometimes a display of opulence backfires—people mistake us for materialists in the garb of *sādhus.* And factually, unless we have sufficient realization, simply wearing silk won't make us preachers.

Śrīla Prabhupāda stressed that our greatest asset is our purity. So, devotees should always look blissful. (Have a look through the real old BTG's—you'll be amazed to see dozens of dazzling devotee photos.) Śrīla Prabhupāda: "It is essential that a *brahmacārī* engaged in spiritual advancement look very healthy and lustrous."[134] If a devotee looks dull and morose we can understand that he is not relishing devotional service, but is contemplating sense gratification. The face is the index of the mind.

We can't fake it, and if we try, we'll look ridiculous. Cutting a profile never made anybody into a *brahmacārī.* But if we've got it, our genuine bliss is the best advertisement for Kṛṣṇa consciousness.

NAKEDNESS

Nakedness is not at all appreciated in Vedic culture.[135] The private parts should remain unexposed at all times. A *brahmacārī* should as much as possible avoid seeing even his own genitals. To see the private parts of the body is not only vulgar, but tends to stimulate unwanted desires. Śrīla Prabhupāda: "To see oneself naked is the beginning of madness."[136] Even if alone in a room, one should not for a moment be exposed. That includes while bathing, while changing, and even while sleeping.

While bathing, wear a *gāmcha*. Simply a *kaupīna* is insufficient. After bathing, hold a dry *gāmcha* with one hand around the now wet one and take off the wet one with the other hand (sounds complex but it's simple—standard practice in India). Rinse and firmly wring out the wet one, then dry yourself with it (most of the water gets absorbed, body heat does the rest). This is the way that Śrīla Prabhupāda bathed. Indeed, millions of Indians still bathe like this every day—the majority of them outdoors, at a well, tank, or river. Still, they never expose their private parts, even to the elements.

To change, keep a dhoti or *gāmcha* wrapped around the waist until the cloth you're changing into is in position. And while sleeping wear at least *kaupīnas* and *gāmcha. Gāmchas* should be at least knee length, for the sake of decency. Those from a Western background may find this all rather peculiar at first. But to remain covered is not at all difficult—one just has to become aware of the necessity. It's all a part of the Vedic heritage, which expounds proper standards of behavior for an actually cultured civilization. Just as on becoming a vegetarian one comes to realize how abominable meat-eating is, or on coming to Kṛṣṇa consciousness a devotee comes to understand how meaningless life without Kṛṣṇa is, so to one who learns to cover himself up, not doing so, even for a few seconds while changing, seems uncouth.

THE GENERAL BEHAVIOR AND DISPOSITION OF A BRAHMACĀRĪ

Every being is an individual. All the rules and regulations in the world can't snuff out a person's individuality. So despite the *brahmacārī's* adherence to a strict regime, there are all kinds of characters in the *brahmacārī-āśrama.* Eccentricity is not uncommon amongst those who strive for the extraordinary, and *brahmacārīs* are no exception. Everyone has idiosyncrasies, and these become more apparent when we live lives of constant endeavor with little or no privacy—there are quite a few singular devotees around! Such variety adds spice to our already interesting lives in Kṛṣṇa consciousness. Zaniness, however, is not the standard. The standard is, as Śrīla Prabhupāda said, that a devotee be a perfect gentleman.

Below are a few guidelines on the behavior of an ideal *brahmacārī.* If you don't exactly fit the description, don't worry—hardly anyone does. We are all struggling with the modes of material nature on different rungs of the ladder of spiritual advancement. But make the effort to reach the standard of excellence. Take lessons and inspiration from the activities and dealings of great devotees like the six Gosvāmīs of Vṛndāvana and Śrīla Prabhupāda. If you observe any good qualities in a devotee, be he a *sannyāsī* or a new *bhakta*, learn from him. Try, try, try.

Submission to and friendship with the guru are the directing principles in the life of a *brahmacārī.*[137] He always tries to avoid doing anything which would displease his guru, who he worships as a pure representative of Śrīla Prabhupāda and the *guru-paramparā.* In his dealings with others he is straightforward and fair, being ever conscious that he is representing his guru. Thus a *brahmacārī* is *suśīlāḥ sādhavaḥ*, a well-behaved saintly person.[138] He does not try to draw attention to himself. He is self-satisfied, jolly, and confident—never morose. So naturally everyone—even the nondevotees—like him. The six Gosvāmīs were dear to both the gentle and the ruffians because they were never envious of anyone. Śrīla Prabhupāda wrote that, "In our common dealings we should maintain friendship with everyone."[139] (Then what to speak of with devotees.)

Nārada Muni describes *brahmacārīs* as *dāsavan nīcaḥ*: very humble, submissive, and obedient, like a slave.[140] If a *brahmacārī* is not obedient, there is no meaning to his being a *brahmacārī*. *Brahmacārīs* should be prepared to work hard, undergo austerities, accept discipline, and surrender. It is somewhat understandable (although not very good) if a householder is not very surrendered. But for a *brahmacārī* not to be so is an aberration. If a *brahmacārī*, especially a junior *brahmacārī*, is not prepared to surrender, be disciplined, and accept authority, he is no *brahmacārī* at all and is not fit to live in an *āśrama*.

Too much independence is not good, especially for *brahmacārīs* newly joining the *āśrama*. A newcomer should be prepared to buckle under and do what he is told without complaining. By following this disciplinary process, the sense of surrender becomes fixed and strong. Such a *brahmacārī* can be relied upon to do well in any conditions.

Brahmacārīs are traditionally meant for service, not to be served, so *brahmacārīs* should not expect or demand service from others. Rather, they should be eager to serve others. Specifically, *brahmacārīs* traditionally act as assistants to *sannyāsīs*. A *brahmacārī* should be reluctant to accept service from others, especially on a regular basis, and certainly should not have a personal servant. An exception may be a *brahmacārī* who has been engaged in devotional service over many years and is physically incapacitated in old age. Even then, such a personal servant should not be a godbrother or one on the level of a godbrother.

The ideal *brahmacārī* dedicates his life for spiritual advancement and always endeavors to be self-controlled and detached from material enjoyment. However, he is not mindlessly fanatical and does not condemn devotees who do not follow as strictly as he does. He is not ignorant or naive or a ball of passion, but conducts himself in the mode of goodness, as a *brāhmaṇa*.

Steadiness is the bedrock of *brahmacārī* life. Having in the beginning accepted training in the principles of Kṛṣṇa consciousness, a serious *brahmacārī* maintains continued, firm adherence to those standards throughout his life.

If a devotee is following all the principles and serving nicely (as all good *brahmacārīs* do), *māyā* will try to trick him into being falsely proud, into thinking himself better than other devotees. We should consider that even if we are doing well now, we have no guarantee that we shall be able to consistently maintain such a high standard. Many devotees before us have advanced dramatically, only to fall due to offenses caused by false pride. Genuine and steady advancement must be accompanied by humility, for pride goes before a fall.

BRAHMACARYA AS STUDENT LIFE

Śrīla Prabhupāda wanted *gurukulas*, to give children the opportunity to easily perfect their lives and go back home, back to Godhead. Śrīla Prabhupāda: "If one practices devotional service from the beginning of his life, surely he will return home, back to Godhead, without a doubt."[141] Whatever deficiencies ISKCON *gurukulas* may have had, they are special because they are centered around Kṛṣṇa. Because Śrīla Prabhupāda saw the modern schools as indoctrinating the helpless children in sense gratification and mental speculation, he called the schools "slaughterhouses."[142]

What about the rest of us, who joined ISKCON in youth or later? Can we become students of Kṛṣṇa consciousness? The answer is yes—we *must* become serious devotee students. Traditionally, *brahmacārīs* studied Vedic knowledge under the guidance of their guru and rendered him menial service. Both elements are there for ISKCON *brahmacārīs* also. The aspects of study and training should never be minimized. The guru accepts service from a disciple simply to make him a candidate worthy of receiving Vedic knowledge. Unless there is an awakening of transcendental knowledge within the heart of the devotee, there is no meaning to the guru-disciple relationship. That knowledge is contained within the scriptures, and Śrīla Prabhupāda has given us, in straightforward language, the deepest mysteries of spiritual understanding in his Bhaktivedanta purports. But the ability of the student to actually comprehend the message of the scriptures depends on his being favored by a bona fide spiritual master.

Gradually, many new books on Kṛṣṇa consciousness are being published in English, and Śrīla Prabhupāda wanted that. However, Śrīla Prabhupāda's books are the basis of our movement. Śrīla Prabhupāda gave us plenty to read. The philosophy is nondifferent from Kṛṣṇa: vast and unlimited. "Even if we read the entire *Bhagavad-gītā* every day, all eighteen chapters, in each reading we shall find a new explanation. That is the nature of transcendental literatures."[143]

Before going on from the *brahmacārī-āśrama* to the *gṛhastha-* or *sannyāsa-āśramas,* the *brahmacārī* should have a proper understanding of Śrīla Prabhupāda's books. Every devotee must have at least a basic understanding of the philosophy. Otherwise his Kṛṣṇa consciousness will not develop properly. If a *brahmacārī* doesn't have a taste for Vedic knowledge, what is the meaning of his being a *brahmacārī?* If, on the other hand, a *brahmacārī* makes a habit of carefully and regularly studying Śrīla Prabhupāda's books, that will be sufficient to make his life successful.

In addition to philosophy, Kṛṣṇa consciousness is a transcendental kaleidoscope of culture, art, and science. Those who take the trouble to learn any aspect will be enriched. Everyone has latent abilities, so why not develop some talents to use in Kṛṣṇa's service? As stated by Nārada Muni, a *brahmacārī* should be *dakṣa*, expert.[144] Śrīla Prabhupāda elaborated on this by stating that a *brahmacārī* should be expert in everything.[145]

As far as possible, every devotee should learn to give class, receive guests, preach, quote Sanskrit *ślokas*, cook, perform fundamental Deity worship, lead a *kīrtana,* sing *bhajanas,* and play the *mṛdaṅga.* And there are other abilities which are useful for all-rounder *brahmacārīs* in the modern age to learn, such as basic vehicle maintenance, computer skills, and elementary accounting.

Devotees should know and apply Vedic etiquette (appropriate use of right and left hands, not stepping over books, etc.) and codes of health and hygiene.* They should be self-reliant in every way, from washing their clothes and keeping themselves and their quarters clean, to looking after themselves in any situation. So devotees who come to our movement have to be trained. The junior *brahmacārīs* of today are the senior *brahmacārīs* of tomorrow. Today's trainee is tomorrow's teacher.

If you have the inclination to excel in any aspect of devotional service, take permission from your authorities and go ahead, get into it. One of the duties of gurus and Kṛṣṇa conscious leaders is to guide the *brahmacārī* according to his inclination so that he will always be productive and happy. So take guidance and become an expert speaker, cook, *pūjārī,* or whatever, for Kṛṣṇa. Learn to play *mṛdaṅga* nicely; learn hundreds of *ślokas.* If from pre-Kṛṣṇa conscious life you have some extra expertise, for instance, in gardening, art, or computers, by all means develop that skill in Kṛṣṇa consciousness. Learn something, do something for Kṛṣṇa, and train others to do it also. Make your life successful in Kṛṣṇa consciousness. Don't go away feeling unfulfilled, thinking that *karmī* life can offer anything which Kṛṣṇa consciousness cannot. Whatever propensity we have can be satisfied in Kṛṣṇa consciousness.

THE BRAHMACĀRĪ-ĀŚRAMA (RESIDENCE)

The *brahmacārī* quarters may be dormitory type or divided into smaller rooms. In either case, it's better if the *brahmacārīs* all stay together in one area. Staying alone or having too much privacy is never recommended for devotees. The tendency is to oversleep or otherwise fall into *māyā.*

Śrīla Prabhupāda once walked into the *brahmacārī* room (10.8 x 3.5 meters) in Hyderabad and said, "Forty *brahmacārīs* can stay in here." The devotees were stunned and thought Śrīla Prabhupāda was joking, but he wasn't.[146]

* A forthcoming book, *Vaiṣṇava Culture, Etiquette and Behavior,* by Bhakti Vikāsa Swami, explains this subject in detail.

The *brahmacārī-āśrama* should, obviously, be far away from the *brahmacāriṇī* and householder areas, and, preferably, close to the temple. There should be adequate toilet and bathing facilities so that everyone can conveniently get to *maṅgala-ārati* on time.

A full set of Śrīla Prabhupāda's books should be available, or better still, there should be a separate library-cum-study. (Too many of our temples still don't provide this important facility. Devotees, especially *brahmacārīs,* give up everything to serve Kṛṣṇa. If at all possible they should have a place where they can go to peacefully absorb themselves in Śrīla Prabhupāda's books.)

In the early days of ISKCON, devotees didn't sleep on beds, but they are standard fittings in many of our *āśramas* nowadays. Beds aren't necessarily a bad thing (although *brahmacārīs* traditionally aren't supposed to use them), but personally I don't see the advantage to having them. Apart from costing money, they take up valuable space and provide a constant temptation to be used. Besides, soft mattresses are bad for health. Sleeping on the floor is conducive to the *brahmacārī* ideals of simplicity and austerity. A *brahmacārī* doesn't need any special arrangement—he can take rest anywhere. A bed is just something else to get attached to. On rising, a *brahmacārī* rolls up his bedding neatly, puts it away (out of sight, out of mind) and sponges the floor where he slept. Śrīla Prabhupāda: "A *brahmacārī* lies down on the floor."[147]

Pictures on the *brahmacārī* room walls (or anywhere else, for that matter) should be properly framed, not just ripped out of a magazine and stuck up haphazardly with sticky tape. Don't sleep with your feet toward them! Mirrors are anathema for *brahmacārīs*, so just keep a small one on the wall so the boys can put their *tilaka* on nicely.

The *brahmacārī-āśrama* must be kept neat and clean. That means sweeping out and washing with water every day. Śrīla Prabhupāda: "If devotees don't clean their rooms every day with water, then they are living like hogs." Don't just leave things lying around; have lockers and use them. If we make a mess, we should clean it up on the spot, not leave it for someone else to tidy up.

Keep a waste bin, use it, and empty it out daily. Keep a laundry basket, too, and place dirty cloth in it, not on top of it, near it, around it or half-in and half-out. Hang washed cloth to dry outside or in a separate room. Towels and *kaupīnas* especially should be out of sight. Keep walls, ceilings, fans, windows, and pictures clean too. Don't make a mess with the *tilaka.* Watch out for cobwebs and accumulated dust in corners and behind cupboards.

Basic rules of communal living should be observed. Items used communally (such as books) should not be taken away. After using, return them to the place where they are kept. And take permission before using anyone's personal possessions.

Bringing *prasāda* into the *brahmacārī-āśrama* invites ants, cockroaches, and mice; and stashing *prasāda* is against the pure devotional principles. The *Bhāgavatam* states, "A saintly mendicant should not even collect foodstuffs to eat later in the same day or the next day. If he disregards this injunction and like the honeybee collects more and more delicious foodstuffs, that which he has collected will indeed ruin him."[148]

Keep the air fresh by burning incense and letting fresh air in as much as possible. Bad smells are horrible, and stale air is unhealthy. Be sure to keep the toilets and bathroom area always clean and disinfected. Unless peak cleanliness is maintained, disease can spread rapidly in communal situations.

There's no real place in the *brahmacārī-āśrama* for *karmī* books, magazines, or newspapers. Those devotees who really have to read such things in relation to their service can do so privately.

In a strict *āśrama,* lights go on and off at fixed times (e.g. 3:30 a.m. and 9:30 p.m.). Best is to awake to a Śrīla Prabhupāda *bhajana* cassette. Late resters and early risers should go quietly, avoiding turning the lights on and only using a flashlight if necessary, and even then being careful not to shine it in others' faces. So-called *brahmacārīs* who unnecessarily stay up late at night making so much noise that others cannot rest properly, and who then sleep in the morning program, are not proper *brahmacārīs* and are not fit to live in an *āśrama.*

On waking, don't lie in your bedding trying to enjoy the stupor of semi-consciousness. Rise immediately and chant Hare Kṛṣṇa. Reluctant risers should be firmly coaxed into action—don't let them rot in their misery. Śrīla Prabhupāda: "One who cannot rise early is not very serious about spiritual life."[149]

Most important of all to make the *brahmacārī* residence actually an *āśrama* is to keep the Kṛṣṇa conscious mood strong. That depends on the devotees themselves. Talk philosophy, chant the holy names, read Śrīla Prabhupāda's books, recite *ślokas.* Don't waste time, and don't talk *prajalpa.* Otherwise the atmosphere will be intolerable.

PERSONAL RELATIONSHIPS

Śrīla Prabhupāda: "Relationships between Godbrothers must be very genuine and pleasing, otherwise the future of our institution is not very hopeful."[150]

Communal living can be a strain, especially when there is pressure to conform to strict regulations, tight schedules, and ideal standards of Kṛṣṇa conscious behavior. Furthermore, life in modern society can be so confusing that many devotees who join the *brahmacārī-āśrama* will have disturbed and complex psychology. In the Western countries especially, many will have been through traumatic or perverted experiences, such as those resulting from failed love affairs, broken homes, homosexuality, molestation, intoxication, and violence.

They come to Kṛṣṇa consciousness seeking peace of mind, love, security—a more natural, pure, and simple life in the shade of Kṛṣṇa's lotus feet. People with many different backgrounds join this movement, so if we are to live peacefully in the society of devotees, we will have to learn to co-exist with all types of persons in all stages of development of Kṛṣṇa consciousness. Due to false ego, we all have the tendency to think that our approach to or vision of Kṛṣṇa consciousness is *the* correct one. But a symptom of a more advanced devotee is his willingness to appreciate the service done by others, without emphasizing their faults.

We have to work at creating a transcendental family atmosphere in our temples so that prospective devotees will automatically feel inclined to surrender to Kṛṣṇa. Affection, intelligence, humility, readiness to listen, sympathy, consideration of others, kind words, and friendly dealings—in other words, mature Kṛṣṇa consciousness—are required. Thoughtfulness—little things like taking the trouble to fold another devotee's cloth after removing it from the line—can make all the difference.

It is a strange phenomenon in our movement that younger devotees are often more enthusiastic than devotees who have been initiated longer. However, it is best not to "get on the case" of a more senior devotee. The real test of steadiness in Kṛṣṇa consciousness is over long years, not a few short months. Generally, preaching to senior devotees should be done by devotees senior or equal to them (in terms of years in the movement, service record, strictness in following the Kṛṣṇa conscious process, etc.).

Be especially thoughtful when dealing with new or struggling devotees. Older men joining the *brahmacārī-āśrama* need special consideration also, for latecomers often find the austerities and high-pressure lifestyle hard to adjust to. Being more mature in years and experience of the world, it may be difficult for them to relate to the more youthful *brahmacārīs.*

After all, Kṛṣṇa consciousness is a voluntary process. This movement can only run on love and trust, on the co-operative spirit. Śrīla Prabhupāda: "The devotee's duty is to be always conscious in his dealings with others, especially with another devotee of the Lord."[151] If we are not careful in dealing with devotees, personal relationships may get strained. Weaker devotees may get discouraged and go away, thus spoiling their great opportunity to perfect their lives in Kṛṣṇa consciousness.

Real friendship between devotees is deep and profound. It is most important that *brahmacārīs* develop great love, trust, and friendship with one another, based on the mood of each wanting to be the servant of the servant of each other. Devotees care for each other and help each other advance. If somehow or other we can establish even one or two deep friendships within this movement, that will be a great help to keep us fixed on the path throughout our lives.

Sometimes, however, devotees may feel lonely, even if living with several nice devotees. They just can't seem to relate to anyone intimately. Sometimes devotees even get married mainly because they are seeking sympathy and close companionship. Inability to relate properly with devotees will certainly hamper our advancement in Kṛṣṇa consciousness, and to overcome such problems we may consult Śrīla Rūpa Gosvāmī's *Nectar of Instruction,* Text 4, in which he explains the six exchanges of love shared by devotees. Kṛṣṇa consciousness is a tried and tested process. It works. So if we experience loneliness, we simply have to make the endeavor to open up to other devotees and share Kṛṣṇa consciousness with them in the manner prescribed by Śrīla Rūpa Gosvāmī. A devotee who is humble from his heart, who expects nothing and desires nothing but the menial service of the Vaiṣṇavas, will certainly have no problems relating to others.

THE BRAHMACĀRĪ LEADER

If at all possible, a *brahmacārī* leader should live with the *brahmacārīs.* He should be a senior, exemplary, and mature devotee. Real *brahmacārīs* are like valuable jewels for our society. They work willingly and hard all day for Kṛṣṇa without any expectation of return, live austerely, are submissive and rarely complain. Often they are the ones who are doing the front line work of our mission, by preaching and distributing books. They are usually young men, maybe two- or three-year devotees, and appreciate older devotees' association for guidance and inspiration. But in our bigger centers, by necessity everything is departmentalized. Older devotees get married or get into specialized service such as management. Often inadvertently, the younger devotees are left without a leader. Although they have been around for some time, know what to do, and can give guidance to others, they still would appreciate and benefit from the association of an *āśrama* leader.

The *brahmacārī* leader can be a senior *brahmacārī,* a *sannyāsī,* or a householder with a renounced and detached attitude, as is suitable for training *brahmacāris.* He can live with or slightly separate from the *brahmacārīs.* (Also, if visiting or resident *sannyāsīs* have their quarters adjacent to the *brahmacārīs,* it will be for their mutual benefit.) The *brahmacārī* leader will have his regular full-time service, but will still keep an eye on the *brahmacārīs.* He'll see that they are getting to the temple programs and keeping everything clean, he will encourage and advise them, and sometimes sit and read with them—he is there, he is available. We all need someone who we respect and trust, who we can reveal our minds in confidence to. Guiding and counseling dedicated devotees is a great service to Lord Caitanya's *saṅkīrtana* movement.

ATTITUDES TOWARD GṚHASTHA MEN

Some stalwart *brahmacārīs* maintain a persistently harsh attitude toward *gṛhasthas,* or even toward *brahmacārīs* less rigid than themselves. Of course, *brahmacārīs* should always preach to each other about the glories of *brahmacārī* life and the dangers of householder life, for such discussions are healthy and help make the mind strong. However, to become unnecessarily critical or to develop a superiority complex are against the principles of pure devotion and are damaging to spiritual advancement. It is not necessarily true that a staunch *brahmacārī* is dearer to Kṛṣṇa than an apparently entangled householder. After all, we are like toys in the hands of *māyā;* if Kṛṣṇa withdraws His protection we will not be able to maintain our vows. Despite all the strictness we may maintain, despite all the austerities we may perform, if we become proud, that is our foolishness. Despite our external display of spiritual advancement, with such delusions of grandeur our actual progress will be very slow.

An interesting point is that the gurus in traditional *gurukulas* were often *gṛhasthas.* An example is Sāndīpani Muni, the guru of Kṛṣṇa. And many personalities far greater than us were householders. Among the twelve *mahājanas*, seven are or were householders. In the Kṛṣṇa consciousness movement today also, many advanced, dedicated devotees are householders.

So, without maintaining any stigmas, we should take good association wherever we find it. Narottama dāsa Ṭhākura sings: "It does not matter whether a devotee is a *gṛhastha* or a *sannyāsī;* if he chants the name 'Gaurāṅga,' I want his association." Therefore *brahmacārīs* should be eager to humbly serve devotee *gṛhasthas* and respect the service they render.

But make sure the association is good. Be cautious in mixing with devotees whose thoughts and conversations are involved only in family affairs and moneymaking, who are in the enjoying mood, or who do not strictly follow the rules and regulations of Kṛṣṇa consciousness. *Brahmacārīs* are not meant for socializing and hanging around *gṛhastha's* homes. And if a householder regularly watches TV and in other ways lives like a *karmī*, avoid his home—it is not a *gṛhastha-āśrama,* but a blind well. (Of course, for preaching, we have to go to *karmīs'* houses, but then we have to be all the more careful. Just to teach us, Śrīla Prabhupāda said, "Whenever I enter a rich man's house, I pray to Kṛṣṇa that I may not fall down.")

And even if householder devotees are good association, it is better that *brahmacārīs* not associate much with them in their homes or with their families. When doing so, a *brahmacārī* must maintain a strong internal resolve, otherwise he may become attracted to the affection and comforts of home life and think, "I could also be enjoying this." Once a *brahmacārī* starts thinking like that, the seed of his downfall is planted.

Brahmacārīs, unlike householder devotees, are able to directly absorb themselves in Kṛṣṇa consciousness without any extraneous distractions. Householders often look to the *sannyāsīs* and *brahmacārīs* for inspiration. *Sannyāsīs* have a special duty to guide and uplift *gṛhasthas.* Humble, blissful *brahmacārīs* will also be appreciated everywhere.

DEALINGS WITH WOMEN DEVOTEES

There is a great difference between ordinary materialistic women and those who have come to take shelter of Kṛṣṇa. Women in ISKCON are all devotees and therefore glorious. Some of them are clearly advanced from their previous lives. They should be regarded with all due respect—from a distance. If they are serious devotees, they will respect your strictness.

Due to lack of training or attachment to women's lib ideas, women devotees may sometimes act improperly with you. Better let it pass, and not make a scene out of it. Women are supposed to be trained in chastity, but modern women aren't. We men also may still be influenced by the lusty exploitative mentality in our dealings with women. So we may also be at fault. If it becomes necessary, have a word with the temple authorities.

In these beginning days of ISKCON we have to be strict but also tolerant, understanding that most Westerners can't adjust their social behavior overnight to resemble that of traditional Indian Vaiṣṇavas. Śrīla Prabhupāda was sensitive about this point and therefore was successful in establishing Kṛṣṇa consciousness in the West.

Brahmacārīs often have a tendency to reject women, but Śrīla Prabhupāda never did that because he was above attraction and repulsion and simply wanted to engage everyone in Kṛṣṇa's service. When a devotee complained to Śrīla Prabhupāda that the presence of women in our movement caused too many problems and suggested that we no longer accept women as full time devotees, Śrīla Prabhupāda replied, "They have come to take shelter of Kṛṣṇa. We cannot turn them away."[152] (Facilities are provided in Western countries for *brahmacāriṇīs* to stay in separate *āśramas.*)

"Regarding the disturbance made by woman devotees, they are also living beings. They also come to Kṛṣṇa. So consciously I cannot deny them. If our male members, the *brahmacārīs* and the *sannyāsīs,* become steady in Kṛṣṇa consciousness, there is no problem. It is the duty of the male members to be very steady and cautious. This can be done by regular chanting like Haridāsa Ṭhākura did. Whenever there is a young woman, we should remember Haridāsa Ṭhākura and beg his mercy to protect us, and we should think that these beautiful *gopīs* are meant for the enjoyment of Kṛṣṇa. It is a dilemma for our society that we cannot deny these girls, and at the same time they are a great dangerous allurement to the young boys."[153]

On being informed that some *brahmacārīs* felt disturbed by the presence of women in the temple, Śrīla Prabhupāda sarcastically suggested that the *brahmacārīs* go to the forest.[154] Previously, *brahmacārīs* used to live in the forest, far away from the agitation of the cities. But that is not possible in the modern age. Indeed, as a consequence of preaching, at least as many women as men will be attracted to Kṛṣṇa consciousness, and we cannot deny their existence, or their right to serve Kṛṣṇa. Rather, anyone who comes to Kṛṣṇa consciousness must be encouraged. However, as long as one is not completely pure, if a male devotee begins with the best intentions to encourage a woman to take to Kṛṣṇa consciousness, the tendency is to become attracted on the emotional and physical levels. Therefore, even though *brahmacārīs* may preach to anyone, it is better that women preach to women.

In 1967, at the 2nd Avenue temple in New York City, Śrīla Prabhupāda announced in one class, "Don't see these girls as objects of sense gratification. See them as associates of Kṛṣṇa."[155] And in the mid-1970's in America, a party of *sannyāsīs* and *brahmacārīs* became overly righteous about the attachments of *gṛhasthas* and women. Tension developed and reached exploding point at the Māyāpura Festival of 1976. In the course of setting everything straight (the way he always did—by preaching Kṛṣṇa consciousness) Śrīla Prabhupāda said that male devotees should address the women as "My dear mother" and the women should see the men as "My dear son."[156]

In a conversation in Seattle in 1968, Śrīla Prabhupāda said, "Now, another thing: Girls should not be taken as inferior. Sometimes, of course, in scripture we say that woman is the cause of bondage. So, that should not be aggravated that women are inferior. The girls who come, we should treat them nicely. After all, anyone who is coming to Kṛṣṇa consciousness, man or woman, is very fortunate. The idea of addressing each other as *Prabhu* means, 'You are my master.' *Prabhu* means 'master.' So everyone shall treat others as 'my master.' This is Vaiṣṇava understanding. In spiritual life there is nothing like this sexism. The more we forget sex life means we are advancing in spiritual life. So this should be the attitude: women, godsisters, should be nicely treated."

In one temple in Brazil, the *brahmacārīs* became so "fired-up" that they wanted to send all the women away. When the GBC, H.H. Hṛdayānanda Gosvāmī, found out, he joked, "Don't be ridiculous. Then the *brahmacārīs* wouldn't have anyone to perform for."

There are certain points in Śrīla Prabhupāda's books concerning women which unless one is a very self-controlled devotee and expert preacher, one should be cautious about repeating in public and in classes, especially if women devotees or guests are present (e.g., quotes stating women to be less intelligent than men, or nine times as lusty, etc.). After all, *māṁ hi pārtha vyapāśritya,* and *kalau śūdra-sambhavaḥ.* Everyone in this age is low born. Men or women, we are all running on Lord Caitanya's and Śrīla Prabhupāda's mercy. We don't want to discourage women who are already devotees, nor those who are potential devotees. Nor do we want to make the *brahmacārīs* artificially proud. Sensitive topics need to be handled by competent devotees.

The Vedic social philosophy states that women are to be protected by men, but that duty is for the *gṛhasthas,* not for *brahmacārīs* or *sannyāsīs.* For a *brahmacārī*, young women mean trouble. However sincere young women devotees may be, when in contact with *brahmacārīs* a kind of energy is produced that is not conducive for devotional advancement. Those who have regular contact with young women devotees, even innocently or for the sake of service, are almost certain to get worn down. They may not even notice the effect of such association, but nevertheless it is like radioactivity: slow, subtle, and irreversible.

A *brahmacārī* should be very cautious if a woman is being "too nice" to him (e.g. keeps giving him *mahā-prasāda*). Service by a woman is a trap for a man.[157] It is women's nature to seek shelter and protection from a man, because it is generally both spiritually and materially beneficial for them to be married. But *brahmacārīs* should know that although men generally improve materially if married, that so-called improvement simply means entanglement in sense gratification; therefore for a man's spiritual progress it is intrinsically better to live without a woman. Acting on the platform of this knowledge, a *brahmacārī* who wants to stay *brahmacārī* has to be free from material compassion for women looking for husbands.

Śrīla Prabhupāda: "The managers of our society should see that all the *brahmacārīs* stay *brahmacārī,* and all the women get married." Devotees: "How is that possible, Śrīla Prabhupāda?" Śrīla Prabhupāda: "That is your management."[158]

Śrīla Prabhupāda noted, "These girls generally come to our society to find out a suitable husband."[159] Naturally, women devotees want to marry the best men devotees. They tend to be more attracted to *brahmacārīs* who are steady, committed, mature, and responsible. Almost perversely, *brahmacārīs* who are serious to stay *brahmacārīs* usually become targets of anxious *brahmacāriṇīs*. For a women to "hunt down" a man who wants to remain committed to *brahmacārī* life could be considered an act of violence against his progressive spiritual development. On the other hand, it can be considered a test that even great sages have to undergo.

If a *brahmacārī* who wants to stay a *brahmacārī* finds that a young woman is becoming friendly toward him, alarm bells should go off in his head and he should extricate himself from that situation. If that is not possible, the next best response is not to respond. To remain polite but cold in the face of advances, and to consistently show disinterest, soon convinces women to direct their conjugal aspirations elsewhere. There is no room for sentiment in such dealings. If the *brahmacārī* allows his heart to flutter and reciprocates with even a little interest, the huntress, being encouraged, will not stop until the quarry's heart is fully pierced with Cupid's arrows.

If, however, a woman remains persistent in her desire for an unwilling *brahmacārī*, the latter may frankly say to her, "Mātājī, I already gave many lifetimes to many women like yourself. Please give me your blessings that I can give this life fully to Kṛṣṇa, without unnecessary disturbances or entanglements." If the *brahmacārī* is serious about his commitment, only a shameless woman would continue to pursue him further.

However, in our temples it is often a practical necessity that men and women engage in devotional service side by side. We can't avoid such situations, although temple authorities should arrange that male and female devotees are kept apart as much as possible. *Brahmacārīs* should maintain Vaiṣṇava respect toward devotee women, without becoming overly familiar or loose, or developing friendships with them. Śrīla Prabhupāda: "*Sannyāsīs* should have 'Keep in a cool place' stamped on their foreheads, just like on the butter package."[160]

DEALINGS WITH NONDEVOTEE WOMEN

Dealing with nondevotee women in the developed countries is an even bigger problem because they have no idea how to behave with *brahmacārīs* at all. Nor is it possible to explain to them. It is very, very dangerous and better to be avoided totally (which is impossible).

There is no stricture that *brahmacārīs* cannot preach to women, but after a woman's interest in Kṛṣṇa consciousness is aroused, it is better that further preaching to her be done by women devotees. Otherwise, if a *brahmacārī* repeatedly preaches to the same woman, the fire and butter principle is sure to act.

Saṅkīrtana devotees often have extensive contact with nondevotee women, so they have no other recourse but to constantly pray for the special mercy of Lord Caitanya to protect them. They should be alert, keeping their minds tightly under control, lest like Ajāmila they be "victimized by the dangerous lustful glance of a prostitute."[161] *Saṅkīrtana* devotees should avoid visiting degraded places such as porno shops and sleazy bars. There are plenty of other places to distribute books. Although we may not be immediately affected, everything we see remains as an impression within the mind. Later on, maybe years later, those experiences may resurface in the consciousness and cause agitation. As Śrīla Prabhupāda said after preaching at a rock concert, "This is no place for a *brahmacārī*."[162]

Saṅkīrtana brahmacārīs who feel agitation from contact with women on *saṅkīrtana* are advised to concentrate on preaching and distributing books to men. If a devotee finds that he is not maintaining his spiritual strength and feels that his position in Kṛṣṇa consciousness is being threatened because of constant contact with nondevotee women, he should discuss with his temple authorities and if necessary adjust his service.

DEALINGS WITH CHILDREN

Apart from those *brahmacārīs* connected with the *gurukula,* most *brahmacārīs* generally won't have a lot of contact with children. *Brahmacārīs* have no business frivolously playing with children or fondling them (fondling children or animals can mean attempting to enjoy their bodies). Any dealings with children should be on the basis of Kṛṣṇa consciousness.

Children look up to whatever example adults set, so especially in the presence of children *brahmacārīs* should be responsible enough to act in an ideal Kṛṣṇa conscious way. Not that joking or light-heartedness are by any means forbidden for a *brahmacārī,* but the tendency of many adults to become childish in the presence of children is beneficial neither for the adults or the children.

If you feel there's a need to correct or chastise a child, better refer to his parents or teachers. After all, children are very sensitive.

DEALINGS WITH FAMILY AND FRIENDS

A Kṛṣṇa conscious person is not interested in associating with nondevotees. But he cannot be totally insensitive to those "near and dear ones" from his pre-devotional days. Usually, parents and others just can't understand why "their boy" "dropped everything" to shave his head and chant, dance, and be happy. Sometimes family members are favorable, sometimes neutral, and sometimes inimical toward Kṛṣṇa consciousness. But in almost all cases, if dealt with considerately, they will gradually adjust to their son's being a "Hare Kṛṣṇa." Sometimes they even become devotees themselves.

So it's best to be patient and try not to antagonize them. If they make a fuss, try to point out some positive aspects of your involvement in Kṛṣṇa consciousness which they may appreciate: that you're happy, living a clean life, and so on. And make sure to give them *prasāda,* as much and as often as possible.

If they remain persistently antagonistic, then there will be no other alternative than to politely but firmly cut off contact with them until they are ready to change their outlook. Ultimately it's your life, to do with as you see fit.

Some advice from Śrīla Prabhupāda: "Regarding your manner of behavior with your parents who are not in Kṛṣṇa consciousness; I may inform you that you should treat four different classes of men in four different ways. A devotee should love God and God's devotees. A devotee should make friendship with devotees. A devotee should try to enlighten innocent persons, and a devotee should reject opposite elements. As father and mother they should be offered proper respect according to social custom, but you cannot accept their non-Godly instructions. Best thing is, to avoid misunderstanding, to remain silent without any affirmation or negation of their instructions. We should try to keep our friendship with everyone in the world, but we cannot sacrifice the principles of Kṛṣṇa consciousness on being employed by some relative of this world. Don't let them know that you do not approve of your parents' instructions, but at the same time you should be very careful in dealing with them. If you object to their instruction and let them know it, then they will feel sorry, sad."[163]

DEALINGS WITH NONDEVOTEES IN GENERAL

The *Bhāgavatam* enjoins that a middle-level devotee recognize two classes of nondevotee and behave with them accordingly.[164] He should show mercy to the innocent (by giving them Kṛṣṇa consciousness) and avoid the inimical.

Our movement is a pioneering one and, especially in the West, sometimes meets with hostility. Of course, we often meet with tolerance also, but rarely with understanding. The culture of respecting *sādhus* just isn't there.

Newer devotees who have yet to attain steadiness in devotional service often experience Kṛṣṇa conscious bliss during the morning program, but once outside the temple compound find it difficult not to lose their consciousness to *māyā.*

Under these circumstances it is not surprising if they develop defensive or negative attitudes toward nondevotees, whose habits, opinions and comments constantly undermine the undeveloped faith of the beginning devotee and threaten his very standing in Kṛṣṇa consciousness.* Of course, not all nondevotees are out-and-out demons or rogues and cannot be so generalized. Nor can we assume that we are really devotees, beyond that we are trying to be so. Still, there is a great difference between *karmīs* (a term Śrīla Prabhupāda used to generally describe materialists in the modern age) and devotees. And for all devotees, aspiring or advanced, association with nondevotees is unpalatable and can be detrimental (unless we are engaging them in Kṛṣṇa's service, which is blissful).

The Nectar of Devotion directs devotees not to be neglectful in ordinary dealings, yet also to rigidly give up the company of nondevotees. One should deal with the material world only as much as necessary, or in other words, only for essential matters. While doing so, we should try to conduct ourselves in such a way that nondevotees may gradually become favorable to Kṛṣṇa consciousness, or at least not inimical toward it.

* See Śrīla Prabhupāda's letter to Lynne Ludwig in *The Science of Self Realization* for a full discussion of these points.

GIVING UP NONDEVOTIONAL ATTACHMENTS

Kṛṣṇa consciousness is the culture of the spiritual world, a continuous festival of multifarious transcendental activities. But we are so unfortunate that we are still attracted to the worldly tidings of sense pleasure.

A real devotee has no business reading nondevotional literature (unless it's directly related to service, e.g. the gardener consulting a gardening book), watching TV, going to the cinema, eating food cooked by nondevotees, following sports, politics, or fashions, learning martial arts, or listening to nondevotional music.* The fickle mind dreams up justifications for engaging in these useless activities, inventing myths of how they can be related to devotional service. But ninety-five percent of the time we indulge in them for our own sense gratification, not for the sake of *bhakti.*

Lord Caitanya warned that eating the food of materialistic people will pollute the mind; thus we will not be able to remember Kṛṣṇa and our life will be spoiled. Grains cooked by nondevotees are especially contaminating. If we can take nice *prasāda,* what is the need for anything else? Even when out traveling, we should take care not to sacrifice our standards for the sake of convenience. Śrīla Prabhupāda: "Food prepared by an unclean, sinful man or woman is extremely infectious."[165]

We also have to be careful what we read. Newspapers and magazines may provide information that is relevant for us, but they also have much information that we do not need. They also usually

---

* Setting the songs of the Vaiṣṇava *ācāryas* to rock music is inappropriate, unnecessary, and a *rasābhāsa. Bhakti-yoga* is the culture of the soul. Traditional devotional tunes, based on the Vedic musical science, naturally help to awaken our dormant feelings for Kṛṣṇa; rock rhythms invoke attachment to sex, drugs and violence. Although rock tunes with Kṛṣṇa conscious lyrics may have some value in attracting those who are not in Kṛṣṇa consciousness (Śrīla Prabhupāda did approve of the *Change of Heart* Album—tasteful and directly Kṛṣṇa conscious lyrics set to soft pop, although he said it should not be played in the temple), they are of little use to devotees who already have the real thing. Śrīla Prabhupāda's recorded lectures, conversations, *bhajanas* and *kīrtanas* are recommended daily listening material for those wishing to achieve and maintain a high standard of Kṛṣṇa consciousness. See *Bg.* 4.26 Translation and Purport in this connection.

have photos of attractive women. Many nondevotional literatures contain subtle sexual connotations, which pollute the mind and mislead the intelligence. Sex literatures, even of the so-called scientific type, are to be rigidly avoided. Just as the consciousness of the cook enters into food, so do the thoughts of the writer enter the writing. We have to be vigilant not to become subtly contaminated.

Wearing *karmī* clothes when there is no clear need to is an expression of mundane attachment. Once Śrīla Prabhupāda admonished some devotees for having long hair and not shaving their heads regularly. Although they gave all kinds of "reasons" for doing so, such as "being good for preaching," Śrīla Prabhupāda detected the real reason: "hippie seeds."[166] The revealing phrase, "hippie seeds," can be applied to anything that is not clearly, authorizedly, and directly meant for the service of Kṛṣṇa.

We may not even realize how it is happening, but these materialistic tendencies subtly poison the consciousness. We are trying to get free from the modes of material nature, but these *karmī* attachments will drag us down. We may say: "Those strong attachments are there, what can I do?" What we can do is work on getting rid of them, instead of surrendering to them and again cultivating them.

If my readers find these restrictions too fanatical or unrealistic I must inform that in pre-1977 ISKCON (when Śrīla Prabhupāda was personally leading and directing us) these were all taboo, practically unheard of amongst devotees. Śrīla Prabhupāda trained us so nicely. It's only since his departure that we've unlearned so many of the things that he painstakingly taught us.

Kṛṣṇa consciousness means new life, a fresh perspective of reality. If we want to be free from the shackles of *māyā,* we can't hold on to the ball-and-chain of mundane involvement. If we really want Kṛṣṇa, we're going to have to snap off these attachments. To maintain interest in even one sphere of illusion will constitute an obstruction, blocking our progress in Kṛṣṇa consciousness. Remember, the real idea of Kṛṣṇa consciousness is to surrender mind, body, and words to Kṛṣṇa. To go beyond a superficial level of Kṛṣṇa consciousness means to get serious.

These mundane attachments have to be replaced with Kṛṣṇa conscious attachments. That is possible by dovetailing our desires in Kṛṣṇa consciousness, not diverting them back to be dovetailed again with *māyā.* How to do it? Simple. We can read Kṛṣṇa conscious literature (Śrīla Prabhupāda gave us so much), sing Kṛṣṇa conscious *bhajanas* (there are so many), perform Kṛṣṇa conscious dramas (there's plenty of scope), discuss Kṛṣṇa conscious philosophy (there's unlimited depth), and cook for Kṛṣṇa (there are thousands of preparations). The Kṛṣṇa connection will purify us. But nondevotional activities are saturated with the modes of passion and ignorance and simply contaminate and disturb the mind. A serious devotee must give them up.

YUKTA-VAIRĀGYA

"Renunciation is the basic principle sustaining the lives of Śrī Caitanya Mahāprabhu's devotees. Seeing this renunciation, Caitanya Mahāprabhu, the Supreme Personality of Godhead, is extremely satisfied."[167]

Śrīla Rūpa Gosvāmī has analyzed the real meaning of renunciation: "When one is not attached to anything, but at the same time accepts everything in relation to Kṛṣṇa, one is rightly situated above possessiveness. On the other hand, one who rejects everything without knowledge of its relationship to Kṛṣṇa is not as complete in his renunciation."[168]

This means that if a devotee has the opportunity to utilize anything in the service of Kṛṣṇa, he should do so, even if such an object is usually used for materialistic purposes. This is called *yukta-vairāgya.* Devotees use all kinds of machines, collect and spend millions of dollars, engage women, form international organizations—all for the service of Kṛṣṇa.

Still, we have to be careful. Śrīla Prabhupāda used to quote the Bengali saying, "Fish, but don't touch the water." There is danger at every step in the material world. If we forget the connection with

Kṛṣṇa, we will become lured into material consciousness again. Śrīla Prabhupāda: "In the material world, all distresses are due to extravagance." Money and power can be intoxicating, management can give rise to the illusion that "I am the doer, I am the controller," and machines can fascinate. We may consider ourselves strong, but Śrīla Prabhupāda knew all our weaknesses.

Therefore he stressed that we must regularly hear and chant about Kṛṣṇa, so as to keep the right perspective. For a devotee to progress, he must hear and chant sufficiently. Even if he is absorbed in service, that is not enough. Hearing and chanting must be there, with quality and in sufficient quantity. By working for work's sake, taking pleasure from manipulating money and machines, one's consciousness may end up like a materialist's. So many devotees in the past have become diverted from the goal of life or lured into unnecessarily opulent living in the name of *yukta-vairāgya*. The distinction between the moods of renunciation and enjoyment may sometimes be very subtle, but the attitude makes the difference between a *karmī* and a devotee—one wants to enjoy, the other wants to serve. Without *vairāgya,* there is no possibility of *yukta-vairāgya*.

The ability to utilize material opulence in Kṛṣṇa's service without becoming affected is possible for advanced devotees. So *brahmacārīs* especially should practice *yukta-vairāgya* with great restraint, under the guidance of an expert spiritual master, tending always toward austerity and self-denial rather than comfortable living, within the parameters approved by Śrīla Prabhupāda:

Books are the Basis
Preaching is the Essence
Utility is the Principle
Purity is the Force.

INDIA

If you can take it, India is a great place for *brahmacārīs*. In India, you don't have to try to be austere—life is automatically austere. If you have an inclination for *tapasya*, you will find the right atmosphere in Bhārata-varṣa. Despite modern India's pathetic attempts to imitate the West, and despite the hellish sex/violence cinema and music syndrome, India is still a lot less sexually agitating than the West. Of course, if someone wants to fall down he can do so anywhere; but the opportunities are less blatant than in the West. There is still some civilization and culture left.

And that is one of the reasons why Śrīla Prabhupāda wanted devotees to come to India. Western devotees are very impressive to Indians. Indians tend to respect Western devotees, especially if they are competent preachers and know how to conduct themselves as *sādhus*. There is great opportunity for Western devotees in India to preach, and to simultaneously pick up some Vedic culture.

They can get a broader perspective of Kṛṣṇa consciousness by experiencing how it is still accepted and practiced by millions. They can derive the benefit of visiting and serving the holy *dhāmas,* especially Māyāpura and Vṛndāvana, learn to conduct themselves as *sādhus,* and pick up devotional skills such as cooking and preaching to persons who are knowledgeable in *śāstra*. They will have to develop tolerance, patience, and self-reliance to cope with the difficulties of life in India. Devotees can learn how to behave with superiors and juniors and how to conduct themselves with gravity. Future *gṛhasthas* can see how family life should be, and how to bring up children.

The real benefit that India has to offer goes to those devotees who come to spend an extended period for service, rather than for just a brief visit. It is not essential or practical that every devotee serve in India; but it would be a great help for *brahmacārīs* to spend a year or two in Bhārata-varṣa before plunging into the *gṛhastha-āśrama.* Especially if one travels and preaches in India, and is a little receptive and intelligent, he can have a lot of Kṛṣṇa conscious fun and adventure, and gain a broad vision of Kṛṣṇa consciousness which will stay with him throughout his life.

All arrangements should be made in consultation with the relevant authorities.

OVERCOMING SEXUAL DESIRE

As Garuḍa is the enemy of snakes, as impersonalism is the enemy of devotion, so lust is the enemy of the conditioned soul. It is the first of three gateways to hell.[169] Lust is so powerful that it may seem impossible to overcome. The *brahmacārī* vows to fight sex desire, and may sometimes think he is winning the battle, only to find himself again plunged into the ocean of material desire.

This is due to previous *saṁskāras* (impressions in the *citta*, subconsciousness). Every activity, thought, and sensual experience of a conditioned soul produces a *saṁskāra*. Each *saṁskāra* becomes added to a stockpile of mental impressions that is not vanquished even at death. Sexual acts, or even thoughts of sex, produce particularly strong *saṁskāras*. These *saṁskāras* influence the disposition (*vṛtti*) of a person and give rise to innumerable *vāsanās* (material desires).

These *saṁskāras*, impressions from previous births, are embedded deep in the subconsciousness, and thus even a devotee seriously practicing *brahmacarya* may still have strong sexual desires. Even an apparently pure *brahmacārī* may have latent sexual desires that can emerge and destroy him at any time, as was the case with Ajāmila.[170] How can we overcome this eternal enemy, this destroyer of knowledge and self-realization?[171] What can we do if we are sexually agitated?

There is a process to overcome sex attraction, and that process is the system of devotional service. The practice of *brahmacarya* is essential in, but subsidiary to, the ultimate purifying process of devotional service. Only by devotional service can material desires be entirely overcome. As with Āyurvedic treatment, the cure for the disease may not be immediate, but it will be complete. The malady is deeply rooted and complex. We have been dominated by sexual desires for millions of lifetimes, and it is not easy to shake them off. To overcome it we will have to take a serious, mature decision to continue with devotional service throughout our lives. That is the only remedy.

First of all, we have to understand that *everyone* is sexually agitated. Apart from completely pure devotees, who are very rare in this world, everyone from Brahmā down to the ants and bugs is disturbed by sexual attraction. Even *sannyāsīs* and other advanced devotees may be subject to such attacks from *māyā* at any time. But because they have practiced controlling these gross desires, they are able to remain steady in Kṛṣṇa consciousness.

We should not become discouraged, thinking that sex desire is impossible to overcome. We must have the conviction that it *is* possible. Prahlāda Mahārāja compares sex agitation to an itch.[172] It irritates, and we want to scratch it. But if we scratch it, it gets worse. Better to tolerate without scratching; then in course of time, the irritation will gradually go away. We have to be realistic that in almost all cases it will take considerable time, patience, and faith to conquer this most basic and overwhelming of all material desires. We have to go on in Kṛṣṇa consciousness, praying to Kṛṣṇa for help in controlling the rascal mind.

In the *Bhagavad-gītā* Kṛṣṇa admits that it is very difficult to curb the restless mind, but assures that it is possible by constant practice and by detachment. Śrīla Prabhupāda: "By training, one can forget sex life."[173] Traditionally, *brahmacārīs* were trained rigidly from birth. That was when the whole atmosphere was much more favorable for spiritual advancement. But we have been brought up in a highly disturbed society, with no training in sense control—rather, the opposite. How is it possible, then, for us to control the mind and senses and be rigid *brahmacārīs*?

No doubt, it is very difficult to control the mind and senses, especially in the modern age. But that doesn't mean we shouldn't try. Unless we at least try, we are not even civilized human beings, what to speak of being spiritual aspirants.

And certainly Kṛṣṇa will help us, if we really want to be helped. Kṛṣṇa has come as Lord Caitanya to help us in our most fallen position with the best of all advice: chant Hare Kṛṣṇa. Everything is possible for those who chant the holy names with sincerity and patience. Chanting cleans the heart. *Ceto-darpaṇa-mārjanam*. Lord Caitanya said, *ihā haite sarva-siddhi haibe sabāra*:

"By chanting the Hare Kṛṣṇa mantra, everyone will get all perfection."[174]

As explained by Śrīla Prabhupāda: "Everyone wants to fulfill lusty desires. So unless one is in the modes of goodness or transcendental, everyone will like. That is the material world, *rajas-tamaḥ*. Just like I am a hungry man. There is foodstuff. I want to eat it. So if I take by force, that is illegal, and if I pay for it, then it is legal. But I am the hungry man, I want it. This is going on. Everyone is lusty. Therefore they say 'legalized prostitution.' They want it.

"So marriage is something legalized, that's all. The passion and the desire is the same, either married or not married. So this Vedic law says, 'Better married. Then you will be controlled.' So he will not be so lusty as without married life. So the *gṛhastha* life is a concession—the same lusty desire under rules and regulation. Without married life he will commit rape in so many ways, so better let him be satisfied with one, both the man and woman, and make progress in spiritual life.

"Everyone in this material world has come with these lusty desires and greediness. Even demigods like Lord Śiva, Lord Brahmā. Lord Brahmā became lusty after his daughter. And Lord Śiva became mad after Mohinī-mūrti. So what to speak of us insignificant creatures? Lusty desire is there. That is the material world.

"Unless one is fully Kṛṣṇa conscious, this lusty desire cannot be checked. It is not possible. That is *tapasya*, that voluntarily we accept some inconvenience. *Tapasā brahmacaryena*. *Tapasya* means first *brahmacarya*, how to avoid sex desire. That is first step. Where is their *tapasya*? It is very difficult to do this *tapasya*. Therefore Caitanya Mahāprabhu has given *harer nāma*. If you chant Hare Kṛṣṇa mantra regularly, you'll be cured. Otherwise, regular *tapasya* is almost impossible nowadays."[175]

We have to chant Hare Kṛṣṇa, not just mechanically, but really calling out to Kṛṣṇa for help to follow all the eight features of *brahmacarya* properly. Śrīla Prabhupāda writes: "If we stick to the principle of chanting the Hare Kṛṣṇa *mahā-mantra* offenselessly, then, by the grace of Śrīla Haridāsa Ṭhākura, we may be saved from the allurement of women. However, if we are not very strict in chanting the Hare Kṛṣṇa *mahā-mantra,* we may at any time fall victim to women."[176]

The *Vedānta-sūtra* (4.4.22) refers to *anāvṛttiḥ śabdāt,* liberation by sound. Chanting loudly and clearly greatly helps in overcoming lust. In traditional *gurukulas*, *brahmacārīs* chant Vedic mantras for hours daily. Along with chanting the Hare Kṛṣṇa *mahā-mantra*, devotees may take up the *sādhana* of loudly chanting verses from *Bhagavad-gītā*, *Śrīmad-Bhāgavatam*, or other scriptures.

Chanting should be accompanied by regular hearing about the realities of material life. The *Śrīmad-Bhāgavatam* narrates the activities of great personalities like Yayāti, Purūravā, and Saubhari who found out after years wasted in attempting to enjoy sex that there is no enjoyment in it at all. Their stories are recorded so that intelligent people can come to the same conclusion simply by hearing about them.

Hearing about Kṛṣṇa's pastimes with the *gopīs* is specifically recommended to vanquish lusty desires in the heart.[177] However, "If you become more lusty by seeing or hearing the pastimes of Kṛṣṇa with Rādhārāṇī, that means you are not fit. Stop it. Don't be foolish."[178]

Hearing accompanied by contemplation leads to realization. The real thing is to become totally disgusted with the thought of sex. But until we reach that stage, we have to carefully control the mind and body by intelligent understanding that sex is not in our interest. Therefore the intelligence should be applied to consider the following points:

The temporary nature of the beauty of young women; the young girls of today are the old women of tomorrow.

The illusory nature of that beauty. Try imagining how beautiful a woman's body would be minus its skin!

Sex does not bring happiness. The nondevotees are having sex, but they are miserable. The devotees are happy, and the more they advance and give up material attachments, the happier they become.

On the contrary, engagement in sex, licit or illicit, inevitably leads to suffering. It is unavoidable. (See "Sex—The Cause of Unlimited Suffering,") Sex desire, although much appreciated by people in general, causes pain to the heart.

Sex is disappointing, firstly because the anticipated delight is never fulfilled in the actual act. In other words, it is not as enjoyable as *māyā* would have us believe.

Sex is frustrating, because desires for it are unlimited, but physical ability to engage in it is limited to a few minutes at a time.

Devotees have higher knowledge and experience of a higher taste. Just as a rich man can never savor the coarse rice relished by the poor man, so even a fallen devotee cannot enjoy the illusory pleasure of sex, even though he tries.

We made a commitment at the time of initiation. For one who knows the difference between right and wrong and has taken a vow not to sin, to willingly engage in illicit sex will bring serious reactions.

The most important reason for refraining from illicit sex, or from even thinking of sex, is that it is not pleasing to guru and Kṛṣṇa.

According to Śrīla Śrīdhara Svāmī, by meditation on the Supreme Lord one can overcome lust and other mental disturbances.[179] More specifically, the *Bhāgavatam* states that sex desire can be overcome by meditation on Kṛṣṇa's eyebrows.[180] This can be very effective. We can meditate on the Deity we are serving, or on pictures of Kṛṣṇa—Kṛṣṇa will help us. Śrīla Prabhupāda also recommended Deity worship for those very troubled by lusty desires. We may think ourselves too impure to go anywhere near the Deities, but this process is prescribed because if one is at all principled, when he comes in the presence of the Deities he must force his mind to stop thinking of sex. And gradually, by performing this intimate service, a conscientious devotee will become so attracted to Kṛṣṇa that all lower desires will become insignificant.

Don't play games with the mind. It is useless to meditate on sense gratification and also hope to give it up.[181] Better than meditating on sex is meditating on the consequences of it. Any sane person should consider the suffering that accrues from sexual activity and resolve not to indulge in it.

Habitually looking at women and thinking of them plunges a person into the ocean of lusty desires and drives him mad. There is no question of spiritual advancement for such a person. Conversely, one who gives up the bad habit of looking at women with lusty intentions will automatically become more peaceful in mind. What to speak of not looking at women, a *brahmacārī* should not even look at animals engaged in sexual affairs, remembering that the great yogi Saubhari Muni fell down by seeing the copulation of fish.[182]

Somehow or other the mind must be wrenched away from sense gratification and fixed on Kṛṣṇa. Tell yourself: "If you want to have sex, you can. It's not difficult to arrange. Everyone is having sex. But if you want Kṛṣṇa, that is something else. So either go ahead, get married, do it, or forget it altogether."

As stated in *Śrīmad-Bhāgavatam* (7.15.22), *asaṅkalpāj jayet kāmam:* By making plans with determination, one should give up lusty desires for sense gratification. *Asaṅkalpāt* can be translated as, "By not making plans for sex; by not thinking about it; by not visualizing it; by not day-dreaming about it." In his commentary, Śrīla Bhaktisiddhānta Sarasvatī Ṭhākura suggests *bhogārhatā-buddhi varjanāt* as a synonym for *asaṅkalpāt*. This basically means, "by giving up the enjoying mentality." Śrīla Viśvanātha Cakravartī Ṭhākura comments: "*Asaṅkalpāt* means that even if lust arises from remembrance or seeing of a woman, a person is determined not to think, 'This woman is to be enjoyed by me;' thus he conquers lust."

One technique to control the mind is to ignore it. "A person who is not disturbed by the incessant flow of desires—that enter like rivers into the ocean, which is ever being filled but is always still—can alone achieve peace, and not the man who strives to satisfy such desires."[183] "By tolerance alone can one conquer desires and avarice."[184]

So many nonsense thoughts enter our minds. If instead of picking up on them we simply ignore them, they will naturally and quickly die, to be replaced by other thoughts. Therefore we have to train our minds to think of Kṛṣṇa. *Sa vai manaḥ kṛṣṇa-pādāravindayoḥ:* Mahārāja Ambarīṣa engaged in various activities of devotional service but first of all he fixed his mind on Kṛṣṇa.[185] Philosophical discussion between devotees, attempting to understand the philosophy of Kṛṣṇa consciousness "from different angles of vision" (as Śrīla Prabhupāda encouraged us to do), gives the mind meaningful subject matter to meditate on and makes it strong. "One should not be lazy in the matter of understanding the philosophical conclusions of devotional service, for such discussions strengthen the mind. Thus one's mind becomes attached to Śrī Kṛṣṇa."[186]

Bhaktivinoda Ṭhākura has suggested that devotees harassed by morbid desires for sexual enjoyment meditate on Kṛṣṇa's pastime of killing Śaṅkhacūḍa. Śaṅkhacūḍa wanted to enjoy with the *gopīs.* Similarly, we should understand that our desire to enjoy sex is demoniac, for all living entities are *prakṛti* and are meant to be enjoyed by Kṛṣṇa. So we should loudly cry out to Kṛṣṇa that, just as He killed the demon Śaṅkhacūḍa, may He please kill our demoniac desires.

There are many suitable prayers to help us overcome sexual agitation. In *Śrīmad-Bhāgavatam* there is a prayer, "May Sanat-kumāra protect me from lusty desires."[187] In the purport Śrīla Prabhupāda writes, "Lusty desires are very strong in everyone, and they are the greatest impediment to the discharge of devotional service. Therefore those who are very much influenced by lusty desires are advised to take shelter of Sanat-kumāra, the great *brahmacārī* devotee." Another nice prayer is found in *Caitanya-caritāmṛta* (*Madhya* 22.16):

kāmādīnāṁ kati na katidhā pālitā durnideśās
teṣāṁ jātā mayi na karuṇā na trapā nopaśāntiḥ
utsṛjyaitān atha yadu-pate sāmprataṁ labdha-buddhis
tvām āyātaḥ śaraṇam abhayaṁ māṁ niyuṅkṣvātma-dāsye

"O my Lord, there is no limit to the unwanted orders of lusty desires. Although I have rendered them so much service, they have not shown any mercy to me. I have not been ashamed to serve them, nor have I even desired to give them up. O my Lord, head of the Yadu dynasty, recently, however, my intelligence has been awakened, and now I am giving them up. Due to transcendental intelligence, I now refuse to obey the unwanted orders of these desires, and I now come to You to surrender myself at Your fearless lotus feet. Kindly engage me in Your personal service and save me." Then there is the classic prayer of Caitanya Mahāprabhu:

ayi nanda-tanuja kiṅkaraṁ
patitaṁ māṁ viṣame bhavāmbudhau
kṛpayā tava pāda-paṅkaja-
sthita-dhūlī-sadṛśaṁ vicintaya

"O son of Nanda Mahārāja (Kṛṣṇa), I am Your eternal servitor, yet somehow or other I have fallen into the ocean of birth and death. Please pick me up from this ocean of death and place me as one of the atoms at Your lotus feet."[188]

We have no other shelter but Kṛṣṇa, as Śrīla Prabhupāda explained: "Our most difficult position is sex. Kṛṣṇa, *māyā,* has given such a propensity—sex—that it will create disturbance. Even though you are rigid and vowed and you are doing nicely, sometimes, especially at night, you are disturbed. Therefore, *suratau*—Kṛṣṇa is the most expert in this conjugal love, therefore we have to admit, surrender to Kṛṣṇa, *suratau paṅgor*. We are very much feeble and very slow and so far as our sex impulse is concerned, here it is especially mentioned Madana-mohana. Sex impulse is called Cupid, Madana. If we become staunch devotees of Kṛṣṇa these material sex impulses will vanish. Because even Cupid becomes attracted by Kṛṣṇa. We are attracted by Cupid, but Cupid is attracted by Kṛṣṇa, therefore Kṛṣṇa is Madana-mohana. That is the only remedy. *Yadāvadhi mama cetaḥ kṛṣṇa-padāravinde.* If you stick to the lotus feet of Kṛṣṇa—'Kṛṣṇa please save me'—then this material thing, sex agitation, will not disturb you. This is the only way. Therefore it is said, 'Madana-mohana.' Our spiritual life is hampered very strongly by this sex impulse, but it is material so we try to tolerate.

"Just tolerate a little, and chant Hare Kṛṣṇa, pray to Kṛṣṇa, 'Please save me from these disturbances.' And we should materially also control. Control means *atyāhāraḥ prayāsaś ca prajalpo niyamāgrahaḥ. Atyāhāraḥ* means too much eating, that is also agitating. So everything can be controlled by Kṛṣṇa's grace. He is Madana-mohana; therefore our first business is to surrender to Madana-mohana and establish our relationship with Him. 'My dear Lord Kṛṣṇa, I have so long forgotten You.' That song is sung by Śrīla Bhaktivinoda Ṭhākura, *mānasa deho geho jo kichu mora, arpiluṅ tuwā pade nanda-kiśora.* This is full surrender. Then Kṛṣṇa answers, *ahaṁ tvāṁ sarva-pāpebhyo mokṣayiṣyāmi mā śucaḥ*. He will protect us, so *tāṁs titikṣasva bhārata.* There are many disturbances. So Kṛṣṇa says, 'Tolerate, and do your business faithfully.' Chant Hare Kṛṣṇa, follow the rules and regulations, and remain fully surrendered at the lotus feet of Madana-mohana, there will be no more disturbance."[189] (Śrīla Prabhupāda also described that unless one is captivated by the beauty of Madana-mohana, then he will be *Madana-dahana,* troubled by the arrows of Cupid.[190] See *Cc. Ādi* 1.19 Purport to understand more about approaching Madana-mohana.)

Perfection is not achieved in a day. We may stumble while climbing a mountain, but we have to re-gather our strength and determination and resume the climb, until we become so adept that we don't slip anymore. Ultimately, we have to develop a superlatively higher taste in Kṛṣṇa consciousness. We have to actually get to the stage where we're always experiencing great bliss.

To get to the top of the mountain and onto the plateau takes much endeavor. What is required is full surrender of mind, body, and words, twenty-four hours a day, forever, and nothing less. It definitely *is* possible, for that is the promise of guru and Kṛṣṇa. But we have to become qualified to receive their mercy.

Lord Kṛṣṇa instructed Uddhava *(S.B.* 11.20.27-29) that a devotee should continue in devotional service without becoming depressed by his inability to immediately overcome sense desire.

These texts and purports are so relevant in this regard that they have been reproduced here in full.

TRANSLATION

Having awakened faith in the narrations of My glories, being disgusted with all material activities, knowing that all sense gratification leads to misery, but still being unable to renounce all sense enjoyment, My devotee should remain happy and worship Me with great faith and conviction. Even though he is sometimes engaged in sense enjoyment, My devotee knows that all sense gratification leads to a miserable result, and he sincerely repents such activities.

PURPORT

The beginning stage of pure devotional service is described here by the Lord. A sincere devotee has practically seen that all material activities lead only to sense gratification and all sense gratification leads only to misery. Thus a devotee's sincere desire is to engage twenty-four hours a day in the loving service of Lord Kṛṣṇa without any personal motivation. The devotee sincerely desires to be established in his constitutional position as the Lord's eternal servitor, and he prays to the Lord to elevate him to this exalted position. The word *anīśvara* indicates that because of one's past sinful activities and bad habits one may not immediately be able to completely extinguish the enjoying spirit. The Lord here encourages such a devotee not to be overly depressed or morose but to remain enthusiastic and to go on with his loving service. The word *nirviṇṇa* indicates that a sincere devotee, although somewhat entangled in the remnants of sense gratification, is completely disgusted with material life and under no circumstances willingly commits sinful activities. In fact, he avoids every kind of materialistic activity. The word *kāmān* basically refers to sex attraction and its by-products in the form of children, home and so forth. Within the material world, the sex impulse is so strong that even a sincere candidate in the loving service of the Lord may sometimes be disturbed by sex attraction or by lingering sentiments for wife and children. A pure devotee certainly feels spiritual affection for all living entities, including the so-called wife and children, but he knows that material bodily attraction leads to no good, for it simply entangles one and one's so-called relatives in a miserable chain reaction of fruitive activities. The word *dṛḍha-niścaya* ("steadfast conviction") indicates that in any circumstance a devotee is completely determined to go on with his prescribed duties for Kṛṣṇa. Thus he thinks, "By my previous shameful life my heart is polluted with many illusory attachments. Personally I have no power to stop them. Only Lord Kṛṣṇa within my heart can remove such inauspicious contamination. But whether the Lord removes such attachments immediately or lets me go on being afflicted by them, I will never give up my devotional service to Him. Even if the Lord places millions of obstacles in my path, and even if because of my offenses I go to hell, I will never for a moment stop serving Lord Kṛṣṇa. I am not interested in mental speculation and fruitive activities; even if Lord Brahmā personally comes before me offering such engagements, I will not be even slightly interested. Although I am attached to material things I can see very clearly that they lead to no good because they simply give me trouble and disturb my devotional service to the Lord. Therefore, I sincerely repent my foolish attachments to so many material things, and I am patiently awaiting Lord Kṛṣṇa's mercy."

The word *prīta* indicates that a devotee feels exactly like the son or subject of the Supreme Personality of Godhead and is very attached to his relationship with the Lord. Therefore, although sincerely lamenting occasional lapses into sense enjoyment, he never gives up his enthusiasm to serve Lord Kṛṣṇa. If a devotee becomes too morose or discouraged in devotional service, he may drift into an impersonal consciousness or give up his devotional service to the Lord. Therefore, the Lord here advises that although one should sincerely repent, he should not become chronically depressed. One should understand that because of his past sins he must occasionally suffer disturbances from the material mind and senses, but one should not therefore become a devotee of detachment, as do the speculative philosophers. Although one may desire detachment to purify one's devotional service to the Lord, if one becomes more concerned with renunciation than with acting for the pleasure of Lord Kṛṣṇa, he is misunderstanding the position of loving devotional service. Faith in Lord Kṛṣṇa is so powerful that in due course of time it will automatically award detachment and perfect knowledge. If one gives up Lord Kṛṣṇa as the central object of one's worship and concentrates more on knowledge and detachment, one will become deviated from one's progress in going back home, back to Godhead. A sincere devotee of the Lord must be sincerely convinced that simply by the strength of devotional service and the mercy of Lord Kṛṣṇa he will achieve everything auspicious in life. One must believe that Lord Kṛṣṇa is all-merciful and that He is the only real goal of one's life. Such determined faith combined with a sincere desire to give up sense enjoyment will carry one past the obstacles of this world.

The words *jāta-śraddhaḥ mat-kathāsu* are most significant here. By faithful hearing of the mercy and glories of the Lord one will gradually be freed from all material desire and clearly see at every moment the utter frustration of sense gratification. Chanting the glories of the Lord with firm faith and conviction is a tremendously powerful spiritual process that enables one to give up all material association.

There is actually nothing inauspicious in the devotional service of the Lord. Occasional difficulties experienced by a devotee are due to his previous material activities. On the other hand, the endeavor for sense gratification is completely inauspicious. Thus sense gratification and devotional service are directly opposed to each other. In all circumstances one should therefore remain the Lord's sincere servant, always believing in His mercy. Then one will certainly go back home, back to Godhead.

TRANSLATION

When an intelligent person engages constantly in worshipping Me through loving devotional service as described by Me, his heart becomes firmly situated in Me. Thus all material desires within the heart are destroyed.

PURPORT

The material senses are engaged in gratifying the concoctions of the mind, causing many types of material desires to become prominent, one after another. One who constantly engages in the devotional service of the Lord by hearing and chanting the Lord's transcendental glories with firm faith gets relief from the harassment of material desires. By serving the Lord one becomes strengthened in the conviction that Śrī Kṛṣṇa is the only actual enjoyer and all others are meant to share the Lord's pleasure through devotional service. A devotee of the Lord situates Śrī Kṛṣṇa on a beautiful throne within his heart and there offers the Lord constant service. Just as the rising sun gradually eliminates all trace of darkness, the Lord's presence within the heart causes all material desires there to weaken and eventually disappear. The words *mayi hṛdi sthite* ("when the heart is situated in Me") indicate that an advanced devotee sees Lord Kṛṣṇa not only within his own heart but within the hearts of all living creatures. Thus a sincere devotee who chants and hears the glories of Śrī Kṛṣṇa should not be discouraged by the remnants of material desires within the heart. He should faithfully wait for the devotional process to naturally purify the heart of all contamination.

The above texts refer to devotees who are fixed in their devotional determination, yet still subject to disturbance. Those who are more neophyte and agitated may try to forcibly suppress their desires. However, such a process cannot ultimately be successful, for desires cannot be overcome unless they are purified. Like pressing on a bump in a carpet, a suppressed desire simply comes up elsewhere. A *brahmacārī* struggling with sex desire may not like to admit his predicament even to himself. But if he clearly has problems with gluttony, anger, or other contaminations, he should know it to be the same enemy—sex desire—manifesting in a different way. It is best for such a *brahmacārī* to admit his difficulty and face up to it with intelligence. Biting the teeth and straining to hold on eventually leads to collapse.

Devotees who feel excessively agitated, whose minds are always disturbed by lusty desires, had better consult a senior devotee for help. Śrīla Rūpa Gosvāmī recommends in his *Upadeśāmṛta* that devotees reveal their minds in confidence to others. Discussing spiritual difficulties with advanced devotees helps in overcoming them.

We should know that there is no easy way out. You can't just take a pill to stop sex desire. There is no instant *mantra, tantra, yantra, kavaca,* or astrological stone that makes material desires vanish. And although mechanical means, such as restricting association with women and dietary control, will help, the real magic formula is Kṛṣṇa consciousness, pure devotional service.

kecit kevalayā bhaktyā
vāsudeva-parāyaṇāḥ
aghaṁ dhunvanti kārtsnyena
nīhāram iva bhāskaraḥ

"Only a rare person who has adopted complete, unalloyed devotional service to Kṛṣṇa can uproot the weeds of sinful actions with no possibility that they will revive. He can do this by discharging devotional service, just as the sun can immediately dissipate fog by its rays."[191]

Śrīla Prabhupāda: "Why are you induced by sex life? Stop it by Kṛṣṇa consciousness. If you devote your whole life in Kṛṣṇa consciousness you will not be agitated by any sex life. If one is actually advanced in Kṛṣṇa consciousness, he will deride, 'Huh! Nonsense! What is this?' That is Kṛṣṇa conscious advancement. The only remedy is Kṛṣṇa consciousness."[192]

There is no other solution. We have to apply ourselves to Kṛṣṇa consciousness very seriously, and when Kṛṣṇa sees our sincerity He will bless us, and gradually all these dirty things will go away. As Śrīla Prabhupāda replied when asked what to do about lust, "You have to become Kṛṣṇa conscious, otherwise there is no solution to this problem."[193] "It is only by the grace of the Supreme Lord that one can be protected from the allurement of lusty material desires. The Lord gives protection to devotees who are always engaged in His transcendental loving service."[194]

As stated by Śrīla Narottama dāsa Ṭhākura, *kāma kṛṣṇa-karmārpaṇe:* lusty desires should be redirected toward the service of Kṛṣṇa. This is practical. A devotee who develops the desire to please Kṛṣṇa, and is constantly absorbed in His service, automatically overcomes material lust.

To maintain a constant service mood requires the steadiness of the mode of goodness. Steady *brahmacarya* is also possible only for those on the platform of goodness. *Ati-brahmacarya,* "extreme *brahmacarya*" may be manifested as artificial austerities or misogyny, but these are symptoms of the mode of passion.

It is a common misconception that lust can be conquered by being nasty to women, but traditional *brahmacārī* training is to learn to respect women. For a person brought up in lust, ugly passions will arise whenever he sees a beautiful young woman. But the sight of the same woman will arouse a respectful feeling for a mother in the heart of a person who has been trained properly. One who feels reverence for women, considering them as mothers, cannot lust after them or want to exploit them.

The tendency for the mind to sink to the lowest depths can be overcome by bringing it to the highest level. Instead of thinking of exploiting the bodies of others by sex life, a *brahmacārī* should meditate on how to bestow the topmost benefit upon all by preaching Kṛṣṇa consciousness. A *brahmacārī* sees the body of a woman as an allurement of *māyā*, but also sees a soul within crying out for Kṛṣṇa.

Narottama dāsa Ṭhākura states that material desires become insignificant if one gets the mercy of Lord Nityānanda. Lord Nityānanda was ordered by Lord Caitanya to preach Kṛṣṇa consciousness to all classes of men, even to the most fallen, which he did under the most difficult circumstances by exhibiting the greatest humility. So if we take on difficulties in preaching service, praying for Lord Nityānanda's mercy, surely He will help us.

Some new devotees experience that they feel more sexual agitation after coming to Kṛṣṇa consciousness than they did before! Philosophically we can understand that it was not that the devotee was more pure before coming to Kṛṣṇa, but that the stockpile of dormant material desires within the heart has become manifested.[195] When a room is cleaned after a long time, all the dust and dirt which was hidden in dark corners comes out. On initial cleaning, the room actually seems to become more dirty. The fact is that the room was full of dirt before, but because there was no proper attempt to clean it, the dirt remained unnoticed. But the end result is that the room becomes clean in a way that it never was before—not superficially, but completely. Similarly, chanting Hare Kṛṣṇa cleans the mirror of the heart. When material desires come out, go on chanting. If the heart is very dirty, the cleansing process may be long and difficult. But the end result, maybe after much endeavor, will be that the heart will be spotlessly clean.*

FALLDOWN

It is very disappointing that devotees, despite professing high ideals, sometimes deviate from the regulative principles, especially by falling into illicit sex. When devotees fall down, especially senior devotees, it causes great disturbance. Of course, that tendency is there in the conditioned souls. Before engagement in sense gratification comes contemplation of the act, which is developed from the seed of sinful desire in the mind. These unwanted desires arise out of the subconsciousness like bubbles surfacing from the bottom of a pond. The expert transcendentalist is adept at ignoring these grotesque thoughts and letting them die. If they are fed, they will grow bigger and bigger and eventually devour the aspiring yogi. Externally a devotee may act as if strong but if internally he harbors desires, then when an opportunity arises to fulfill those desires, the internal is likely to become external.

Even for a devotee seriously trying to lead a pure life, it is not surprising if he is attacked by gross desires, because it is the business of *māyā* to disturb him. The modern age is especially difficult for *brahmacārīs*, because even while walking on the street

---

* In this connection, *Cc. Madhya-līlā*, Chapter 12, "The Cleansing of the Guṇḍicā Temple," is very instructive.

they will see so many dressed-up women, cinema advertisements, and billboards, all specifically designed to invoke lusty desires. Modern cities throng with thousands of women trying to outdo each other in being provocative. Traditionally, *brahmacārīs* would keep their eyes downcast while walking on a public path, so as to avoid seeing the distractions of *māyā.* This may not be practical in today's cities, but still *brahmacārīs* have to be very careful to control their eyes while moving in *māyā's* kingdom. It is not surprising if the mind becomes agitated, but if a *brahmacārī* persistently cannot control his mind, he had better get married before he falls down into illicit sex.

A gross falldown may also happen accidentally, that is, without previous contemplation. Unexpectedly, a devotee may find himself in a situation where *māyā* is presenting herself to him, and due to insufficient spiritual strength he succumbs. Therefore a *brahmacārī* is cautious at every step of his life, so as to avoid danger. Kṛṣṇadāsa Kavirāja Gosvāmī has cautioned devotees not to fall into "the whirlpools of unfortunate situations. If one falls into such positions, he is finished."[196] However, we also have to preach in this most contaminated world. Therefore we should always stay tight in the association of devotees, and keep strong by hearing and chanting with full attention. Śrīla Prabhupāda: "If you chant always Hare Kṛṣṇa, read my books, and preach this philosophy sincerely, then Kṛṣṇa will provide you with all facility, and you will not fall down into material entanglement."[197]

For preaching we must take risks, but not to the extent that our minds become greatly agitated. We must know the limits of our strength in Kṛṣṇa consciousness, and work within those limits. Śrīla Prabhupāda: "That is our real mission, to deliver the world by preaching Kṛṣṇa's message to others, but even higher realization, the highest realization, is to save oneself."[198]

However, an inadvertent, temporary fall down is not a disqualification for devotional service—Kṛṣṇa forgives. The devotee must pick himself up quickly and carry on. But we must know that falldowns, even mental, are damaging to our devotional service. If there is no attempt for rectification, we can expect Kṛṣṇa to reciprocate such insincerity by withdrawing His mercy. Thus the privilege of devotional service is lost.

MASTURBATION

In our endeavor to become Kṛṣṇa conscious, *māyā* is always trying to knock us back. Even for a sincere devotee who has made considerable progress, *māyā* doesn't hesitate to use her lowest and grossest weapon: sex. Sometimes devotees—even responsible devotees who have no intentions of physically engaging in illicit sex—become weak. On lying down, they submit to the mad mind, and even against their own will[199] indulge in mental fantasies and masturbation.

This is a difficult problem, especially if it becomes a habit. If this contemplation is not stopped at an early stage, then it will likely go from thinking, to feeling, to willingly engaging in sex. Such a person usually ends up getting married, or worse, falls into illicit sex and becomes a debaucher. A devotee with this habit will always feel guilty, and may literally go crazy.

Guilty feelings sometimes impel a devotee to hide this problem from those who care about his devotional advancement. However, to rectify this faulty mentality requires confidential counseling from one's guru, local authority, or any other trusted devotee.

Admitting to this takes courage and can understandably be embarrassing. But if a devotee suffering from this malady is at all to overcome it, he must seek advice from a senior devotee who he can completely trust. Particularly, the spiritual master is the topmost well-wisher of the disciple, so no *anarthas* should be kept secret from him if the disciple really wants to weed them out for good.

However, even with the best of help, it may not be easy to overcome this painful predicament. The only real solution is to surrender to Kṛṣṇa. "This divine energy of Mine, consisting of the three modes of material nature, is difficult to overcome. But one who has surrendered to Me can easily cross beyond it."[200] We have to take shelter of Madana-mohana (See lengthy quote from Śrīla Prabhupāda's lecture in "Overcoming Sex Desire").

Take heart though, for "Impossible is a word in a fool's dictionary."[201] With sincere endeavor and the help of others this degrading habit can be broken.

A practical tip to Kṛṣṇa-ize the mind at night is to read the Kṛṣṇa book with devotees before retiring, and thus go to sleep thinking of Kṛṣṇa's pastimes. Some devotees go to sleep listening to a cassette of Śrīla Prabhupāda's transcendental voice purifying their mind.

In the following letter, Śrīla Prabhupāda seems to be addressing this problem: "You are finding some difficulty with sex desire and have asked guidance from me to instruct you how to handle this problem of the material body. First of all I think you should know that such problems are not very unnatural because in the body the conditioned soul is very prone to failure. But also we must remember that such failure will not discourage us from executing the most important mission of our life, to become fully Kṛṣṇa conscious. So whatever fall down has been, you should be regretful about it, but it is not so serious nor is it a permanent disqualification. But you must try to check yourself from such artificial things and take full shelter of the lotus feet of Kṛṣṇa. I think that for such checking, marriage is the only solution. It is understood that everyone has some nasty habits, but by sticking to Kṛṣṇa consciousness, chanting our required rounds loudly, and tending the Deities, these items will surely save you. So always be seriously engaged in serving Kṛṣṇa and pray to Kṛṣṇa to help you with your frailties. But I think that marriage is the solution with no other alternative. If you are married you can continue to practice all the items of worship and with more peace of mind, so such solution, along with redoubled efforts to serve nicely and be very pleasing to Kṛṣṇa, these things will help you. It is my open advice for everyone that one who is disturbed by sex must take the responsibility of married life."[202]

HOMOSEXUALITY

Neither heterosexuality nor homosexuality are "natural." Heterosexual desire is a perverted reflection of our original love for Kṛṣṇa and homosexuality is another twist. Śrīla Prabhupāda: "The homosexual appetite of a man for another man is demoniac and is not for any sane man in the ordinary course of life."[203]

Due to the influence of Kali-yuga, homosexuality is now a common problem. As Kali-yuga advances we will have to accommodate more and more people with past perverse lives and give them the opportunity for purification. If homosexuals sincerely come to Kṛṣṇa consciousness, what advice should we give them?

In the Vedic culture, heterosexual desires can be accommodated within the *gṛhastha-āśrama,* but there is no scope for accommodating homosexual desires. Śrīla Prabhupāda recommended marriage (to a woman!) for a disciple with homosexual desires. This advice may not seem very practical, for the homosexual's attraction is to men rather than women. But homosexual or heterosexual, the disease is lust. Homosexuality means that the lust has increased to an abnormally high degree. Marriage means to channel that lust in a manner acceptable within the Vedic culture.

Anyway, homosexuals coming to Kṛṣṇa consciousness will need special guidance from senior devotees. The homosexual must be understood as an individual person and be given proper facility after frank discussion. He should understand his condition to be especially fallen, but should be confident that by Kṛṣṇa consciousness, all difficulties can be overcome. And other devotees should be sympathetic and understanding with such sincere souls.

As with any conditioned soul accepted for devotional service, sheltering homosexuals in the *āśrama* is a risk. As with a heterosexual, we shall first have to see if a homosexual is sufficiently self-controlled before he may be allowed to stay in the *āśrama*, remembering that, whereas heterosexual *brahmacārīs* are sheltered from the objects of their attraction in the *brahmacārī-*

āśrama, the homosexual is surrounded by them. We must be compassionate, but we cannot sacrifice our standards of purity.

PREACHING ABOUT CELIBACY

Preaching to nondevotees should generally not be about celibacy, but about the need to become Kṛṣṇa conscious. If they take up Kṛṣṇa consciousness then everything else will follow. Newcomers to Kṛṣṇa consciousness are sometimes discouraged by so many restrictions, especially those on sex. They should be encouraged to chant, take *prasāda,* and associate with devotees. If they want sex, that is not forbidden—in the *gṛhastha-āśrama.* On the other hand, if a young man is ready to be a *brahmacārī,* by all means encourage him.

At least among committed devotees, preaching about celibacy must go on. Śrīla Prabhupāda: "The whole world is engaging in this vagina problem. These things should be regularly discussed. This is *kīrtana.* If these things are not discussed in our movement, then everything will grow weak. There should be one class after another. Everything is in the books."[204]

It is undoubtedly difficult to promote celibacy in a world atmosphere where everything is related to sex and women. The whole world today is absorbed in gross sense gratification, of which the ultimate expression is sex. Moreover, so-called scientists and doctors openly state that losing semen is not harmful to health.

If people ask why we are celibate, we can explain to them that it is a prerequisite for self-realization. The mind must be controlled, but it never can be if it is agitated by sex indulgence. One cannot be a transcendentalist, whether a yogi, *jñānī,* or devotee, without being celibate.[205]

Celibacy has been accepted by priests and monks in leading Hindu, Buddhist, and Christian traditions since time immemorial. Jesus, Buddha, Śaṅkarācārya, and countless others accepted the vow of celibacy. Celibacy is not an old-fashioned, cranky idea, but a dynamic, vital principle for achieving a success so sublime that ordinary people cannot conceive of it at all.

Furthermore, the practice of celibacy has not been limited to the sphere of religion. As Dr. R.W. Bernard notes in his book *Science Discovers the Physiological Value of Continence*:[206]
"The greatest intellectual geniuses in both ancient and modern times led continent lives, and there is yet to be recorded one individual who freely expended seminal fluid who ever amounted to anything. In most cases, individuals who have achieved have been forced by necessity to abstain from sexual indulgence, as Cervantes, who wrote *Don Quixote* while in prison, or Dante who wrote his *Divine Comedy* while in exile. Milton wrote *Paradise Lost* when blind and when he did not indulge in sex. Sir Isaac Newton, active in intellect until the age of 80, led a continent life from birth, and so did Leonardo da Vinci and Michelangelo, both of whom retained their creative genius (until) an advanced age."

Other famous celibates include Pythagoras, Plato, Aristotle, Spinoza, Kant, Beethoven, and Herbert Spencer. Many other philosophers, artists, and scientists have preferred to sublimate the sex drive so as to increase their creativity and concentrate their energy on intellectual pursuits.

This stands as evidence against the standard Freudian objection that celibates become frustrated and should therefore be allowed to indulge.* It is true that restricting the body without being able to control the mind could lead to psychosis. Without developing a higher consciousness, celibacy will be torture. But many non-celibates also suffer frustration, anxiety, or physical disease, caused directly or indirectly by sex. Celibate or non-celibate, the real problem is sex.

Furthermore, those with knowledge of the laws of karma understand that indulgence in sex entangles the conditioned souls ever more deeply in material bondage. The ultimate solution, then, is neither to accept nor reject sex, but to rise above it altogether to come to the spiritual platform. A fully Kṛṣṇa conscious person can be fully celibate or can have a dozen children, but either way his

* It is interesting to note that although Sigmund Freud's theories were instrumental in increasing promiscuity, he himself found it necessary at a certain point to abstain from conjugal relations so as to devote his life to his work.

consciousness is never contaminated. But for the neophyte transcendentalist, sexual agitation is a major disturbance in his meditation on the Absolute Truth.

Therefore, aspiring devotees who are capable of doing so are advised to remain completely celibate—if they can control their minds. Otherwise, devotees may get married and engage in restricted sex during part of their lives.

Nevertheless, sex is risky. Even within marriage, if sex is engaged in at the wrong time, in the wrong place, in the wrong consciousness, or without having undergone the required purificatory rituals, both man and woman become punishable by the laws of nature. Yet the pushing of sex desire is so strong that, even knowing all this, we become impelled to commit sinful acts. *Kāma eṣa krodha eṣa*. Therefore it is best to remain *brahmacārīs,* strictly avoiding contact with women so as not to be victimized.

Devotees must be convinced of the necessity of sense control. We must know that sense control is in our real self-interest. Without becoming free from sense gratification, especially sex, no one can achieve perfection in Kṛṣṇa consciousness. *Brahmacarya* is that essential training and practice in sense control and detachment, through which perfection is finally attained. We must be determined to follow the principles of *brahmacarya,* otherwise we cannot make any progress.

In preaching, another approach is to explain the deleterious effects of sex, animal slaughter, gambling, and intoxication on society. Crime, war, floods, droughts, famine, cancer, AIDS, and multifarious other problems are scourging the world. Learned professors write big scholarly treatises suggesting how to overcome the problems, but the problems remain. People do not know that they are reaping the poisonous harvest of sinful activities, especially of cow killing and illicit sex. However, even a hundred years ago, sense control was considered a virtue and excessive sense indulgence a vice.

It was only after "Man from monkeys" Darwin and "Let loose" Freud that the old barriers collapsed. Free sex flourished. Gradually, divorce, "living together," unmarried mothers, birth control, abortion, and homosexuality—all formerly banned and considered despicable—became socially acceptable. Nowadays austerity for spiritual advancement is considered despicable. The resultant society is a disaster, and getting worse. Now even child abuse and incest have become everyday affairs. The materialists express their horror, but probably after some time they will legalize and encourage these types of sinful activities as well.

It is quite possible because the whole society is made up of *varṇa-saṅkara*—children begotten in lust. John Lennon observed that, "Most children are born over a bottle of whisky on Saturday night." The degraded consciousness of such unwanted by-products is unimaginable. Born in the mode of ignorance, they are totally blind to the necessity of sense control. They are constantly involved in all kinds of abominable activities, considering them quite normal, and never for a moment imagine that the reactions to sinful activity are the cause of all chaos in human society.

STAYING BRAHMACĀRĪ

If one can stay a *brahmacārī* without being unduly agitated by sex desire, that is by far the best situation from which to aim at going back to Godhead. Without the heavy burden of family responsibilities, the distractions of social life, and the ever-present opportunity for sense gratification, the *brahmacārī* can live simply and peacefully and dedicate his whole life and energy to understanding Kṛṣṇa. Without having to cater to the expectations of often-materialistic relatives, his only obligation is to please his guru, Hari, and the Vaiṣṇavas. No need to get a job, no need to get a home, no need to go shopping for saris—simple, easy, and nice. So even if there is some difficulty or occasional mental agitation, if you can at all do it, stay *brahmacārī!* Avoid family life! Just see the example of Nārada Muni and the Haryaśvas.[207]

Śrīla Prabhupāda: *"Brahmacārī* life is the easiest *āśrama* to practice Kṛṣṇa consciousness from. So little is required. A little *prasāda.* A little service. And six feet of space to lay down your head at night and rest so you can continue to serve guru and Kṛṣṇa another day."[208]

"A *gṛhastha* has many responsibilities. A *brahmacārī* has no responsibility. His only responsibility is to serve Kṛṣṇa. The real business of human life is to take the responsibility of spiritual advancement. So if one remains *brahmacārī*, he has no disturbance in that responsibility. But if he becomes a *gṛhastha*, disturbance is there. You cannot take wholeheartedly the spiritual responsibility."[209]

Opting to remain celibate is a great decision. It is called *bṛhad-vrata* ("the great vow of perpetual celibacy"), for it is not at all easy to follow. Mahājana Bhīṣmadeva was awarded his name (meaning "terrible") by the demigods upon his adopting this vow,[210] for it is indeed a very difficult task to undertake. But for those who adhere firmly to this vow, it practically guarantees liberation.[211]

Brahmacarya is a path followed by only a few, and rarely understood or appreciated. Those who decide to remain lifelong celibates may have to face doubts expressed by those who believe such a determination to be impossible to keep. And considering that several apparently stalwart devotees have fallen into the clutches of women, it may well seem impractical for others to try to maintain such rigid vows. However, the failure or setback of some does not portend failure for all. Although throughout history some renunciates have fallen victim to woman, yet others have resisted female charms and thus gone on to achieve perfection. Our *ācāryas* have never stopped encouraging devotees to aspire for the highest ideal despite the inevitability that some will slip along the way. That most *brahmacārīs* eventually marry certainly does not mean that those determined to remain celibate cannot succeed.

Seriously committed *brahmacārīs* try to avoid the unnecessary entanglement of family life by dedicating their lives to guru and Kṛṣṇa. Even if householders are doubtful about the chances of such *brahmacārīs* surviving, they need not cynically and unnecessarily try to break the spirit and enthusiasm of *brahmacārīs* by telling them that they are fighting a hopeless battle. Such discouraging words may be due to enviousness on the part of such householders, who take perverse pleasure in prodding *brahmacārīs* to totter and fall.

Sometimes *brahmacārīs* are accused of hypocrisy: that for all their caution in dealing with women, they are not free from sex desire, and should therefore just get married. However, it is understood that the *brahmacārī* is not free from sex desire. If he were, he would not be in this material world. Nevertheless, he is following the path by which sex desire is overcome. It is not an easy path, and may take many years of careful practice to become perfect. That a *brahmacārī* still has sex desire is not an indictment, nor does it mean that he must get married. That he is committed to fight against *māyā* is praiseworthy, even if his progress is slow. Of course, those whose minds constantly dwell on sex are not *brahmacārīs* at all and have no business being in that *āśrama*.

Śrīla Prabhupāda: "My open advice is that if any one can remain a *brahmacārī*, it is very nice, but there is no need of artificial *brahmacārīs*. In *Bhagavad-gītā* it is stated that one who exhibits outwardly as self-restrained, but inwardly he thinks of sense gratification, he is condemned as a false pretender. We do not want any false pretenders in numbers, but we want a single sincere soul."[212]

The relevant verse is *Gītā* 3.6: "One who restrains the senses of action but whose mind dwells on sense objects certainly deludes himself and is called a pretender."

Those who unnecessarily scorn the glorious *brahmacārī-āśrama* like to cite this verse. However, the next verse of *Gītā* (3.7) describes actual *brahmacārīs*: "On the other hand, if a sincere person tries to control the active senses by the mind and begins *karma-yoga* (in Kṛṣṇa consciousness) without attachment, he is by far superior." Kṛṣṇa here speaks of controlling the senses by the mind. Those *brahmacārīs* who try to control the senses by force, by accepting a regimen of severe austerities, almost always fail and collapse miserably into sense gratification. Those who are naturally averse to sense indulgence, for whom living without comforts is pleasurable, who do not have to be coaxed into *sādhana* and service, are more suited for staying *brahmacārī*. One can remain *brahmacārī* whose desire to satisfy guru and Kṛṣṇa is stronger than his desire to satisfy his senses.

Such level-headed *brahmacārīs* try to control the active senses by the mind by applying in life what they have heard from *śāstra*. Those who can come to the platform of realization simply by hearing are most likely to remain *brahmacārīs* for life, whereas those who do not realize what they hear will have to make their own experiences in the *gṛhastha-āśrama*.

Those intending to remain lifelong *brahmacārīs* should particularly read and discuss those portions from *śāstra* that emphasize the value of remaining free from sex. (The second part of this book provides a comprehensive reader.) *Śāstric* descriptions of sexual entanglement are unreservedly factual and strong, and are welcomed by renunciates who want to break their material attachments. Those who want to maintain such attachments may dislike such descriptions, but that is simply their misfortune. Those who become enlivened by such strong statements are fit candidates for trying to remain as *brahmacārīs*. Those who become discouraged, thinking the challenge to overcome sexual attraction to be too tough, are not going to make it.

Notwithstanding the opinions of others, the lifelong *brahmacārī* goes on hearing and discussing such descriptions so as to maintain sharp spiritual intelligence. He must be firmly convinced that material life is no better than a ditch into which people pass stool. He does not feel *brahmacarya* to be an oppressively difficult struggle, but counts his blessings daily for remaining safe from family life.

The lifelong *brahmacārī* must have a positive, hopeful outlook, born of faith in Kṛṣṇa. Those with a critical, negative mentality cannot remain *brahmacārī*. The lifelong *brahmacārī* also has to develop an inner toughness and self-sufficiency. He maintains his determination even in non-ideal circumstances such as getting little personal association with advanced Vaiṣṇavas. His inner resolve is that of a *sannyāsī*, although he has not formally accepted that role. That resolve is to do whatever is necessary to make sure this is his last birth in the material world.

A *brahmacārī* who wants to remain as such has to understand that there will always be women in this world, that he cannot run away from the world, and that he must therefore adjust his consciousness to be absorbed in Kṛṣṇa. *Brāhme carati iti brahmacarya*. Avoidance of women can be practiced to a certain extent, but the real avoidance is to not let the mind indulge in thoughts of sense enjoyment. To one who is actually enjoying *brahma-sukha* (spiritual happiness), the question, "Should I get married or not?" will hardly enter his head, and if it does, he immediately rejects it without dwelling on it or being disturbed by it.

Along with the great endeavor to conquer sex desire, devotees who want to stay *brahmacārī* must cultivate a mood of selflessness. Most householders are practically compelled to give more importance to their immediate familial duties than to the mission of Kṛṣṇa consciousness. The *brahmacārī's* freedom from such obligations is not meant for living a foppish, lazy life but for cultivating selflessness in the service of Kṛṣṇa and his devotees. This is a vital key to staying *brahmacārī*. A so-called *brahmacārī* who is selfish and attached should get realistic and get married.

Simply a show of *brahmacarya* is not sufficient, nor can it last. *Brahmacarya* means *brāhme carati*, not "nonsense *carati*." A nonsense person dressed in saffron is not a *brahmacārī*. A real *brahmacārī* is absorbed in service, and is surrendered and determined. "*Brahmacārī* means strictly following."[213] "*Brahmacārī* life can be continued only by deep absorption in Kṛṣṇa consciousness."[214] "*Brahmacārī* means don't be attached. If you can, avoid all this nonsense. That is *brahmacārī*. Try to avoid, better. If not, enter (family life)."[215] Those who are not fully into it are in the wrong *āśrama*. Better they go home and become honest householders, rather than making a show of renunciation that they are not fit for.

"Renunciation is not cheap, but has to be pursued as a lifelong plan. Within this plan, discretion is the better part of valor. Lord Caitanya cautioned the young Raghunātha dāsa Gosvāmī that the ocean of material existence is very wide and not easily crossed. Just by impetuously jumping into the ocean and making a few mad strokes, we cannot expect to reach Kṛṣṇaloka." (Satsvarūpa dāsa Gosvāmī)

Some unmarried devotees are clearly unfit for remaining *brahmacārīs*. Those who are not very serious about spiritual life, or who are strongly inclined toward sense gratification, or whose minds are so agitated that they often become upset even over trifles, are obviously in the wrong *āśrama*. They are not to be condemned, for everyone is at a different stage of development and it cannot be expected that everyone will immediately take to full Kṛṣṇa consciousness.

On the other hand, those who are serious to stay *brahmacārī* should definitely be encouraged to do so, and not just married off for the sake of expediency. Our movement needs many examples of devotees who have stuck to Kṛṣṇa consciousness staunchly without feeling the need for increased sense gratification. Later on some of the most exemplary long-term *brahmacārīs* may take *sannyāsa.*

Sannyāsa means to be finished with sex life forever, to be saved from family life and to save others from family life. *Sannyāsīs* give the greatest service to humanity by traveling everywhere and preaching the message of Kṛṣṇa unrestrictedly. The *sannyāsa-āśrama* is the ideal for the other three *āśramas,* which are all meant to lead one to this fourth, crest-jewel of all *āśramas.* Traditionally, *brahmacārīs* act as assistants to *sannyāsīs,* so to serve and take the association of *sannyāsīs* will definitely be a great help for remaining a *brahmacārī.*

However, it is not that after several years a *brahmacārī* necessarily has to opt either for householder life or *sannyāsa*. The *brahmacārī-āśrama* is not just for children. Many spiritual institutions in India have senior *brahmacārīs* who are highly respected for their spiritual qualities. Śrīla Prabhupāda wrote that *brahmacārī* and *sannyāsa* life are in essence the same and that it was therefore not necessary for every *brahmacārī* to take *sannyāsa*.[216]

Indeed, in many ways the *brahmacārī-āśrama* is the best for spiritual advancement and developing Vaiṣṇava qualities. It facilitates the essential quality of humility, for the *brahmacārī* has neither the possessions of a *gṛhastha* nor the status of a *sannyāsī*, both of which can foster false pride. *Brahmacārī* life is generally considerably more simple and austere than that of *sannyāsīs* in the modern day. *Brahmacārīs* can remain less entangled than *sannyāsīs* in the social affairs of householders, who prefer to go to *sannyāsīs* for blessings and advice, and who like to call *sannyāsīs* to their homes and feed them. The *brahmacārī-āśrama* is also intrinsically the best for nurturing surrender to guru.

Therefore, more important than formally taking *sannyāsa* is the firm decision to stay *brahmacārī*, with determination never to engage in sex life again. With such a conviction, a *brahmacārī* practices Kṛṣṇa consciousness with deep faith and commitment. If one wants to stay *brahmacārī,* a whimsical approach will not do. What is required is firm, steady service; regular, potent *sādhana;* and a deep vision of Kṛṣṇa consciousness acquired from intensive study of Śrīla Prabhupāda's books.

AND IF YOU ARE THINKING ABOUT GETTING MARRIED...

If you are thinking about getting married, stop it. Much better just to remain *brahmacārī.* If all you've heard about getting married doesn't help you understand that you shouldn't, read on. (It would have been nicer not to have such a section in this book. But many *brahmacārīs* eventually get married, and some guidance is needed for them.)

Having received the great benediction of a human birth, and the even more rarely achieved gift of association with devotees, we stand poised on the threshold of eternity. Will we be intelligent enough to perfect our lives by fully surrendering to Kṛṣṇa, or will we have to come back again to taste the bitter fruits of material life?

We want Kṛṣṇa. That's why we have taken to Kṛṣṇa consciousness. But to get Kṛṣṇa, the supreme pure, we have to become pure. Hence, there is the process of devotional service. But it takes time. No one is becoming a pure devotee overnight. We want Kṛṣṇa, but we are held back by multifarious material desires, especially the powerful sex urge, which haunts us like a repeating nightmare.

Therefore the Vedic social system is arranged for gradual purification. Of the four *āśramas,* three are specifically meant for renunciation. And because we conditioned souls have so many material desires, in the *gṛhastha-āśrama* scope is given for limited "enjoyment," coupled with the continuous performance of auspicious activities.

In youth the senses are very strong. A conditioned soul may be seriously seeking self-realization, but is not ready for full renunciation. He has the facility to enjoy(?) family life during early manhood, while keeping in contact with Kṛṣṇa consciousness. When old age approaches he must again take up a life of penance.

Lifelong *brahmacarya* is for those *brahmacārīs* who never consider marriage as an option. If thoughts of marriage or sex start to linger in the mind of a *brahmacārī*, if he feels dissatisfied with his status as a menial servant, or is anxious about his future security, it is an indication that he is probably in the wrong *āśrama* and should prepare himself for marriage. He should honestly face the question, "I may be able to avoid marriage now, but will I be able to remain single throughout life?"

Sometimes it is said that family life is the safe path[217] and *brahmacarya* the easy path. *Brahmacārī* life is by nature simple and in that sense easy. Although somewhat austere, it frees its practitioners from unnecessary material entanglements and the problems that go along with them. Thus a *brahmacārī* remains largely problem-free. A genuine *brahmacārī* has few problems, and especially does not have serious mental problems. A *brahmacārī* with many problems should go to the *āśrama* for working out problems, namely the *gṛhastha-āśrama,* which is by nature full of problems. Indeed, although *brahmacārī* life is considered austere because it tends toward zero sense gratification, the difficulties a *gṛhastha* has to undergo to maintain his little sense gratification are often more than those a *brahmacārī* voluntarily accepts.

Thus the *gṛhastha-āśrama* is said to be safe but problematic, whereas the *brahmacārī-āśrama* is relatively problem-free but can be risky. But in another way the *brahmacārī* is more safe, because he has no opportunity to indulge in sex, whereas a householder may do so at any time. The safety of a householder is that if he is going to indulge in sex, he may do so licitly with his wife, whereas a *brahmacārī* who fails to control his senses can only do so illicitly. *Brahmacārī* life is safe, then, only if the *brahmacārī* is sufficiently controlled to be a real *brahmacārī*. If he is too much agitated by lusty desires, he is unsafe in the *brahmacārī-āśrama*, and should become safe by entering householder life.

However, it is naive to think that getting married is a cure for sex desire. It's not that easy. Rather, those who are not self-controlled within marriage increase their attachment for sex by indulging in it. Thus, the safety of family life is not without its perils, and is hard-earned.

The best practice of *brahmacarya*, therefore, is to persevere and remain free from sex. It is not necessary or compulsory that everyone get married. But for one who cannot maintain the firm determination to stay *brahmacārī,* and is agitated so severely by material desires that he cannot concentrate properly on service, it may be better for him to get married and be done with it rather than totter on the mental platform indefinitely. An unsteady *brahmacārī* can battle on and try to become more fixed, but unless he soon does so, it may be difficult for him to avoid marriage.

From the philosophical standpoint, for a *brahmacārī* to marry doesn't seem to make a lot of sense. The purpose of this movement is to get disentangled from the material world, so to deliberately get re-entangled appears to be self-defeating.

Of course, getting married is not an offense, and is a reality for most devotees. But a would-be *gṛhastha* should know what he is getting into. Marriage is often approached whimsically, without enough serious consideration and preparation. It is better to be informed about the responsibilities of married life, and to have a clear picture of what lies ahead after marriage.

Brahmacārīs should have a mature and proper understanding of what being a *gṛhastha* means. Otherwise, they may have a romantic misconception of the *gṛhastha-āśrama*, which is actually based on the commitment to responsibly maintain a Kṛṣṇa conscious family. *Brahmacārīs* contemplating marriage should carefully study Śrīla Prabhupāda's extensive instructions on *gṛhastha* duties, so as not to be bewildered on this point.

Brahmacārīs in the illusion that family life is nice are advised to read "The Forest of Material Enjoyment."[218] Unfortunately, the power of *māyā* is such that even upon reading such descriptions of the horrors of family life, those who are inclined toward it think that such descriptions are exaggerated, or would not apply in their case. Be warned: When the scriptures describe the miseries of family life, it is not just theoretical or in reference to mundane marriages only. Licit or illicit, the fleeting delight of sex is always accompanied by suffering. *Brahmacārī*s who doubt this may ask any sober householder what he thinks about family life. Almost all of them will advise to stay *brahmacārī* if possible.

Family life is always troublesome, and in today's unsettled and complex world, getting married is a greater risk than ever before. Marriage as an institution has suffered greatly, and devotees' marriages have been no exception.

The attempt to make family life smooth and comfortable takes up much of the time and energy of most householders, yet is nevertheless rarely achieved. The minuscule joys of family life, earned with many difficulties, increase as more children are born. To maintain a wife and family is not easy. In Kali-yuga a man who can simply maintain a wife and a family is considered to be a highly successful person. If the wife is demanding or not very compatible with the husband, the suffering increases more and more without respite.

Therefore marriage should not be entered into lightly, but with caution, reserve, and sobriety. If a man is not prepared to take full responsibility, he shouldn't get married. Whimsically messing up peoples' lives, thinking, "Well, I'll just check it out, and if I don't like it, I'll drop it," is one of the symptoms of Kali-yuga mentioned in the *Śrīmad-Bhāgavatam.* The scriptural recommendations about non-attachment are not a wholesale license for irresponsibility. Non-attachment does not mean that a husband should whimsically leave his wife (or vice versa). If they are so unattached then why did they marry in the first place?

Many ISKCON devotees have entered into marriage without the sense of commitment demanded by Vedic standards. The resultant divorce rate is even worse than that of the *karmīs,* although Śrīla Prabhupāda did not want any divorce at all. This is Kali-yuga marriage. As soon as there is a disagreement between husband and wife (as there almost inevitably will be), or if one partner finds the other not sufficiently sexually attractive, then there is separation and divorce. This continues to be a major problem within our society and a cause of losing many devotees to *māyā.* As long as this divorce syndrome continues in ISKCON, it will be very difficult to substantiate to the world our claims of an alternative, better way of life. Devotees have to become responsible.

The father must be responsible to maintain his dependents both materially and spiritually, without abandoning them whimsically if there is some problem. But the social situation is so unstable that many materially solvent men become paupers overnight. Nor is there any guarantee that one's children are going to be serious about Kṛṣṇa consciousness—the lure of gross sense gratification has already claimed scores of ISKCON children.

The father is responsible for: seeing that the wife, children, and other dependents are properly clothed, housed, fed, and educated, and that their health needs are taken care of; arranging the marriages of the children and especially of the daughters, and, most important; ensuring they get training and guidance in Kṛṣṇa consciousness.

There are quite a few senior *gṛhastha* devotees whose marriages have been more or less successful, so *gṛhasthas*-to-be and newly married couples would be well advised to consult them. In any marriage the going will not always be smooth, so if you can get some sympathetic help, take it.

Now, when to get married and how to go about it? Better not leave it too late. Marriage does not have to be a last gasp rescue attempt for an agitated wreck of a *brahmacārī*—much better if it can be planned and entered into in a sober manner. The traditional Vedic system is that at about the age of twenty, after about fifteen years in the *gurukula,* a *brahmacārī* sits with his guru to decide whether or not he should be married. Even if the guru directs him toward householder life, the *brahmacārī* may spend a few more years in the *gurukula* before getting married, without mental agitation caused by uncertainty.

Śrīla Prabhupāda recommended that men be married by 25, when in the prime of life and able to easily beget healthy children. Remember, when you get toward fifty, you will have to think about renunciation again. So by that time your first progeny should be grown up. "I understand that you do not want to get married now, but if you marry at all, you should marry now. Because after the age of 30, marriage is not so pleasing."[219]

A *brahmacārī* who has reached his mid-thirties would be well advised to remain a life-long *brahmacārī.* Even with difficulty, if by performing humble service and by keeping strong association, he can avoid getting entangled so late in life, then that will be more suitable for spiritual life than becoming a middle-aged bridegroom.

Before getting married, however, it is best to get at least five good years in the *brahmacārī-āśrama.* A solid training in renunciation and sense control is a firm foundation for household life. When a *brahmacārī* is confident that he can remain a *brahmacārī* even when living with a woman, then he is ready to enter the *gṛhastha-āśrama.* "Remain a *brahmacārī*" means that he will continue to be attached to austerity. He will never give up chanting at least sixteen rounds, following the four regulative principles, rising early, taking only *prasāda,* etc. His unavoidably increased contact with women, money, sense gratification, and social life will not be the cause of his falldown.

Otherwise, (we've seen it happen so often) a man prematurely married fails to control his senses and tumbles into a dark well. His

Kṛṣṇa consciousness becomes covered over, he loses the ability to understand what is actually beneficial for him, and his family life becomes almost exactly like that of a *karmī.*

So spend some time as a *brahmacārī.* Go through the rigors and ecstasies of book distribution, study Śrīla Prabhupāda's books conscientiously, travel, preach, have some transcendental adventure and fun.

Then, how to go about getting a suitable partner. This should be done prudently. It is best to take a little time, and not rush into marrying. The Vedic system is that a third party arranges the marriage—the boy and girl would not even see each other till the wedding day. Moderners will protest, but the stability of arranged marriages in India is still far greater than that of "love marriages" in the West. *Brahmacārīs* whose parents are not Kṛṣṇa conscious may consult some senior *gṛhasthas* for help in arranging a suitable match. *(Sannyāsīs* and gurus should not be approached as marriage counselors; it is not meant for them.) A *brahmacārī* should not hang around the *brahmacāriṇīs* and check them out, thus encouraging looseness. Also, before marriage, the would-be husband must make adequate arrangements for income and accommodation. (Śrīla Prabhupāda has given much advice on marriage and how to enter into it in *Śrīmad-Bhāgavatam,* Canto 3, Chapters 21-24.)

Brahmacārīs should not have any stigma against *gṛhasthas* or against *brahmacārīs* planning to get married. It is not necessarily true that a *brahmacārī* is any less serious because he is thinking of entering householder life. The *brahmacārī* who can remain as a *brahmacārī* respects *brahmacārīs* who get married, knowing that their purpose is to come to the transcendental platform.

A final point: Make up your mind. Do not flip-flop, changing back and forth from saffron to white cloth like a chameleon.

Śrīla Prabhupāda wrote many letters to devotees who were considering whether or not to get married, and some quotations have been reproduced in the appendices so that devotees presently in the same predicament can take advantage of his advice.

THE AUTHOR

Born in Britain in 1957, the author joined ISKCON in London in 1975 and was initiated that year, with the name Ilāpati dāsa, by the founder-*Ācārya,* His Divine Grace A. C. Bhaktivedanta Swami Prabhupāda.

From 1977 to 1979 Ilāpati dāsa was based in India, mostly traveling in West Bengal distributing Śrīla Prabhupāda's books. He spent the following ten years helping to pioneer ISKCON's preaching in Bangladesh, Burma, Thailand, and Malaysia.

In 1989 he was granted the order of *sannyāsa,* receiving the name Bhakti Vikāsa Swami, and again made his base in India. Since then he has preached Kṛṣṇa consciousness throughout the subcontinent—lecturing in English, Hindi, and Bengali—and also spending a few months each year preaching in the western hemisphere. His television lectures in Hindi have been viewed by millions worldwide.

Bhakti Vikāsa Swami writes extensively on Kṛṣṇa conscious topics. His books have been translated into over twenty languages, with more than four hundred thousand in print.

A BRAHMACĀRĪ READER:

ŚRĪLA PRABHUPĀDA AND OTHERS ON BRAHMACARYA, MARRIAGE, THE DANGERS OF SEXUAL ATTRACTION, AND RELATED TOPICS ESPECIALLY RELEVANT FOR BRAHMACĀRĪS.

Following is a series of quotes extracted from Śrīla Prabhupāda's books, letters, recorded lectures and conversations, and from reliable anecdotes, which complement the subject matter of this book.

There are many important *ślokas* relating to control of the senses and the mind in the *Bhagavad-gītā,* and several long sections in the *Bhāgavatam,* which are very important for *brahmacārīs.* To save space, these have not been printed in this book. References to them are given below.

Gītā verses:

2.58–71
3.34, 36–43
4.26, 34
5.21–23
6.4–7, 13, 14, 16–19, 26, 34–36
8.28 18.36–38

Important passages from *Śrīmad-Bhāgavatam:*

Canto 3, Chapters 30 and 31, especially Chapter 31, verses 32–42
Canto 4, Chapters 25–29, "The Story of King Purañjana."
Canto 5, Chapter 5, verses 1–13
Canto 5, Chapters 13 and 14
Canto 7, Chapter 12, verses 1–16
Canto 9, Chapter 19, verses 1–17
Canto 11, Chapter 26, verses 1–24

Śrī Caitanya-caritāmṛta, Antya-līlā, Chapter 3: "The Punishment of Junior Haridāsa," is also very instructive.

Recommended further reading regarding the value of celibacy: Brain Gain, by H.H. Danavir Goswami, 2005: Rupanuga Vedic College, Kansas City, USA.

QUOTES FROM ŚRĪMAD-BHĀGAVATAM

The whole material creation is moving under the principle of sex life. In modern civilization, sex life is the focal point for all activities. (1.1.1)

One cannot enter into the kingdom of God unless one is perfectly cleared of all sins. The material sins are products of our desires to lord it over material nature. It is very difficult to get rid of such desires. Women and wealth are very difficult problems for the devotee making progress on the path back to Godhead. Many stalwarts in the devotional line fell victim to these allurements and thus retreated from the path of liberation. But when one is helped by the Lord Himself, the whole process becomes as easy as anything by the divine grace of the Lord.

To become restless in the contact of women and wealth is not an astonishment, because every living being is associated with such things from remote time, practically immemorial, and it takes time to recover from this foreign nature. But if one is engaged in hearing the glories of the Lord, gradually he realizes his real position. By the grace of God such a devotee gets sufficient strength to defend himself from the state of disturbances, and gradually all disturbing elements are eliminated from his mind. (1.2.17)

In the system of *varṇāśrama-dharma,* which is the beginning of actual human life, small boys after five years of age are sent to become *brahmacārīs* at the guru's *āśrama,* where these things are systematically taught to boys, be they king's sons or sons of ordinary citizens. The training was compulsory, not only to create good citizens of the state, but also to prepare the boy's future life for spiritual realization. The irresponsible life of sense enjoyment was unknown to children of the followers of the *varṇāśrama* system. Without being self-controlled, without being disciplined and without being fully obedient, no one can become successful in following the instructions of the spiritual master, and without doing so, no one is able to go back to Godhead. (1.5.24)

The main purpose of *varṇāśrama-dharma* is to awaken knowledge and detachment. The *brahmacārī-āśrama* is the training ground for the prospective candidates. In this *āśrama* it is instructed that this material world is not actually the home of the living being. The conditioned souls under material bondage are prisoners of matter, and therefore self-realization is the ultimate aim of life. The whole system of *varṇāśrama-dharma* is a means to detachment. One who fails to assimilate this spirit of detachment is allowed to enter into family life with the same spirit of detachment. Therefore, one who attains detachment may at once adopt the fourth order, namely, renounced, and thus live on charity only, not to accumulate wealth, but just to keep body and soul together for ultimate realization. Household life is for one who is attached, and the *vānaprastha* and *sannyāsa* orders of life are for those who are detached from material life. The *brahmacārī-āśrama* is especially meant for training both the attached and detached. (1.9.26)

It is essential that one practice self-control by celibacy without the least desire for sex indulgence. For a man desiring to improve the condition of his existence, sex indulgence is considered suicidal, or even worse. Therefore, to live apart from family life means to become self-controlled in regard to all sense desires, especially sex desires. (2.1.16)

The grossest type of *anartha* which binds the conditioned soul in material existence is sex desire, and this sex desire gradually develops in the union of the male and female. When the male and female are united, the sex desire is further aggravated by the accumulation of buildings, children, friends, relatives and wealth. When all these are acquired, the conditioned soul becomes overwhelmed by such entanglements, and the false sense of egoism, or the sense of "myself" and "mine" becomes prominent, and the sex desire expands to various political, social, altruistic, philanthropic and many other unwanted engagements, resembling the foam of the sea waves, which becomes very prominent at one time and at the next moment vanishes as quickly as a cloud in the sky. The conditioned soul is encircled by such products, as well as products of sex desire, which is summarized in three headings, namely profit, adoration and distinction. All conditioned souls are mad after these different forms of sex desire, and one shall see for himself how much he has been freed from such material hankerings based primarily on the sex desire. As a person feels his hunger satisfied after eating each morsel of foodstuff, he must similarly be able to see the degree to which he has been freed from sex desire. The sex desire is diminished along with its various forms by the process of *bhakti-yoga* because *bhakti-yoga* automatically, by the grace of the Lord, effectively results in knowledge and renunciation, even if the devotee is not materially very well educated. Knowledge means knowing things as they are, and if by deliberation it is found that there are things which are at all unnecessary, naturally the person who has acquired knowledge leaves aside such unwanted things. When the conditioned soul finds by culture of knowledge that material necessities are unwanted things, he becomes detached from such unwanted things. This stage of knowledge is called *vairāgya* or detachment from unwanted things. We have previously discussed that the transcendentalist is required to be self-sufficient and should not beg from the rich blind persons to fulfill the bare necessities of life. Śukadeva Gosvāmī has suggested some alternatives for the bare necessities of life, namely the problem of eating, sleeping and shelter, but he has not suggested any alternative for sex satisfaction. One who has the sex desire still with him should not at all try to accept the renounced order of life. For one who has not attained to this stage, there is no question of a renounced order of life. So by the gradual process of devotional service under the guidance of a proper spiritual master, and following the principles of the *Bhāgavatam,* one must be able to at least to control the gross sex desire before one accepts the renounced order of life factually.

So purification means getting free gradually from sex desire. (2.2.12)

From the Lord's genitals originate water, semen, generatives, rains and the procreators. His genitals are the cause of a pleasure that counteracts the distress of begetting.

The genitals and the pleasure of begetting counteract the distresses of family encumbrances. One would cease to generate altogether if there were not by the grace of the Lord, a coating, a pleasure-giving substance, on the surface of the generative organs. This substance gives a pleasure so intense that it counteracts fully the distress of family encumbrances. A person is so captivated by this pleasure-giving substance that he is not satisfied by begetting a single child, but increases the number of children, with great risk in regard to maintaining them, simply for this pleasure-giving substance. This pleasure-giving substance is not false, however, because it originates from the transcendental body of the Lord. In other words, the pleasure-giving substance is a reality, but it has taken on an aspect of pervertedness on account of material contamination. In this material world, sex life is the cause of many distresses on account of material contact. Therefore, the sex life in the material world should not be encouraged beyond the necessity. (2.6.8 Text & Purport)

The spiritual world, which consists of three fourths of the Lord's energy, is situated beyond this material world, and it is especially meant for those who will never be reborn. Others, who are attached to family life and who do not strictly follow celibacy vows, must live within the three material worlds.

The climax of the system of *varṇāśrama-dharma* or *sanātana-dharma* is clearly expressed here in this particular verse of *Śrīmad-Bhāgavatam.* The highest benefit that can be awarded to a human being is to train him to be detached from sex life, particularly because it is only due to sex indulgence that the conditioned life of material existence continues birth after birth. Human civilization in which there is no control of sex life is a fourth-class civilization because in such an atmosphere there is no liberation of the soul encaged in the material body. Birth, death, old age and disease are related to the material body, and they have nothing to do with the spirit soul. But as long as the bodily attachment for sensual enjoyment is encouraged, the individual spirit soul is forced to continue the repetition of birth and death on account of the material body, which is compared to garments, subjected to the law of deterioration.

In order to award the highest benefit of human life, the *varṇāśrama* system trains the follower to adopt the vow of celibacy beginning from the order of *brahmacārī.* The *brahmacārī* life is for students who are educated to follow strictly the vow of celibacy. Youngsters who have had no taste of sex life can easily follow the vow of celibacy, and once fixed in the principle of such a life, one can very easily continue to the highest perfectional stage, attaining the kingdom of the three-fourths energy of the Lord. It is already explained that in the cosmos of three-fourths energy of the Lord there is neither death nor fear, and one is full of the blissful life of happiness and knowledge. A householder attached to family life can easily give up such a life of sex indulgence if he has been trained in the principles of the life of a *brahmacārī.* A householder is recommended to quit home at the end of fifty years (*pañcaśordhvaṁ vanaṁ vrajet*) and live a life in the forest; then, being fully detached from family affection, he may accept the order of renunciation as a *sannyāsī* fully engaged in the service of the Lord. Any form of religious principles in which the followers are trained to pursue the vow of celibacy is good for the human being because only those who are trained in that way can end the miserable life of material existence. The principles of *nirvana,* as recommended by Lord Buddha, are also meant for ending the miserable life of material existence. And this process, in the highest degree, is recommended here in the *Śrīmad-Bhāgavatam,* with clear perception of ideal perfection, although basically there is no difference between the process of Buddhists, Śaṅkarites and Vaiṣṇavites. For promotion to the highest status of perfection, namely freedom from birth and death, anxiety and fearfulness, not one of these processes allows the follower to break the vow of celibacy.

The householders and persons who have deliberately broken the vow of celibacy cannot enter into the kingdom of deathlessness. The pious householders or the fallen yogis or the fallen transcendentalists can be promoted to the higher planets within the material world (one fourth of the energy of the Lord), but they will fail to enter into the kingdom of deathlessness. *Abṛhad-vratas* are those who have broken the vow of celibacy. *The vānaprasthas,* or those retired from family life, and the *sannyāsīs,* or renounced persons, cannot break the vow of celibacy if they want success in the process. The *brahmacārīs, vānaprasthas* and *sannyāsīs* do not intend to take rebirth (*apraja*), nor are they meant for secretly indulging in sex life. Such a fall down by the spiritualist may be compensated by another chance for human life in good families of learned *brāhmaṇas* or of rich merchants for another term of elevation, but the best thing is to attain the highest perfection of deathlessness as soon as the human form of life is attained; otherwise the whole policy of human life will prove to be a total failure. Lord Caitanya was very strict in advising His followers in this matter of celibacy. For a transcendentalist, therefore, who at all wants to be promoted to the kingdom beyond material miseries, it is worse than suicide to deliberately indulge in sex life, especially in the renounced order of life. Sex life in the renounced order of life is the most perverted form of religious life, and such a misguided person can only be saved if, by chance, he meets a pure devotee. (2.6.20 Text & Purport)

To exhibit His personal ways of austerity and penance, He appeared in twin forms as Nārāyaṇa and Nara in the womb of Mūrti, the wife of Dharma and the daughter of Dakṣa. Celestial beauties, the companions of Cupid, went to try to break His vows, but they were unsuccessful, for they saw that many beauties like them were emanating from Him, the Personality of Godhead.

The Lord, being the source of everything that be, is the origin of all austerities and penances also. Great vows of austerity are undertaken by sages to achieve success in self-realization. Human life is meant for such *tapasya,* with the great vow of celibacy, or *brahmacarya.* In the rigid life of *tapasya,* there is no place for the association of women. And because human life is meant for *tapasya* for self-realization, factual human civilization, as conceived by the system of *sanātana-dharma* or the school of four castes and four orders of life, prescribes rigid disassociation from woman in three stages of life. In the order of gradual cultural development, one's life may be divided into four divisions: celibacy, household life, retirement and renunciation. During the first stage of life, up to twenty-five years of age, a man may be trained as a *brahmacārī* under the guidance of a bona fide spiritual master just to understand that woman is the real binding force in material existence. If one wants to get freedom from the material bondage of conditional life, he must get free from the attraction for the form of a woman. Woman, or the fair sex, is the enchanting principle for the living entities, and the male form, especially in the human being, is meant for self-realization. The whole world is moving under the spell of womanly attraction, and as soon as a man becomes united with a woman, he at once becomes a victim of material bondage under a tight knot. The desires for lording it over the material world, under the intoxication of a false sense of lordship, specifically begin just after the man's unification with a woman. The desires for acquiring a house, possessing land, having children and becoming prominent in society, the affection for community and the place of birth, and the hankering for wealth, which are all like phantasmagoria or illusory dreams, encumber a human being, and he is thus impeded in his progress toward self-realization, the real aim of life. The *brahmacārī,* or a boy from the age of five years, especially from the higher castes, namely from the scholarly parents (the *brāhmaṇas*), the administrative parents (the *kṣatriyas*), or the mercantile or productive parents (the *vaiśyas*), is trained until twenty-five years of age under the care of a bona fide guru or teacher, and under strict observance of discipline he comes to understand the values of life along with taking specific training for a livelihood. The *brahmacārī* is then allowed to go home and enter householder life and get married to a suitable woman. But there are many *brahmacārīs* who do not go home to become householders but continue the life of *naiṣṭhika-brahmacārīs,* without any connection with women. They accept the order of *sannyāsa,* or the renounced order of life, knowing well that combination with women is an unnecessary burden that checks self-realization. Since sex desire is very strong at a certain stage of life, the guru may allow the *brahmacārī* to marry; this license is given to a *brahmacārī* who is unable to continue the way of *naiṣṭhika-brahmacarya,* and such discriminations are possible for the bona fide guru. A program of so-called family planning is needed. The householder who associates with woman under scriptural restrictions after a thorough training of *brahmacarya* cannot be a householder like cats and dogs. Such a householder, after fifty years of age, would retire from the association of women as a *vānaprastha* to be trained to live alone without the association of woman. When the practice is complete, the same retired householder becomes a *sannyāsī,* strictly separate from woman, even from his married wife. Studying the whole scheme of disassociation from women, it appears that a woman is a stumbling block for self-realization. (2.7.6 Text & Purport)

Those who are serious about gaining release from material bondage should not be entangled in the false relationship of family bondage. (3.12.5)

The human being is a social animal, and his unrestricted mixing with the fair sex leads to downfall. Such social freedom of man and woman, especially among the younger section, is certainly a great stumbling block on the path of spiritual progress. Material bondage is due only to sexual bondage, and therefore unrestricted association of man and woman is surely a great impediment. (3.12.28)

During student life the *brahmacārīs* were given full instructions about the importance of the human form of life. Thus the basic education was designed to encourage the student in becoming free from family encumbrances. Only students unable to accept such a vow in life were allowed to go home and marry a suitable wife. Otherwise, the student would remain a perfect *brahmacārī,* observing complete abstinence from sex for his whole life. It all depended on the quality of the student's training. (3.12.42)

When a man or woman is afflicted by the lust of sex desire, it is to be understood as sinful contamination. (3.14.16)

The three perfections of liberation are religiosity, economic development and sense gratification; for a conditioned soul, the wife is considered to be the source of liberation because she offers her service to the husband for his ultimate liberation. Conditional material existence is based on sense gratification, and if someone has the good fortune to get a good wife, he is helped by the wife in all respects. If one is disturbed in his conditional life, he becomes more and more entangled in material contamination. A faithful wife is supposed to co-operate with her husband in fulfilling all material desires so that he can then become comfortable and execute spiritual activities for the perfection of life. If, however, the husband is progressive in spiritual advancement, the wife undoubtedly shares in his activities, and thus both the wife and the husband profit in spiritual perfection. It is essential, therefore, that girls as well as boys be trained to discharge spiritual duties so that at the time of co-operation both will be benefited. The training of the boy is *brahmacarya,* and the training of the girl is chastity. A faithful wife and spiritually trained *brahmacārī* are a good combination of advancement of the human mission. (3.14.17)

Of the four orders of human society—the student or *brahmacārī* order, the householder, or *gṛhastha* order, the retired or *vānaprastha* order, and the renounced, or *sannyāsa* order—the householder is on the safe side. The bodily senses are considered plunderers of the fort of the body. The wife is supposed to be the commander of the fort, and therefore whenever there is an attack on the body by the senses, it is the wife who protects the body from being smashed. The sex demand is inevitable for everyone, but one who has a fixed wife is saved from the onslaught of the sense enemies. A man who possesses a good wife does not create a disturbance in society by corrupting virgin girls.

Without a fixed wife, a man becomes a debauchee of the first order and is a nuisance in society—unless he is a trained *brahmacārī, vānaprastha* or *sannyāsī.* Unless there is rigid and systematic training of the brahmacārī by the expert spiritual master, and unless the student is obedient, it is sure that the so-called *brahmacārī* will fall prey to the attack of sex. There are so many instances of fall down, even for great yogis like Viśvāmitra.

A *gṛhastha* is saved, however, because of his faithful wife. Sex life is the cause of material bondage, and therefore it is prohibited in three *āśramas* and is allowed only in the *gṛhastha-āśrama.* The *gṛhastha* is responsible for producing first-quality *brahmacārīs, vānaprasthas* and *sannyāsīs.* (3.14.20)

Sex life is the background of material existence. Here also it is repeated that demons are very fond of sex life. The more one is free from the desires for sex, the more he is promoted to the level of the demigods; the more one is inclined to enjoy sex, the more he is degraded to the level of demoniac life. (3.20.23)

Brahmacarya (following the rules and regulations of celibacy) is required for perfection of self-realization and mystic power. (3.21.4)

Here are some descriptions of a *brahmacārī-yogī.* In the morning, the first duty of a *brahmacārī* seeking spiritual elevation is *huta-hutāśana,* to offer sacrificial oblations to the Supreme Lord. Those engaged in *brahmacarya* cannot sleep until seven or nine o'clock in the morning. They must rise early in the morning, at least one and a half hours before the sun rises, and offer oblations, or in this age, they must chant the holy name of the Lord, Hare Kṛṣṇa. As referred to by Lord Caitanya, *kalau nāsty eva nāsty eva nāsty eva gatir anyathā:* there is no other alternative, no other alternative, no other alternative, in this age, to chanting the holy name of the Lord. The *brahmacārī* must rise early in the morning and, after placing himself, should chant the holy name of the Lord. From the features of the sage, it appeared that he had undergone great austerities; that is the sign of one observing *brahmacarya,* the vow of celibacy. If one lives otherwise, it will be manifest in the lust visible in his face and body. The word *vidyotamānam* indicates that the *brahmacārī* feature showed in his body. That is the certificate that one has undergone great austerity in yoga.

One who hears the transcendental sound vibration of the holy name of the Lord, Hare Kṛṣṇa also improves in health. We have actually seen that many *brahmacārīs* and *gṛhasthas* connected with the International Society for Krishna Consciousness have improved in health, and a luster has come to their faces. It is essential that a *brahmacārī* engaged in spiritual advancement look very healthy and lustrous. (3.21.47)

The principle of *brahmacarya* is celibacy. There are two kinds of *brahmacārīs.* One is called *naiṣṭhika-brahmacārī,* which means one who takes a vow of celibacy for his whole life, whereas the other, the *upakurvāṇa-brahmacārī,* is a *brahmacārī* who takes the vow of celibacy up to a certain age; then, with the permission of his spiritual master, he enters married life. *Brahmacarya* is student life, the beginning of life in the spiritual orders, and the principle of *brahmacarya* is celibacy. Only a householder can indulge in sense gratification or sex life, not a *brahmacārī.* (3.22.14)

A *brahmacārī* practices celibacy, controlling his sex life. One cannot enjoy unrestricted sex life and practice yoga; this is rascaldom. So-called yogis advertise that one can go on enjoying as one likes and simultaneously become a yogi, but this is totally unauthorized. It is very clearly explained here that one must observe celibacy. *Brahmacarya* means that one leads his life simply in relationship with Brahman, or in full Kṛṣṇa consciousness. Those who are too addicted to sex life cannot observe the regulations which will lead them to Kṛṣṇa consciousness. Sex life should be restricted to persons who are married. A person whose sex life is restricted in marriage is also called a *brahmacārī.* (3.28.4)

It is stated in this verse that the charming eyebrows of the Lord are so fascinating that they cause one to forget the charms of sense attraction. The conditioned souls are shackled to material existence because they are captivated by the charms of sense gratification, especially sex life. The sex-god is called *Makara-dhvaja.* The charming brows of the Supreme Personality of Godhead protect the sages and devotees from being charmed by material lust and sex attraction. Yāmunācārya, a great *ācārya,* said that ever since he had seen the charming pastimes of the Lord, the charms of sex life had become abominable for him, and the mere thought of sex enjoyment would cause him to spit and turn his face. Thus if anyone wants to be aloof from sex attraction, he must see the charming smile and fascinating eyebrows of the Supreme Personality of Godhead. (3.28.32)

Men and women whose lives were built upon indulgence in illicit sex life are put into many kinds of miserable conditions in the hells known as Tāmisra, Andha-tāmisra and Raurava.

Materialistic life is based on sex life. The existence of all the materialistic people, who are undergoing severe tribulation in the struggle for existence, is based on sex. Therefore in the Vedic civilization, sex life is allowed only in a restricted way; it is for the married couple and only for begetting children. But when sex life is indulged in for sense gratification illegally and illicitly, both the man and the woman await severe punishment in this world or after death. In this world also they are punished by virulent diseases like syphilis and gonorrhea, and in the next life, as we see in this passage of *Śrīmad-Bhāgavatam,* they are put into different kinds of hellish conditions to suffer. In *Bhagavad-gītā,* First Chapter, illicit sex life is also very much condemned, and it is said that one who produces children by illicit sex life is sent to hell. It is confirmed here in the *Bhāgavatam* that such offenders are put into hellish conditions of life in Tāmisra, Andha-tāmisra and Raurava. (3.30.28 Text & Purport)

If, therefore, the living entity again associates with the path of unrighteousness, influenced by sensually minded people engaged in the pursuit of sexual enjoyment and the gratification of the palate, he again goes to hell as before. (3.31.32 Text)

He becomes devoid of truthfulness, cleanliness, mercy, gravity, spiritual intelligence, shyness, austerity, fame, forgiveness, control of the mind, control of the senses, fortune and all such opportunities. (3.31.33 Text)

One should not associate with a coarse fool who is bereft of the knowledge of self-realization and who is no more than a dancing dog in the hands of a woman. (3.31.34 Text)

The infatuation and bondage which accrue to a man from attachment to any other object is not as complete as that resulting from attachment to a woman or to the fellowship of men who are fond of women. (3.31.35 Text)

At the sight of his own daughter, Brahmā was bewildered by her charms and shamelessly ran up to her in the form of a stag when she took the form of a hind. (3.31.36 Text)

Amongst all kinds of living entities begotten by Brahmā, namely men, demigods and animals, none but the sage Nārāyaṇa is immune to the attraction of *māyā* in the form of woman. (3.31.37 Text)

Just try to understand the mighty strength of My *māyā* in the shape of woman, who by the mere movement of her eyebrows can keep even the greatest conquerors of the world under her grip. (3.31.38 Text)

One who aspires to reach the culmination of yoga and has realized his self by rendering service unto Me should never associate with an attractive woman, for such a woman is declared in the scripture to be the gateway to hell for the advancing devotee. (3.31.39 Text)

The woman created by the Lord is the representation of *māyā,* and one who associates with such *māyā* by accepting services must certainly know that this is the way of death, just like a blind well covered with grass. (3.31.40 Text)

A living entity who, as a result of attachment to a woman in his previous life, has been endowed with the form of a woman, foolishly looks upon *māyā* in the form of a man, her husband, as the bestower of wealth, progeny, house and other material assets. (3.31.41 Text)

A woman, therefore, should consider her husband, her house and her children to be the arrangement of the external energy of the Lord for her death, just as the sweet singing of the hunter is death for the deer. (3.31.42 Text)

(The purports to all these verses *(S.B.* 3.31.32-42) are also highly instructive and are essential reading for *brahmacārīs.* Due to space considerations they have not been included here).

A *gṛhastha* is a person who lives with family, wife, children and relatives but has no attachment for them. He prefers to live in family life rather than as a mendicant or *sannyāsī,* but his chief aim is to achieve self-realization, or to come to the standard of Kṛṣṇa consciousness. (3.32.1)

It is best to remain alone as a *brahmacārī*, *sannyāsī* or *vānaprastha* and cultivate Kṛṣṇa consciousness throughout one's whole life. Those who are unable to remain alone are given license to live in household life with wife and children, not for sense gratification but for cultivation of Kṛṣṇa consciousness. (3.33.12)

It is a woman's nature to want to decorate herself with ornaments and nice dresses and accompany her husband to social functions, meet friends and relatives, and enjoy life in that way. This propensity is not unusual, for woman is the basic principle of material enjoyment. Therefore in Sanskrit the word for woman is *strī*, which means "one who expands the field of material enjoyment." (4.3.9)

An important word in this verse is *ūrdhva-retasaḥ,* which means *brahmacārīs* who have never discharged semen. Celibacy is so important that even though one does not undergo any austerities, penances or ritualistic ceremonies prescribed in the Vedas, if one simply keeps himself a pure *brahmacārī,* not discharging his semen, the result is that after death he goes to the Satyaloka. Generally, sex life is the cause of all miseries in the material world. In the Vedic civilization sex life is restricted in various ways. Out of the whole population of the social structure, only the *gṛhasthas* are allowed restricted sex life. All others refrain from sex. The people of this age especially do not know the value of not discharging semen. As such, they are variously entangled with material qualities and suffer an existence of struggle only. The word *ūrdhva-retasaḥ* especially indicates the Māyāvādī *sannyāsīs,* who undergo strict principles of austerity. (4.11.5)

Gṛhastha life is inauspicious because *gṛhastha* means consciousness for sense gratification, and as soon as there is sense gratification, one's position is always full of dangers. (4.22.13)

Desires for fruitive activities are strongly rooted, but the trees of desire can be uprooted completely by devotional service because devotional service employs superior desires. To try to stop desires is impossible. One has to desire the Supreme in order not to be engaged in inferior desires.

There is no artificial attempt to stop desire. Desire becomes a source of spiritual enjoyment under the protection of the toes of the lotus feet of the Lord. It is stated herein by the Kumāras that the lotus feet of Lord Kṛṣṇa are the ultimate reservoir of all pleasure. One should therefore take shelter of the lotus feet of the Lord instead of trying unsuccessfully to stop desires for material enjoyment. As long as one is unable to stop the desire for material enjoyment, there is no possibility of becoming liberated from the entanglement of material existence. It may be argued that the waves of a river are incessantly flowing and that they cannot be stopped, but the waves of the river flow toward the sea. When the tide comes over the river, it overwhelms the flowing of the river, and the river itself becomes overflooded, and the waves from the sea become more prominent than the waves from the river. Similarly, a devotee with intelligence plans so many things for the service of the Lord in Kṛṣṇa consciousness that stagnant material desires become overflooded by the desire to serve the Lord. As confirmed by Yāmunācārya, since he has been engaged in the service of the lotus feet of the Lord, there is always a current of newer and newer desires flowing to serve the Lord, so much that the stagnant desire of sex life becomes very insignificant. Yāmunācārya even says that he spits on such desires. *Bhagavad-gītā* (2.59) also confirms: *paraṁ dṛṣṭvā nivartate.* The conclusion is that by developing a loving desire for the service of the lotus feet of the Lord, we subdue all material desires for sense gratification. (4.22.39)

One who is advanced in devotional service is never attracted by sex life, and as soon as one becomes detached from sex life and proportionately attached to the service of the Lord, he actually experiences living in the Vaikuṇṭha planets. (4.23.29)

Sometimes even Lord Brahmā and Lord Śiva are subject to being attracted by sex at any time. (4.24.11)

It is sometimes understood that a person becomes lusty just by hearing the tinkling of bangles on the hands of women or the tinkling of ankle bells, or just by seeing a woman's sari. Thus it is concluded that woman is the complete representation of *māyā*. Although Viśvāmitra Muni was engaged in practicing mystic yoga with closed eyes, his transcendental meditation was broken when he heard the tinkling of bangles on the hands of Menakā. In this way Viśvāmitra Muni became a victim of Menakā and fathered a child who is universally celebrated as Śakuntalā. The conclusion is that no one can save himself from the attraction of woman, even though he be an exalted demigod or an inhabitant of the higher planets. Only a devotee of the Lord, who is attracted by Kṛṣṇa, can escape the lures of woman. Once one is attracted by Kṛṣṇa, the illusory energy of the world cannot attract him. (4.24.12)

When one sees the opposite sex, naturally the sex impulse increases. It is said that if a man in a solitary place does not become agitated upon seeing a woman, he is to be considered a *brahmacārī.* But this practice is almost impossible. The sex impulse is so strong that even by seeing, touching or talking, coming into contact with, or even thinking of the opposite sex—even in so many subtle ways—one becomes sexually impelled. Consequently, a *brahmacārī* or *sannyāsī* is prohibited to associate with women, especially in a secret place. The *śāstras* enjoin that one should not even talk to a woman in a secret place. (4.25.17)

Every living entity is a hero in two ways. When he is victim of the illusory energy, he works as a great hero in the material world, as a great leader, politician, businessman, industrialist, etc. and his heroic activities contribute to the material advancement of civilization. One can also become a hero by being master of the senses, a *gosvāmī.* Material activities are false heroic activities, whereas restraining the senses from material engagement is great heroism. However great a hero one may be in the material world, he can be immediately conquered by the lumps of flesh and blood known as the breasts of women. In the history of material activities there are many examples like the Roman hero Antony, who became captivated by the beauty of Cleopatra. Similarly, a great hero in India named Baji Rao became a victim of a woman during the time of Maharashtrian politics, and he was defeated. From history we understand that formerly politicians used to employ beautiful girls who were trained as *viṣa-kanyā*. These girls had poison injected into their bodies from the beginning of their lives so that in due course of time they would become so immune to the poison and so poisonous themselves that simply by kissing a person they could kill him. These poisonous girls were engaged to see an enemy and kill him with a kiss. Thus there are many instances in human history of heroes who have been curbed simply by women. Being part and parcel of Kṛṣṇa, the living entity is certainly a great hero, but due to his own weakness he becomes attracted to the material features. (4.25.25)

Everyone has lusty desires within, and as soon as one is agitated by the movement of a beautiful woman's eyebrows, the Cupid within immediately throws his arrow at the heart. Thus one is quickly conquered by the eyebrows of a beautiful woman. When one is agitated by lusty desires, his senses are attracted by all kinds of *viṣaya* (enjoyable things like sound, touch, form, smell and taste). These attractive sense objects oblige one to come under the control of a woman. In this way the conditional life of a living entity begins. Conditional life means being under the control of a woman or a man. Thus living entities live in bondage to one another, and thus they continue this conditional material life illusioned by *māyā*. (4.25.30)

My dear girl, your face is so beautiful with your nice eyebrows and eyes and with your bluish hair scattered about. In addition, very sweet sounds are coming from your mouth. Nonetheless, you are so covered with shyness that you do not see me face to face. I therefore request you, my dear girl, to smile and kindly raise your head to see me.

Such a speech is typical of a living entity attracted by the opposite sex. This is called bewilderment occasioned by becoming conditioned by material nature. When thus attracted by the beauty of the material energy, one becomes very eager to enjoy. This is elaborately described in this instance of Purañjana's becoming attracted by the beautiful woman. In conditional life the living entity is attracted by a face, eyebrows or eyes, a voice or anything. In short, everything becomes attractive. When a man or a woman is attracted by the opposite sex, it does not matter whether the opposite sex is beautiful or not. The lover sees everything beautiful in the face of the beloved and thus becomes attracted. This attraction causes the living entity to fall down in this material world. (4.25.31 Text & Purport)

According to Vedic instructions, there are two paths for human activities. One is called *pravṛtti-mārga*, and the other is called *nivṛtti-mārga*. The basic principle for either of these paths is religious life. In animal life there is only *pravṛtti-mārga*. *Pravṛtti-mārga* means sense enjoyment, and *nivṛtti-mārga* means spiritual advancement. In the life of animals and demons, there is no conception of *nivṛtti-mārga*, nor is there any actual conception of *pravṛtti-mārga*. *Pravṛtti-mārga* maintains that even though one has the propensity for sense gratification, he can gratify his senses according to the directions of the Vedic injunctions. For example, everyone has the propensity for sex life, but in demoniac civilization sex is enjoyed without restriction. According to Vedic culture, sex is enjoyed under Vedic instructions. Thus the Vedas give direction to civilized human beings to enable them to satisfy their propensities for sense gratification.

In the *nivṛtti-mārga*, however, on the path of transcendental realization, sex is completely forbidden. The social orders are divided into four parts—*brahmacarya, gṛhastha, vānaprastha and sannyāsa*—and only in the householder life can the *pravṛtti-mārga* be encouraged or accepted according to Vedic instructions. In the orders of *brahmacarya, vānaprastha* and *sannyāsa*, there are no facilities for sex. (4.25.39)

So-called love within this material world is nothing but sexual satisfaction. (4.25.42)

A living entity is never satisfied with a woman unless he is trained in the system of *brahmacarya.* Generally a man's tendency is to enjoy many women, and even at the very end of life the sex impulse is so strong that even though one is very old he still wants to enjoy the company of young girls. Thus because of the strong sex impulse the living entity becomes more and more involved in this material world. (4.25.44)

In this way, King Purañjana was captivated by his nice wife and was thus cheated. Indeed, he became cheated in his whole existence in the material world. Even against that poor foolish king's desire, he remained under the control of his wife, just like a pet animal that dances according to the order of its master.

The word *vipralabdhaḥ* is very significant in this verse. *Vi* means "specifically," and *pralabdha* means "obtained." Just to satisfy his desires, the king got the queen, and thus he became cheated by material existence. Although he was not willing to do so, he remained a pet animal under the control of material intelligence. Just as a pet monkey dances according to the desires of its master, the king danced according to the desires of the queen. In *Śrīmad-Bhāgavatam* (5.5.2) it is said, *mahat-sevāṁ dvāram āhur vimukteḥ:* if one associates with a saintly person, a devotee, one's path of liberation becomes clear. But if one associates with a woman or with a person who is too much addicted to a woman, his path of bondage becomes completely clear.

On the whole, for spiritual advancement, one must give up the company of women. This is what is meant by the order of *sannyāsa*, the renounced order. Before taking *sannyāsa*, or completely renouncing the material world, one has to practice avoiding illicit sex. Sex life, licit or illicit, is practically the same, but through illicit sex one becomes more and more captivated. By regulating one's sex life there is a chance that one may eventually be able to renounce sex or renounce the association of women. If this can be done, advancement in spiritual life comes very easily.

How one becomes captivated by the association of one's dear wife is explained in this chapter by Nārada Muni. Attraction for one's wife means attraction for the material qualities.

As long as we are attached to society, family and love of the material world, there is no question of knowledge. Nor is there a question of devotional service. (4.25.62 Text & Purport)

Simple food like rice, *dāl, capātīs,* vegetables, milk and sugar constitute a balanced diet, but sometimes it is found that an initiated person, in the name of *prasāda,* eats very luxurious foodstuff. Due to his past sinful life he becomes attracted by Cupid and eats good food voraciously. It is clearly visible that when a neophyte in Kṛṣṇa consciousness eats too much, he falls down. Instead of being elevated to pure Kṛṣṇa consciousness, he becomes attracted by Cupid. The so-called *brahmacārī* becomes agitated by women, and the *vānaprastha* may again become captivated into having sex with his wife. (4.26.13)

An effeminate husband, simply being attracted by the external beauty of his wife, tries to become her most obedient servant. Śrīpāda Śaṅkarācārya has therefore advised that we not become attracted by a lump of flesh and blood. The story is told that at one time a man, very much attracted to a beautiful woman, wooed the woman in such a way that she devised a plan to show him the ingredients of her beauty. The woman made a date to see him, and before seeing him she took a purgative, and that whole day and night she simply passed stool, and she preserved that stool in a pot. The next night, when the man came to see her, she appeared very ugly and emaciated. When the man inquired from her about the woman with whom he had an engagement, she replied "I am that very woman." The man refused to believe her, not knowing that she had lost all her beauty due to the violent purgative that caused her to pass stool day and night. When the man began to argue with her, the woman said that she was not looking beautiful because she was separated from the ingredients of her beauty. When the man asked how she could be so separated, the woman said "Come on, and I will show you." She then showed him the pot filled with liquid stool and vomit. Thus the man became aware that a beautiful woman is simply a lump of matter composed of blood, stool, urine and similar other disgusting ingredients. This is the actual fact, but in a state of illusion, man becomes attracted by illusory beauty and becomes a victim of *māyā.* (4.26.23)

Karmīs work very hard simply to enjoy sex. Modern human society has improved the materialistic way of life simply by inducing unrestricted sex life in many different ways. This is most prominently visible in the Western world. (4.26.26)

A systematic family life as enjoined in the Vedas is better than an irresponsible sinful life. If a husband and wife combine together in Kṛṣṇa consciousness and live together peacefully, that is very nice. However, if a husband becomes too much attracted by his wife and forgets his duty in life, the implications of materialistic life will again resume. Śrīla Rūpa Gosvāmī has therefore recommended *anāsaktasya viṣayān* (*Bhakti-rasāmṛta-sindhu* 1.2.255). Without being attached by sex, the husband and wife may live together for the advancement of spiritual life. The husband should engage in devotional service, and the wife should be faithful and religious according to the Vedic injunctions. Such a combination is very good. However, if the husband becomes too much attracted to the wife due to sex, the position becomes very dangerous. Women in general are very much sexually inclined. Indeed it is said that a woman's sex desire is nine times stronger than a man's. It is therefore a man's duty to keep a woman under his control by satisfying her, giving her ornaments, nice food and clothes, and engaging her in religious activities. Of course, a woman should have a few children and in this way not be disturbing to the man. Unfortunately, if the man becomes attracted to the woman simply for sex enjoyment, then family life becomes abominable.

The great politician Cāṇakya Paṇḍita has said: *bhāryā rūpavatī śatruḥ*—a beautiful wife is an enemy. Of course every woman in the eyes of her husband is very beautiful. Others may see her as not very beautiful, but the husband, being very much attracted to her, sees her always as very beautiful. If the husband sees the wife as very beautiful, it is to be assumed that he is too much attracted to her. This attraction is the attraction of sex. The whole world is captivated by the two modes of material nature *rajo-guṇa and tamo-guṇa,* passion and ignorance. Generally women are very much passionate and are less intelligent; therefore somehow or other a man should not be under the control of their passion and ignorance. By performing *bhakti-yoga,* or devotional service, a man can be raised to the platform of goodness. If a husband situated in a mode of goodness can control his wife, who is in passion and ignorance, the woman is benefited. Forgetting her natural inclination for passion and ignorance, the woman becomes obedient and faithful to her husband, who is situated in goodness. Such a life becomes very welcome. The intelligence of the man and woman may then work very nicely together, and they can make a progressive march toward spiritual realization. Otherwise, the husband, coming under the control of the wife, sacrifices his quality of goodness and becomes subservient to the qualities of passion and ignorance. In this way the whole situation becomes polluted. The conclusion is that a household life is better than a sinful life devoid of responsibility, but if in the household life the husband becomes subordinate to the wife, involvement in materialistic life again becomes prominent. In this way a man's material bondage becomes enhanced. Because of this, according to the Vedic system, after a certain age a man is recommended to abandon his family life for the stages of *vānaprastha* and *sannyāsa*. (4.27.1)

Thinking of a woman always within one's heart is tantamount to lying down with a woman on a valuable bedstead. (4.27.4)

In this verse Śrīla Govinda dāsa actually says that there is no bliss in the enjoyment of youthful life. In youth a person becomes very lusty to enjoy all kinds of sense objects. The sense objects are form, taste, smell, touch and sound. The modern scientific method, or advancement of scientific civilization, encourages the enjoyment of these five senses. The younger generation is very pleased to see a beautiful form, to hear radio messages of material news and sense gratificatory songs, to smell nice scents, nice flowers, and to touch the soft body or breasts of a young woman and gradually touch the sex organs. All of this is also very pleasing to the animals; therefore in human society there are restrictions in the enjoyment of the five sense objects. If one does not follow, he becomes exactly like an animal.

Thus in this verse it is specifically stated, *kāma-kaśmala-cetasaḥ:* the consciousness of King Purañjana was polluted by lusty desires and sinful activities. In the previous verse it is stated that Purañjana, although advanced in consciousness, lay down on a very soft bed with his wife. This indicates that he indulged too much in sex. The words *navaṁ vayaḥ* are also significant in this verse. They indicate the period of youth from age sixteen to thirty. These thirteen or fifteen years of life are years in which one can very strongly enjoy the senses. When one comes to this age he thinks that life will go on and that he will simply continue enjoying his senses, but, "Time and tide wait for no man." The span of youth expires very quickly. One who wastes his life simply by committing sinful activities in youth immediately becomes disappointed and disillusioned when the brief period of youth is over. The material enjoyments of youth are especially pleasing to a person who has no spiritual training. If one is trained only according to the bodily conception of life, he simply leads a disappointed life because bodily sense enjoyment finishes within forty years or so. After forty years, one simply leads a disillusioned life because he has no spiritual knowledge. For such a person, the expiration of youth occurs in half a moment. Thus King Purañjana's pleasure, which he took in lying down with his wife, expired very quickly. (4.27.5)

Śrīla Narottama dāsa Ṭhākura states:

karma-kāṇḍa, jñāna-kāṇḍa, kevala viṣera bhāṇḍa,
amṛta baliyā yebā khāya
nānā yoni sadā phire, kadarya bhakṣaṇa kare,
tāra janma adhaḥ-pāte yāya

"Fruitive activities and mental speculation are simply cups of poison. Whoever drinks of them, thinking them to be nectar, must struggle very hard life after life, in different types of bodies. Such a person eats all kinds of nonsense and becomes condemned by his activities of so-called sense enjoyment."

Thus the field of action and reactions, by which one's descendants are increased, begins with sex life. Purañjana increased his whole family by begetting sons who in their turn begot grandsons. Thus the living entity, being inclined toward sexual gratification, becomes involved in many hundreds and thousands of actions and reactions. In this way he remains within the material world simply for the purpose of sense gratification and transmigrates from one body to another. His process of reproducing so many sons and grandsons results in so-called societies, nations, communities and so on. All these communities, societies, dynasties and nations simply expand from sex life. As stated by Prahlāda Mahārāja: *yan maithunādi-gṛhamedhi-sukhaṁ hi tuccham (S.B.* 7.9.45). A *gṛhamedhī* is one who wants to remain within this material existence. This means that he wants to remain within this body or society and enjoy friendship, love and community. His only enjoyment is in increasing the number of sex enjoyers. He enjoys sex and produces children, who in their turn marry and produce grandchildren. The grandchildren also marry and in their turn produce great-grandchildren. In this way the entire earth becomes overpopulated, and then suddenly there are reactions provoked by material nature in the form of war, famine, pestilence and earthquakes, etc. Thus the entire population is again extinguished simply to be re-created. This process is explained in *Bhagavad-gītā* (8.19) as repeated creation and annihilation: *bhūtvā bhūtvā pralīyate.* Due to a lack of Kṛṣṇa consciousness, all this creation and annihilation is going on under the name of human civilization. This cycle continues due to man's lack of knowledge of the soul and the Supreme Personality of Godhead. (4.27.9)

The great sage Nārada Muni was a *naiṣṭhika-brahmacārī*—that is, he never had sex life. He was consequently an ever-green youth. Old age, *jarā*, could not attack him.

It requires great strength to resist a woman's attraction. It is difficult for old men, and what to speak of the young. Those who live as *brahmacārīs* must follow in the footsteps of the great sage Nārada Muni, who never accepted the proposals of Jarā. Those who are too much sexually addicted become victims of *jarā*, and very soon their lifespan is shortened. Without utilizing the human form of life for Kṛṣṇa consciousness the victims of *jarā* die very soon in this world. (4.27.21)

When a man is young, he does not care for old age, but enjoys sex to the best of his satisfaction, not knowing that at the end of life his sexual indulgence will bring on various diseases, which so much disturb the body that one will pray for immediate death. The more one enjoys sex during youth, the more he suffers in old age. (4.28.1)

At the fag end of life, when the invalidity of old age attacks a man, his body becomes useless for all purposes. Therefore Vedic training dictates that when a man is in his boyhood he should be trained in the process of *brahmacarya:* that is, he should be completely engaged in the service of the Lord and should not in any way associate with women. (4.28.3)

Due to his contaminated association with women, a living entity like King Purañjana eternally suffers all the pangs of material existence and remains in the dark region of material life, bereft of all remembrance for many, many years.

This is a description of material existence. Material existence is experienced when one becomes attached to a woman and forgets his real identity as the eternal servant of Kṛṣṇa (*naṣṭa-smṛtiḥ*). In this way, in one body after another, the living entity perpetually suffers the threefold miseries of material existence. To save human civilization from the darkness of ignorance, this movement was started. The main purpose of the Kṛṣṇa consciousness movement is to enlighten the forgetful living entity and remind him of his original Kṛṣṇa consciousness. In this way the living entity can be saved from the catastrophe of ignorance as well as bodily transmigration. As Śrīla Bhaktivinoda Ṭhākura has sung:

anādi karama-phale, paḍi' bhavārṇava-jale,
taribāre nā dekhi upāya
ei viṣaya-halāhale, divā-niśi hiyā jvale,
mana kabhu sukha nāhi pāya

"Because of my past fruitive activities, I have now fallen into an ocean of nescience. I cannot find any means to get out of this great ocean, which is indeed like an ocean of poison. We are trying to be happy through sense enjoyment, but actually that so-called enjoyment is like food that is too hot and causes burning in the heart. I feel a burning sensation constantly, day and night, and thus my mind cannot find satisfaction."

Material existence is always full of anxiety. People are always trying to find many ways to mitigate anxiety, but because they are not guided by a real leader, they try to forget material anxiety through drink and sex indulgence. Foolish people do not know that by attempting to escape anxiety by drink and sex, they simply increase their duration of material life. It is not possible to escape material anxiety in this way.

The word *pramadā-saṅga-dūṣitaḥ* indicates that apart from all other contamination, if one simply remains attached to a woman, that single contamination will be sufficient to prolong one's miserable material existence. Consequently, in Vedic civilization one is trained from the beginning to give up attachment for women. The first stage of life is *brahmacārī*, the second stage *gṛhastha*, the third stage *vānaprastha*, and the fourth stage *sannyāsa*. All these stages are devised to enable one to detach himself from the association of women. (4.28.27)

We can definitely see that to advance in Kṛṣṇa consciousness one must control his bodily weight. If one becomes too fat, it is to be assumed that he is not advancing spiritually. Śrīla Bhaktisiddhānta Sarasvatī Ṭhākura severely criticized his fat disciples. The idea is that one who intends to advance in Kṛṣṇa consciousness must not eat very much. Devotees used to go to forests, high hills or mountains on pilgrimages, but such severe austerities are not possible in these days. One should instead eat only *prasāda* and no more than required. According to the Vaiṣṇava calendar, there are many fasts, such as Ekādaśī and the appearance and disappearance days of God and His devotees. All of these are meant to decrease the fat within the body so that one will not sleep more than desired and will not become inactive and lazy. Overindulgence in food will cause a man to sleep more than required. This human form of life is meant for austerity and austerity means controlling sex, food intake, etc. In this way time can be saved for spiritual activity, and one can purify himself both externally and internally. Thus both body and mind can be cleansed. (4.28.36)

By too much attachment for women one becomes a woman in the next life, but a person who associates with the Supreme Personality of Godhead or His representative becomes free from all material attachments and is thus liberated. (4.29.1)

The desires for sexual satisfaction are meant for the *arvāk,* the lowest among men. (4.29.14)

My dear king, please search out that deer who is engaged in eating grass in a very nice flower garden along with his wife. That deer is very much attached to his business, and he is enjoying the sweet singing of the bumblebees in his garden. Just try to understand his position. He is unaware that before him is a tiger, which is accustomed to living at the cost of another's flesh. Behind the deer is a hunter, who is threatening to pierce him with sharp arrows. Thus the deer's death is imminent.

Here is an allegory in which the king is advised to find a deer that is always in a dangerous position. Although threatened from all sides, the deer simply eats grass in a nice flower garden, unaware of the danger all around him. All living entities, especially human beings, think themselves very happy in the midst of families. As if living in a flower garden and hearing the sweet humming of bumblebees, everyone is centered around his wife, who is the beauty of family life. The bumblebees' humming may be compared to the talk of children. The human being, just like the deer, enjoys his family without knowing that before him is the factor of time, which is represented by the tiger. The fruitive activities of a living entity simply create another dangerous position and oblige him to accept different types of bodies. For a deer to run after a mirage of water in the desert is not unusual. The deer is also very fond of sex. The conclusion is that one who lives like a deer will be killed in due course of time. Vedic literatures therefore advise that we should understand our constitutional position and take to devotional service before death comes. According to the *Bhāgavatam* (11.9.29):

labdhvā sudurlabham idaṁ bahu-sambhavānte
mānuṣyam arthadam anityam apīha dhīraḥ
tūrṇaṁ yateta na pated anumṛtyu yāvan
niḥśreyasāya viṣayaḥ khalu sarvataḥ syāt

After many births we have attained this human form; therefore before death comes, we should engage ourselves in the transcendental loving service of the Lord. That is the fulfillment of human life. (4.29.53 Text & Purport)

My dear king, woman, who is very attractive in the beginning but in the end very disturbing, is exactly like the flower, which is attractive in the beginning and detestable at the end. With woman, the living entity is entangled with lusty desires, and he enjoys sex, just as one enjoys the aroma of a flower. He thus enjoys a life of sense gratification—from his tongue to his genitals—and in this way the living entity considers himself very happy in family life. United with his wife, he always remains absorbed in such thoughts. He feels great pleasure in hearing the talks of his wife and children, which are like the sweet humming of bumblebees that collect honey from flower to flower. He forgets that before him is time, which is taking away his life-span with the passing of day and night. He does not see the gradual diminishing of his life, nor does he care about the superintendent of death, who is trying to kill him from behind. Just try to understand this. You are in a precarious position and are threatened from all sides.

Materialistic life means forgetting one's constitutional position as the eternal servant of Kṛṣṇa, and this forgetfulness is especially enhanced in the *gṛhastha-āśrama.* In the *gṛhastha-āśrama* a young man accepts a young wife who is very beautiful in the beginning, but in due course of time, after giving birth to many children and becoming older and older, she demands many things from the husband to maintain the entire family. At such a time the wife becomes detestable to the very man who accepted her in her younger days. One becomes attached to the *gṛhastha-āśrama* for two reasons only—the wife cooks palatable dishes for the satisfaction of her husband's tongue, and she gives him sexual pleasure at night. A person attached to the *gṛhastha-āśrama is* always thinking of these two things—palatable food and sex enjoyment. The talks of the wife, which are enjoyed as a family recreation, and the talks of the children both attract the living entity. He thus forgets that he has to die some day and has to prepare for the next life if he wants to be put into a congenial body.

The deer in the flower garden is an allegory used by the great sage Nārada to point out to the king that the king himself is similarly entrapped by such surroundings. Actually everyone is surrounded by such a family life, which misleads one. The living entity thus forgets that he has to return home, back to Godhead. He simply becomes entangled in family life. Prahlāda Mahārāja has therefore hinted: *hitvātma-pātaṁ gṛham andha-kūpaṁ vanaṁ gato yad dharim āśrayeta.* Family life is considered a blind well (*andha-kūpam*) into which a person falls and dies without help. Prahlāda Mahārāja recommends that while one's senses are there and one is strong enough, he should abandon the *gṛhastha-āśrama* and take shelter of the lotus feet of the Lord, going to the forest of Vṛndāvana. According to Vedic civilization, one has to give up family life at a certain age (the age of fifty), take *vānaprastha* and eventually remain alone as a *sannyāsī.* That is the prescribed method of Vedic civilization known as *varṇāśrama-dharma.* When one takes *sannyāsa* after enjoying family life, he pleases the Supreme Lord Viṣṇu.

One has to understand one's position in family or worldly life. That is called intelligence. One should not remain always trapped in family life to satisfy his tongue and genitals in association with a wife. In such a way, one simply spoils his life. According to Vedic civilization, it is imperative to give up the family at a certain stage, by force if necessary. Unfortunately, so-called followers of Vedic life do not give up their family even at the end of life, unless they are forced by death. There should be a thorough overhauling of the social system, and society should revert to the Vedic principles, that is, the four *varṇas* and the four *āśramas*. (4.29.54 Text & Purport)

My dear king, just try to understand the allegorical position of the deer. Be fully conscious of yourself, and give up the pleasure of hearing about promotion to heavenly planets by fruitive activity. Give up household life, which is full of sex, as well as stories about such things, and take shelter of the Supreme Personality of Godhead through the mercy of the liberated souls. In this way, please give up your attraction for material existence.

Being in the *gṛhastha-āśrama* means being under the control of one's wife. One has to give up all this and put himself in the *āśrama* of the *paramahaṁsa,* that is, put himself under the control of the spiritual master.

The whole world is in *māyā,* being controlled by women. Not only is one controlled by the woman who is one's wife, but one is also controlled by so many sex literatures. That is the cause of one's being entangled in the material world. One cannot give up this abominable association through one's own effort, but if one takes shelter of a bona fide spiritual master who is a *paramahaṁsa,* he will gradually be elevated to the platform of spiritual life. (4.29.55 Text & Purport)

The basic flaw in modern civilization is that boys and girls are given freedom during school and college to enjoy sex life. (4.31.1)

How a beautiful woman's movements and gestures, her hair and the structure of her breasts, hips and other bodily features attract the minds not only of men but of demigods also is very finely described in this statement. The words *divija* and *manuja* specifically emphasize that the attraction of feminine gestures is powerful everywhere within this material world, both on this planet and in the higher planetary systems. It is said that the standard of living in the higher planetary systems is thousands and thousands of times higher than the standard of living on this planet. Therefore the beautiful bodily features of the women there are also thousands and thousands of times more attractive than the features of the women on earth. The creator has constructed women in such a way that their beautiful voices and movements and the beautiful features of their hips, their breasts, and the other parts of their bodies attract the members of the opposite sex, both on earth and on other planets, and awaken their lusty desires. When one is controlled by Cupid or the beauty of women, he becomes stunned like matter such as stone. Captivated by the material movements of women, he wants to remain in this material world. Thus one's promotion to the spiritual world is checked simply by seeing the beautiful bodily structure and movements of women. Śrī Caitanya Mahāprabhu has therefore warned all devotees to beware of the attraction of beautiful women and materialistic civilization. Śrī Caitanya Mahāprabhu even refused to see Pratāparudra Mahārāja because he was a very opulent person in the material world. Lord Caitanya said in this connection, *niṣkiñcanasya bhagavad-bhajanonmukhasya:* those who are engaged in the devotional service of the Lord because they are very serious about going back home, back to Godhead, should be very careful to avoid seeing the beautiful gestures of women and should also avoid seeing persons who are very rich.

niṣkiñcanasya bhagavad-bhajanonmukhasya
pāraṁ paraṁ jigamiṣor bhava-sāgarasya
sandarśanaṁ viṣayiṇām atha yoṣitāṁ ca
hā hanta hanta viṣa-bhakṣaṇato 'py asādhu

"Alas, for a person who is seriously desiring to cross the material ocean and engage in the transcendental loving service of the Lord without material motives, seeing a materialist engaged in sense gratification or seeing a woman who is similarly interested is more abominable than drinking poison willingly." (*Caitanya-caritāmṛta, Madhya* 11.8) One who is serious about going back home, back to Godhead, should not contemplate the attractive features of women and the opulence of rich men. Such contemplation will check one's advancement in spiritual life. Once a devotee is fixed in Kṛṣṇa consciousness, however, these attractions will not agitate his mind. (5.2.6)

nūnaṁ pramattaḥ kurute vikarma
yad indriya-prītaya āpṛṇoti
na sādhu manye yata ātmano 'yam
asann api kleśada āsa dehaḥ

When a person considers sense gratification the aim of life, he certainly becomes mad after materialistic living and engages in all kinds of sinful activity. He does not know that due to his past misdeeds he has already received a body which, although temporary, is the cause of his misery. Actually the living entity should not have taken on a material body, but he has been awarded the material body for sense gratification. Therefore I think it not befitting an intelligent man to involve himself again in the activities of sense gratification by which he perpetually gets material bodies one after another. (5.5.4 Text)

puṁsaḥ striyā mithunī-bhāvam etaṁ
tayor mitho hṛdaya-granthim āhuḥ
ato gṛha-kṣetra-sutāpta-vittair
janasya moho 'yam ahaṁ mameti

The attraction between male and female is the basic principle of material existence. On the basis of this misconception, which ties together the hearts of the male and female, one becomes attracted to his body, home, property, children, relatives and wealth. In this way one increases life's illusions and thinks in terms of "I and mine." (5.5.8)

A *gṛhastha, vānaprastha, sannyāsī* and *brahmacārī* should be very careful when associating with women. One is forbidden to sit down in a solitary place even with one's mother, sister or daughter. In our Kṛṣṇa consciousness movement it has been very difficult to disassociate ourselves from women in our society, especially in Western countries. We are therefore sometimes criticized, but nonetheless we are trying to give everyone a chance to chant the Hare Kṛṣṇa *mahā-mantra* and thus advance spiritually. If we stick to the principle of chanting the Hare Kṛṣṇa *mahā-mantra* offenselessly, then, by the grace of Śrī Haridāsa Ṭhākura, we may be saved from the allurement of women. However, if we are not very strict in chanting the Hare Kṛṣṇa *mahā-mantra,* we may at any time fall victim to women. (5.6.3)

In this material world, family life is an institution of sex. *Yan maithunādi-gṛhamedhi-sukham* (*S.B.* 7.9.45). Through sex, the father and mother beget children, and the children get married and go down the same path of sexual life. After the death of the father and mother, the children get married and beget their own children. Thus generation after generation these things go on in the same way without anyone's attaining liberation from the embarrassment of material life. No one accepts the spiritual processes of knowledge and renunciation, which end in *bhakti-yoga*. Actually human life is meant for *jñāna* and *vairāgya,* knowledge and renunciation. Through these one can attain the platform of devotional service. Unfortunately people in this age avoid the association of liberated people (*sādhu-saṅga*) and continue in their stereotyped way of family life. Thus they are embarrassed by the exchange of money and sex. (5.13.14)

Being cheated by them, the living entity in the forest of the material world tries to give up the association of these so-called yogis, *svāmīs* and incarnations and come to the association of real devotees, but due to misfortune he cannot follow the instructions of the spiritual master or advanced devotees; therefore he gives up their company and again returns to the association of monkeys who are simply interested in sense gratification and women. He derives satisfaction by association with sense gratifiers and enjoying sex and intoxication. Looking into the faces of other sense gratifiers, he becomes forgetful and thus approaches death.

Sometimes a foolish person becomes disgusted with bad association and comes to the association of devotees and *brāhmaṇas* and takes initiation from a spiritual master. As advised by the spiritual master, he tries to follow the regulative principles, but due to misfortune he cannot follow the instructions of the spiritual master. He therefore gives up the company of devotees and goes to associate with sinful people who are simply interested in sex and intoxication. Those who are so-called spiritualists are compared to monkeys. Outwardly, monkeys sometimes resemble *sādhus* because they live naked in the forest and pick fruits, but their only desire is to keep many female monkeys and enjoy sex life. Sometimes so-called spiritualists seeking a spiritual life come to associate with Kṛṣṇa conscious devotees, but they cannot execute the regulative principles or follow the path of spiritual life. Consequently they leave the association of devotees and go to associate with sense gratifiers, who are compared to monkeys. Again they revive their sex and intoxication and looking at one another's faces, they are thus satisfied. In this way they pass their lives up to the point of death. (5.13.17 Text and Purport)

When the living entity becomes exactly like a monkey jumping from one branch to another, he remains in the tree of household life without any profit but sex. Thus he is kicked by his wife just like the he-ass. Unable to gain release, he remains helplessly in that position. Sometimes he falls victim to an incurable disease, which is like falling into a mountain cave. He becomes afraid of death, which is like the elephant in the back of that cave, and he remains stranded, grasping at the twigs and branches of a creeper.

The precarious condition of a householder's life is described herein. A householder's life is full of misery, and the only attraction is sex with the wife who kicks him during sexual intercourse, just as the she-ass does her mate. Due to continuous sex life, he falls victim to many incurable diseases. At that time, being afraid of death, which is like an elephant, he remains hanging from the twigs and branches of the tree, just like a monkey. (5.13.18 Text and Purport)

My dear king, family members in this material world go under the names of wife and children, but actually they behave like tigers and jackals. A herdsman tries to protect his sheep to the best of his ability, but the tigers and foxes take them away by force. Similarly, although a miserly man wants to guard his money very carefully, his family members take away all his assets forcibly, even though he is very vigilant.

One Hindi poet has sung: *din kā dakinī rāt kā bāghinī pālak pālak rahu cuse.* During the daytime, the wife is compared to a witch, and at night she is compared to a tigress. Her only business is sucking the blood of her husband both day and night. During the day there are household expenditures, and the money earned by the husband at the cost of his blood is taken away. At night, due to sex pleasure, the husband discharges blood in the form of semen. In this way, he is bled by his wife both day and night, yet he is so crazy that he very carefully maintains her. Similarly the children are also like tigers, jackals and foxes. As tigers, jackals and foxes take away lambs despite the herdsman's vigilant protection, children take away the father's money, although the father supervises the money himself. Thus family members may be called wives and children, but actually they are plunderers. (5.14.3 Text and Purport)

Every year the plowman plows over his grain field, completely uprooting all weeds. Nonetheless, the seeds lie there and, not being completely burned, again come up with the plants sown in the field. Even after being plowed under, the weeds come up densely. Similarly, the *gṛhastha-āśrama* (family life) is a field of fruitive activity. Unless the desire to enjoy family life is completely burned out, it grows up again and again. Even though camphor may be removed from a pot, the pot nonetheless retains the aroma of camphor. As long as the seeds of desire are not destroyed, fruitive activities are not destroyed.

Unless one's desires are completely transferred to the service of the Supreme Personality of Godhead, the desire for family life continues, even after one has taken *sannyāsa.* Sometimes in our society, ISKCON, a person out of sentiment may take *sannyāsa,* but because his desires are not burned completely, he again takes to family life, even at the risk of losing his prestige and disgracing his good name. These strong desires can be burned out completely when one fully engages in the service of the Lord in devotional service. (5.14.4 Text and Purport)

Sometimes, as if blinded by the dust of a whirlwind, the conditioned soul sees the beauty of the opposite sex, which is called *pramadā.* Being thus bewildered, he is raised upon the lap of a woman, and at that time his good senses are overcome by the force of passion. He thus becomes almost blind with lusty desire and disobeys the rules and regulations governing sex life. He does not know that his disobedience is witnessed by different demigods, and he enjoys illicit sex in the dead of night, not seeing the future punishment awaiting him.

In *Bhagavad-gītā* (7.11) it is said: *dharmāviruddho bhūteṣu kāmo 'smi bharatarṣabha.* Sex is allowed only for the begetting of children, not for enjoyment. One can indulge in sex to beget a good child for the benefit of the family, society and world. Otherwise, sex is against the rules and regulations of religious life. A materialistic person does not believe that everything is managed in nature, and he does not know that if one does something wrong, he is witnessed by different demigods. A person enjoys illicit sex, and due to his blind, lusty desire, he thinks that no one can see him, but this illicit sex is thoroughly observed by the agents of the Supreme Personality of Godhead. Therefore the person is punished in so many ways. Presently in Kali-yuga there are many pregnancies due to illicit sex, and sometimes abortions ensue. These sinful activities are witnessed by the agents of Supreme Personality of Godhead, and a man and woman who create such a situation are punished in the future by the stringent laws of material nature (*daivī hy eṣā guṇamayī mama māyā duratyayā*). Illicit sex is never excused, and those who indulge in it are punished life after life. As confirmed in *Bhagavad-gītā* (16.20):

āsurīṁ yonim āpannā
mūḍhā janmani janmani
mām aprāpyaiva kaunteya
tato yānty adhamāṁ gatim

"Attaining repeated birth among the species of demoniac life, such persons can never approach Me. Gradually they sink down to the most abominable type of existence."

The Supreme Personaality of Godhead does not allow anyone to act against the stringent laws of material nature: therefore illicit sex is punished life after life. Illicit sex creates pregnancies, and these unwanted pregnancies lead to abortion. Those involved become implicated in these sins, so much so that they are punished in the same way the next life. Thus in the next life they also enter the womb of a mother and are killed in the same way. All these things can be avoided by remaining on the transcendental platform of Kṛṣṇa consciousness. In this way one does not commit sinful activity. Illicit sex is the most prominent sin due to lusty desire. When one associates with the mode of passion, he is implicated in suffering life after life. (5.14.9 Text and Purport)

The conditioned soul is sometimes attracted to the little happiness derived from sense gratification. Thus he has illicit sex or steals another's property. At such a time he may be arrested by the government or chastised by the woman's husband or protector. Thus simply for a little material satisfaction, he falls into a hellish condition and is put into jail for rape, kidnapping, theft and so forth.

Material life is such that due to indulgence in illicit sex, gambling, intoxication and meat-eating, the conditioned soul is always in a dangerous condition. Meat-eating and intoxication excite the senses more and more, and the conditioned soul falls victim to women. In order to keep women, money is required, and to acquire money, one begs, borrows or steals. Indeed, he commits abominable acts that cause him to suffer both in this life and in the next. Consequently illicit sex must be stopped by those who are spiritually inclined or who are on the path of spiritual realization. Many devotees fall down due to illicit sex. They may steal money and even fall down from the highly honored renounced order. Then for a livelihood they accept menial services and become beggars. It is therefore said in the *śāstras, yan maithunādi-gṛhamedhi-sukhaṁ hi tuccham:* materialism is based on sex, whether licit or illicit. Sex is full of dangers even for those who are addicted to household life. Whether one has a license for sex or not, there is great trouble. *Bahu-duḥkha-bhāk:* after one indulges in sex, many volumes of miseries ensue. One suffers more and more in material life. A miserly person cannot properly utilize the wealth he has, and similarly a materialistic person misuses the human form. Instead of using it for spiritual emancipation, he uses the body for sense gratification. Therefore he is called a miser. (5.14.22 Text and Purport)

Sometimes the conditioned soul is attracted by illusion personified (his wife or girlfriend) and becomes eager to be embraced by a woman. Thus he loses his intelligence as well as knowledge of life's goal. At that time, no longer attempting spiritual cultivation, he becomes overly attached to his wife or girlfriend and tries to provide her with a suitable apartment. Again, he becomes very busy under the shelter of that home and is captivated by the talks, glances and activities of his wife and children. In this way he loses his Kṛṣṇa consciousness and throws himself in the dense darkness of material existence.

When the conditioned soul is embraced by his beloved wife, he forgets everything about Kṛṣṇa consciousness. The more he becomes attached to his wife, the more he becomes implicated in family life. One Bengali poet, Bankim Chandra, says that to the eyes of the lover the beloved is always very beautiful, even though ugly. This attraction is called *deva-māyā.* The attraction between man and woman is the cause of bondage for both. Actually both belong to the *parā prakṛti,* the superior energy of the Lord, but both are actually *prakṛti* (female). However, because both want to enjoy one another, they are sometimes described as *puruṣa* (male). Actually neither is *puruṣa,* but both can be superficially described as *puruṣa.* As soon as man and woman are united, they become attached to home, hearth, land, friendship and money. In this way they are both entrapped in material existence. The word *bhuja-latā-upagūḍha,* meaning "being embraced by beautiful arms which are compared to creepers," describes the way the conditioned soul is bound within this material world. The products of sex life—sons and daughters—certainly follow. This is the way of material existence. (5.14.28 Text and Purport)

The pseudo *svāmīs, yogīs* and incarnations who do not believe in the Supreme Personality of Godhead are known as *pāṣaṇḍīs.* They themselves are fallen and cheated because they do not know the real path of spiritual advancement, and whoever goes to them is certainly cheated in his turn. When one is thus cheated, he sometimes takes shelter of the real followers of Vedic principles (*brāhmaṇas* or those in Kṛṣṇa consciousness) who teach everyone how to worship the Supreme Personality of Godhead according to the Vedic rituals. However, being unable to stick to these principles, these rascals again fall down and take shelter among *śūdras* who are very expert in making arrangements for sex indulgence. Sex is very prominent among animals like monkeys, and such people who are enlivened by sex may be called descendants of monkeys.

By fulfilling the process of evolution from the aquatics to the animal platform, a living entity eventually reaches the human form. The three modes of material nature are always working in the evolutionary process. Those who come to the human form through the quality of *sattva-guṇa* were cows in their last animal incarnation. Those who come to the human form through the quality of *rajo-guṇa* were lions in their last animal incarnation. And those who come to the human form through the quality of *tamo-guṇa* were monkeys in their last animal incarnation. In this age, those who come through the monkey species are considered by modern anthropologists like Darwin to be descendants of monkeys. We receive information herein that those who are simply interested in sex are actually no better than monkeys. Monkeys are very expert in sexual enjoyment, and sometimes sex glands are taken from monkeys and placed in the human body so that a human being can enjoy sex in old age. In this way modern civilization has advanced. Many monkeys in India were caught and sent to Europe so that sex glands could serve as replacements for those of old people. Those who actually descend from the monkeys are interested in expanding their aristocratic families through sex. In the Vedas there are also certain ceremonies especially meant for sexual improvement and promotion to higher planetary systems, where the demigods are enjoying sex. The demigods are also very much inclined toward sex because that is the basic principle of material enjoyment.

First of all, the conditioned soul is cheated by so-called *svāmīs, yogīs* and incarnations when he approaches them to be relieved of material miseries. When the conditioned soul is not satisfied with them, he comes to devotees and pure *brāhmaṇas* who try to elevate him for final liberation from material bondage. However, the unscrupulous conditioned soul cannot rigidly follow the principles prohibiting illicit sex, intoxication, gambling and meat-eating. Thus he falls down and takes shelter of people who are like monkeys. In the Kṛṣṇa consciousness movement these monkey disciples, being unable to follow the strict regulative principles, sometimes fall down and try to form societies based on sex. This is proof that such people are descendants of monkeys, as confirmed by Darwin. In this verse, it is therefore clearly stated: *yathā vānara-jāteḥ.* (5.14.30)

Entanglement in family life is the root cause of material attachment, indefatigable desires, moroseness, anger, despair, fear and the desire for false prestige, all of which result in the repetition of birth and death. (5.18.14 Text)

Any women who seeks a material husband for her protection, or any man who desires to become the husband of a woman, is under illusion. (5.18.19)

A man or woman who indulges in sexual intercourse with an unworthy member of the opposite sex is punished after death by the assistants of Yamarāja in the hell known as Taptasūrmi. There such men and women are beaten with whips. The man is forced to embrace a red-hot iron form of a woman and the woman is forced to embrace a similar form of a man. Such is the punishment for illicit sex.

Generally a man should not have sexual relations with any woman other than his wife. According to Vedic principles, the wife of another man is considered one's mother, and sexual relations are strictly forbidden with one's mother, sister and daughter. If one indulges in illicit sexual relations with another man's wife, that activity is considered identical with having sex with one's mother. This act is most sinful. The same principle holds for a woman also; if she enjoys sex with a man other than her husband, the act is tantamount to having sexual relations with her father or son. Illicit sex life is always forbidden, and any man or woman who indulges in it is punished in the manner described in this verse. (5.26.20 Text and Purport)

A person who indulges in sex indiscriminately—even with animals—is taken after death to the hell known as Vajrakaṇṭaka-śālmalī. In this hell there is a silk-cotton tree full of thorns as strong as thunderbolts. The agents of Yamarāja hang the sinful man on that tree and pull him down forcibly so that the thorns very severely tear his body.

The sexual urge is so strong that sometimes a man indulges in sexual relations with a cow, or a woman indulges in sexual relations with a dog. Such men and women are put into the hell known as Vajrakaṇṭaka-śālmalī. The Kṛṣṇa consciousness movement forbids illicit sex. From the description of these verses, we can understand what an extremely sinful act illicit sex is. Sometimes people disbelieve these descriptions of hell but whether one believes or not, everything must be carried out by the laws of nature, which no one can avoid. (5.26.2 Text and Purport)

Only a rare person who has adopted complete, unalloyed devotional service to Kṛṣṇa can uproot the weeds of sinful actions with no possibility that they will revive. He can do this simply by discharging devotional service, just as the sun can immediately dissipate fog by its rays. (6.1.15 Text)

The fault of illicit connection with women is that it makes one lose all brahminical qualities. In India there is still a class of servants, called *śūdras,* whose maidservant wives are called *śūdrāṇīs.* Sometimes people who are very lusty establish relationships with such maidservants and sweeping women, since in the higher statuses of society they cannot indulge in the habit of woman hunting, which is strictly prohibited by social convention. Ajāmila, a qualified *brāhmaṇa* youth, lost all his brahminical qualities because of his association with a prostitute. (6.1.21)

This fallen *brāhmaṇa,* Ajāmila, gave trouble to others by arresting them, by cheating them in gambling or by directly plundering them. This was the way he earned his livelihood and maintained his wife and children.

This verse indicates how degraded one becomes simply by indulging in illicit sex with a prostitute. Illicit sex is not possible with a chaste or aristocratic woman, but only with unchaste *śūdras.* The more society allows prostitution and illicit sex, the more impetus it gives to cheaters, thieves, plunderers, drunkards and gamblers. Therefore we first advise all the disciples in our Kṛṣṇa consciousness movement to avoid illicit sex, which is the beginning of all abominable life and which is followed by meat-eating, gambling and intoxication, one after another. Of course, restraint is very difficult, but it is quite possible if one fully surrenders to Kṛṣṇa, since all these abominable habits gradually become distasteful for a Kṛṣṇa conscious person. If illicit sex is allowed to increase in society, however, the entire society will be condemned, for it will be full of rogues, thieves, cheaters and so forth. (6.1.22 Text and Purport)

My dear king, if a sinful person engages in the service of a bona fide devotee of the Lord and thus learns how to dedicate his life unto the lotus feet of Kṛṣṇa, he can be completely purified. One cannot be purified merely by undergoing austerity, penance, *brahmacarya* and the other methods of atonement I have previously described. (6.1.16 Text)

Long ago, when he saw the scene of the drunken *śūdra* and the prostitute, Ajāmila, who was a perfect *brahmacārī,* was affected. Nowadays such sin is visible in so many places, and we must consider the position of a *brahmacārī* student who sees such behavior. For such a *brahmacārī* to remain steady is very difficult unless he is extremely strong in following the regulative principles. Nevertheless, if one takes to Kṛṣṇa consciousness very seriously, he can withstand the provocation created by sin. In our Kṛṣṇa consciousness movement we prohibit illicit sex, intoxication, meat-eating and gambling. In Kali-yuga, a drunk, half-naked woman embracing a drunk man is a very common sight, especially in Western countries, and restraining oneself after seeing such things is very difficult. Nevertheless, if by the grace of Kṛṣṇa one adheres to the regulative principles and chants the Hare Kṛṣṇa mantra, Kṛṣṇa will certainly protect him. Indeed, Kṛṣṇa says that His devotee is never vanquished (*kaunteya pratijānīhi na me bhaktaḥ praṇaśyati*). Therefore all the disciples practicing Kṛṣṇa consciousness should obediently follow the regulative principles and remain fixed in chanting the holy name of the Lord. There need be no fear. Otherwise one's position is very dangerous, especially in this Kali-yuga. (6.1.61)

Unless one is very strong in knowledge, patience and proper bodily, mental and intellectual behavior, controlling one's lusty desires is extremely difficult. Thus after seeing a man embracing a young woman and practically doing everything required for sex life, even a fully qualified *brāhmaṇa,* as described above, could not control his lusty desires and restrain himself from pursuing them. Because of the force of materialistic life, to maintain self-control is extremely difficult unless one is specifically under the protection of the Supreme Personality of Godhead through devotional service. (6.1.62)

As stated in *Śrīmad-Bhāgavatam, yan maithunādi-gṛhamedhi-sukhaṁ hi tuccham;* people are attached to household life for sex only. They are always harassed in many ways by their material engagements, and their only happiness is that after working very hard all day, at night they sleep and indulge in sex. *Nidrayā hriyate naktaṁ vyavāyena ca vā vayaḥ:* at night, materialistic householders sleep or indulge in sex life. *Divā cārthehayā rājan kuṭumba-bharaṇena vā:* during the day they are busy trying to find out where money is, and if they get money they spend it to maintain their families. (6.3.25)

It should be noted that although such a facility for sexual intercourse is achieved by the grace of the Supreme Personality of Godhead, this facility is not offered to advanced devotees, who are free from material desires (*anyābhilāṣitā-śūnyam*). In this connection it may be noted that if the American boys and girls engaged in the Kṛṣṇa consciousness movement want to advance in Kṛṣṇa consciousness to achieve the supreme benefit of loving service to the Lord, they should refrain from indulging in this facility for sex life. Therefore we advise that one should at least refrain from illicit sex. Even if there are opportunities for sex life, one should voluntarily accept the limitation of having sex only for progeny, not for any other purpose. Kardama Muni was also given the facility for sex life, but he had only a slight desire for it. Therefore after begetting children in the womb of Devahūti, Kardama Muni became completely renounced. The purport is that if one wants to return home, back to Godhead, one should voluntarily refrain from sex life. Sex should be accepted only as much as needed, not unlimitedly.

Therefore although sex life is the topmost enjoyment in the material world and although one may have an opportunity for sexual enjoyment by the grace of God, this entails a risk of committing offenses. (6.4.52)

To be a householder is very risky unless one is trained and the wife is a follower of her husband. (6.18.40)

A woman's face is as attractive and beautiful as a blossoming lotus flower during autumn. Her words are very sweet, and they give pleasure to the ear, but if we study a woman's heart, we can understand it to be extremely sharp, like the blade of a razor. In these circumstances, who could understand the dealings of a woman?

Woman is now depicted very well from the materialistic point of view by Kaśyapa Muni. Women are generally known as the fair sex, and especially in youth, at the age of sixteen or seventeen, women are very attractive to men. Therefore a woman's face is compared to a blooming lotus flower in autumn. Just as a lotus is extremely attractive in autumn, a woman at the threshold of youthful beauty is extremely attractive. In Sanskrit a woman's voice is called *nārī-svara* because woman generally sing and their singing is very attractive. At the present moment, cinema artists, especially female singers, are especially welcome. Some of them earn fabulous amounts of money simply by singing. Therefore, as taught by Śrī Caitanya Mahāprabhu, a woman's singing is dangerous because it can make a *sannyāsī* fall a victim to the woman. *Sannyāsa* means giving up the company of women, but if a *sannyāsī* hears the voice of a woman and sees her beautiful face, he certainly becomes attracted and is sure to fall down. There have been many examples. Even the great sage Viśvāmitra fell a victim to Menakā. Therefore a person desiring to advance in spiritual consciousness must be especially careful not to see a woman's face or hear a woman's voice. To see a woman's face and appreciate its beauty or to hear a woman's voice and appreciate her singing as very nice is a subtle fall down for a *brahmacārī* or *sannyāsī.* Thus the description of woman's features by Kaśyapa Muni is very instructive.

When a woman's bodily features are attractive, when her face is beautiful and when her voice is sweet, she is naturally a trap for a man. The *śāstras* advise that when such a woman comes to serve a man, she should be considered to be like a dark well covered by grass. In the fields there are many such wells, and a man who does not know about them drops through the grass and falls down. Thus there are many such instructions. Since the attraction of the material world is based on attraction for women, Kaśyapa Muni thought, "Under the circumstances, who can understand the heart of a woman?" Cāṇakya Pandita has also advised, *viśvāso naiva kartavyaḥ strīṣu rāja-kuleṣu ca:* "There are two persons one should not trust—a politician and a woman." These, of course, are authoritative *śāstric* injunctions, and we should therefore be very careful in our dealings with women.

Sometimes our Kṛṣṇa consciousness movement is criticized for mingling men and women, but Kṛṣṇa consciousness is meant for anyone. Whether one is a man or woman does not matter. Lord Kṛṣṇa personally says, *striyo vaiśyās tathā śūdrās te 'pi yānti parāṁ gatim:* whether one is a woman, *śūdra* or *vaiśya,* not to speak of being a *brāhmaṇa* or *kṣatriya,* everyone is fit to return home, back to Godhead, if he strictly follows the instructions of the spiritual master and Kṛṣṇa. We therefore request all members of the Kṛṣṇa consciousness movement—both men and women—not to be attracted by bodily features but only to be attracted by Kṛṣṇa. Then everything will be all right. Otherwise there will be danger. (6.18.41 Text and Purport)

To satisfy their own interests, women deal with men as if the men were most dear to them, but no one is actually dear to them. Women are supposed to be very saintly, but for their own interest they can kill even their husbands, sons or brothers, or cause them to be killed by others.

A woman's nature has been particularly well studied by Kaśyapa Muni. Women are self-interested by nature, and therefore they should be protected by all means so that their natural inclination to be too self-interested will not be manifested. Women need to be protected by men. A woman should be cared for by her father in her childhood, by her husband in her youth and by her grown sons in her old age. This is the injunction of Manu, who says that a woman should not be given independence at any stage. Women must be cared for so that they will not be free to manifest their natural tendency for gross selfishness. There have been many cases, even in the present day, in which women have killed their husbands to take advantage of their insurance policies. This is not a criticism of women but a practical study of their nature. Such natural instincts of a woman or man are manifested only in the bodily conception of life. When either a man or a woman is advanced in spiritual consciousness, the bodily conception of life practically vanishes. We should see all women as spiritual units (*aham brahmāsmi*), whose only duty is to satisfy Kṛṣṇa. Then the influences of the different modes of material nature, which result from one's possessing a material body, will not act. (6.18.42 Text and Purport)

If a bona fide listener hears of Kṛṣṇa's pastimes with the *gopīs*, which seem to be lusty affairs, the lusty desires in his heart, which constitute the heart disease of the conditioned soul, will be vanquished, and he will become a most exalted devotee of the Lord. (7.1.30)

Before entering household life, one should be trained as a *brahmacārī,* living under the care of the guru, whose place is known as the *gurukula. Brahmacārī guru-kule vasan dānto guror hitam* (*S.B.* 7.12.1). From the beginning, a *brahmacārī* is trained to sacrifice everything for the benefit of the guru. A *brahmacārī* is advised to go begging alms door to door, addressing all women as mother, and whatever he collects goes to the benefit of the guru. In this way, he learns how to control his senses and sacrifice everything for the guru. When he is fully trained, if he likes he is allowed to marry. Thus he is not an ordinary *gṛhastha* who has learned only how to satisfy his senses. A trained *gṛhastha* can gradually give up household life and go to the forest to become increasingly enlightened in spiritual life and at last take *sannyāsa.* Prahlāda Mahārāja explained to his father that to be freed from all material anxieties one should go to the forest. *Hitvātma-pātaṁ gṛham andha-kūpam.* One should give up his household, which is a place for going further down into the darkest regions of material existence. The first advice, therefore, is that one must give up household life (*gṛham andha-kūpam*). However, if one prefers to remain in the dark well of household life because of uncontrolled senses, he becomes increasingly entangled by ropes of affection for his wife, children, servants, house, money and so on. Such a person cannot obtain liberation from material bondage. Therefore children should be taught from the very beginning of life to be first class *brahmacārīs.* Then it will be possible for them to give up household life in the future. (7.6.9)

How can a person who is most affectionate to his family, the core of his heart being always filled with their pictures, give up their association? Specifically, a wife is always kind and sympathetic and always pleases her husband in a solitary place. Who could give up the association of such a dear and affectionate wife? Small children talk in broken language, very pleasing to hear, and their affectionate father always thinks of their sweet words. How could he give up their association? One's elderly parents and one's sons and daughters are also very dear. A daughter is especially dear to her father, and while living at her husband's house she is always in his mind. Who could give up that association? Aside from this, in household affairs there are many decorated items of household furniture, and there are also animals and servants. Who could give up such comforts? The attached householder is like a silkworm, which weaves a cocoon in which it becomes imprisoned, unable to get out.

Simply for the satisfaction of two important senses—the genitals and the tongue—one is bound by material conditions. How can one escape?

In household affairs the first attraction is the beautiful and pleasing wife, who increases household attraction more and more. One enjoys his wife with two prominent sense organs, namely the tongue and the genitals. The wife speaks very sweetly. This is certainly an attraction. Then she prepares very palatable foods to satisfy the tongue, and when the tongue is satisfied one gains strength in the other sense organs, especially the genitals. Thus the wife gives pleasure in sexual intercourse. Household life means sex life (*yan maithunādi-gṛhamedhi-sukhaṁ hi tuccham*). This is encouraged by the tongue. Then there are children. A baby gives pleasure by speaking sweet words in broken language, and when the sons and daughters are grown up one becomes involved in their education and marriage. Then there are one's own father and mother to take care of, and one also becomes concerned with the social atmosphere and with pleasing his brothers and sisters. A man becomes increasingly entangled in household affairs, so much so that leaving them becomes almost impossible. Thus the household becomes *gṛham andha-kūpam,* a dark well into which the man has fallen. For such a man to get out is extremely difficult unless he is helped by a strong person, the spiritual master, who helps the fallen person with the strong rope of spiritual instructions. A fallen person should take advantage of this rope, and then the spiritual master, or the Supreme Personality of Godhead, Kṛṣṇa, will take him out of the dark well. (7.6.13 Text and Purport)

Oh my Lord, because of lusty desires from the very beginning of one's birth, the functions of one's senses, mind, life, body, religion, patience, intelligence, shyness, opulence, strength, memory and truthfulness are vanquished.

As stated in *Śrīmad-Bhāgavatam, kāmaṁ hṛd-rogam.* Materialistic life means that one is afflicted by a formidable disease called lusty desire. Liberation means freedom from lusty desires, because it is only due to such desires that one must accept repeated birth and death. As long as one's lusty desires are unfulfilled, one must take birth after birth to fulfill them. Because of material desires, therefore, one performs various types of activities and receives various types of bodies with which to try to fulfill desires that are never satisfied. The only remedy is to take to devotional service, which begins when one is free from all material desires; *anyābhilāṣitā-śūnyam. Anya-abhilāṣitā* means "material desire," and *śūnyam* means "free from." The spiritual soul has spiritual activities and spiritual desires, as described by Śrī Caitanya Mahāprabhu: *mama janmani janmanīśvare bhavatād bhaktir ahaitukī tvayi.* Unalloyed devotion to the service of the Lord is the only spiritual desire. To fulfill this spiritual desire, however, one must be free from all material desires. (7.10.8)

śrī-nārada uvāca
brahmacārī guru-kule
vasan dānto guror hitam
ācaran dāsavan nīco
gurau sudṛḍha-sauhṛdaḥ

Nārada Muni said: A student should practice completely controlling his senses. He should be submissive and should have an attitude of firm friendship for the spiritual master. With a great vow, the *brahmacārī* should live at the *gurukula*, only for the benefit of the guru. (7.12.1 Text)

[There are five main points in this verse. (1) *vasan:* the *brahmacārī* should reside in the *āśrama* of the guru; (2) *dāntaḥ:* he should learn sense control; (3) *guroḥ hitam:* he must act only for the benefit of his guru; (4) *ācaran dāsa-vat nīcaḥ:* he should behave as a menial servant; (5) *gurau su-dṛḍha sauhṛdaḥ:* he should have an attitude of firm friendship for the spiritual master.]

A *brahmacārī* should be quite well behaved and gentle and should not eat or collect more than necessary. He must always be active and expert, fully believing in the instructions of the spiritual master and the *śāstra.* Fully controlling his senses, he should associate only as much as necessary with women or those controlled by women.

A *brahmacārī* should be very careful not to mix with women or with men addicted to women. Although when he goes out to beg alms it is necessary to talk with women and with men very much attracted to women, this association should be very short, and he should talk with them only about begging alms, and not more. A *brahmacārī* should be very careful in associating with men who are attached to women. (7.12.6 Text and Purport)

A *brahmacārī,* or one who has not accepted the *gṛhastha-āśrama* (family life), must rigidly avoid talking with women or about women, for the senses are so powerful that they may agitate even the mind of a *sannyāsī,* a member of the renounced order of life.

Brahmacarya essentially means the vow not to marry but to observe strict celibacy (*bṛhad-vrata*). A *brahmacārī* or *sannyāsī* should avoid talking with women or reading literature concerning talks between man and woman. The injunction restricting association with women is the basic principle of spiritual life. Associating or talking with women is never advised in any of the Vedic literatures. The entire Vedic system teaches one to avoid sex life so that one may gradually progress from *brahmacarya* to *gṛhastha,* from *gṛhastha* to *vānaprastha,* and from *vānaprastha* to *sannyāsa* and thus give up material enjoyment, which is the original cause of bondage to this material world. The word *bṛhad-vrata* refers to one who has decided not to marry, or in other words, not to indulge in sex life throughout this entire life. (7.12.7 Text and Purport)

Woman is compared to fire, and man is compared to a butter pot. Therefore a man should avoid associating even with his own daughter in a secluded place. Similarly, he should also avoid association with other women. One should associate with women only for important business and not otherwise.

If a butter pot and fire are kept together, the butter within the pot will certainly melt. Woman is compared to fire, and man in compared to a butter pot. However advanced one may be in restraining the senses, it is almost impossible for a man to keep himself controlled in the presence of a woman, even if she is his own daughter, mother or sister. Indeed, his mind is agitated even if one is in the renounced order of life. Therefore, Vedic civilization carefully restricts mingling between men and women. If one cannot understand the basic principle of restraining association between man and woman, he is to be considered an animal. That is the purport of this verse. (7.12.9 Text and Purport)

As long as a living entity is not completely self-realized—as long as he is not independent of the misconception of identifying with his body, which is nothing but a reflection of the original body and senses—he cannot be relieved of the duality between man and woman. Thus there is every chance that he will fall down because his intelligence is bewildered.

Here is another important warning that a man must save himself from attraction to woman. No one should think himself perfect and forget the *śāstric* instruction that one should be very careful about associating even with his daughter, mother or sister, not to speak of other women. (7.12.10 Text and Purport)

In this human form of life, man and woman unite for the sensual pleasure of sex, but by actual experience we have observed that none of them are happy.

As stated by Prahlāda Mahārāja, *yan maithunādi-gṛhamedhi-sukhaṁ hi tuccham.* Man and woman both seek sexual enjoyment, and when they are united by the ritualistic ceremony of marriage, they are happy for some time, but finally there is dissension, and thus there are so many cases of separation and divorce. Although every man and woman is actually eager to enjoy life through sexual unity, the result is disunity and distress. Marriage is recommended to give men and women a concession for restricted sex life, which is also recommended in *Bhagavad-gītā* by the Supreme Personality of Godhead. *Dharmāviruddho bhūteṣu kāmo 'smi:* sex life not against the principles of religion is Kṛṣṇa. Every living entity is always eager to enjoy sex life because materialistic life consists of eating, sleeping, sex and fear. (7.13.26 Text and Purport)

Sex is not at all necessary, although one who absolutely requires it is allowed to enter *gṛhastha* life, or household life, which is also regulated by the *śāstras* and guru... we should not create a so-called comfortable situation, but must prepare to undergo austerity. This is how a human being should actually live to fulfill life's ultimate goal. (7.14.1 Text and Purport)

Every husband is too much attached to his wife. (7.14.12)

My dear king, a self-satisfied person can be happy even with only drinking water. However, one who is driven by the senses, especially by the tongue and genitals, must accept the position of a household dog to satisfy his senses.

Because of greed for the sake of the senses, the spiritual strength, education, austerity and reputation of a devotee or *brāhmaṇa* who is not self-satisfied dwindle, and his knowledge gradually vanishes." (7.15.18-19 Text and Purport)

In this world of duality, family life is the cause that spoils one's spiritual life or meditation. Specifically understanding this fact, one should accept the order of *sannyāsa* without hesitation. (From *smṛti* literature, quoted in 7.15.30 Purport)

There is no harm if one thinks that he is unfit for *sannyāsa;* if he is very much agitated sexually, he should go to the *āśrama* where sex is allowed, namely the *gṛhastha-āśrama.* That one has been found to be very weak in one place does not mean that he should stop fighting the crocodile of *māyā.* One should take shelter of the lotus feet of Kṛṣṇa, and at the same time one can be a *gṛhastha* if he is satisfied with sexual indulgence. There is no need to give up the fight. Śrī Caitanya Mahāprabhu therefore recommended, *sthāne sthitāḥ śruti-gatāṁ tanu-vān-manobhiḥ.* One may stay in whichever *āśrama* is suitable for him; it is not essential that one take *sannyāsa.* If one is sexually agitated, he can enter the *gṛhastha-āśrama.* But one must continue fighting. For one who is not in a transcendental position, to take *sannyāsa* artificially is not a very great credit. If *sannyāsa* is not suitable, one may enter the *gṛhastha-āśrama* and fight *māyā* with great strength. But one should not give up the fighting and go away. (8.2.30)

Those who maintain a demoniac mentality are bewildered by the beauty of a woman, but those who are advanced in Kṛṣṇa consciousness or even those on the platform of goodness are not bewildered. (8.12.15)

The attractive features of a woman are appreciated by those who are affected by lusty desires. (8.12.16)

When a man and woman exchange feelings of lust, both of them are victimized, and thus they are bound to this material world in various ways. (8.12.22)

Śrīla Viśvanātha Cakravartī Ṭhākura remarks that Mohinī-mūrti dragged Lord Śiva to so many places, especially to where the great sages lived, to instruct the sages that their Lord Śiva had become mad for a beautiful woman. Thus although they were all great sages and saintly persons, they should not think themselves free, but should remain extremely cautious about beautiful women. No one should think himself liberated in the presence of a beautiful woman. (8.12.34)

If one is trained to protect his semen by observing celibacy, naturally he is not attracted by the beauty of woman. If one can remain a *brahmacārī,* he saves himself so much trouble in material existence. Material existence means enjoying the pleasure of sexual enjoyment (*yan maithunādi-gṛhamedhi-sukhaṁ hi tuccham*). If one is educated about sex life and is trained to protect his semen, he is saved from the danger of material existence. (8.12.35)

There are two kinds of *brahmacārīs.* One may return home, marry and become a householder, whereas the other, known as *bṛhad-vrata,* takes a vow to remain a *brahmacārī* perpetually. The *bṛhad-vrata brahmacārī* does not return from the place of the spiritual master; he stays there, and later he directly takes *sannyāsa.* (9.4.1)

A person desiring liberation from material bondage must give up the association of persons interested in sex life and should not employ his senses externally (in seeing, hearing, talking, walking and so on). One should always stay in a secluded place, completely fixing his mind at the lotus feet of the unlimited Personality of Godhead, and if one wants any association at all, he should associate with persons similarly engaged.

Saubhari Muni, giving conclusions derived from his practical experience, instructs us that persons interested in crossing to the other side of the material ocean must give up the association of persons interested in sex life and accumulating money.

One who desires complete freedom from material bondage can engage himself in the transcendental loving service of the Lord. He must not associate with *viṣayī*—materialistic persons or those interested in sex life. Every materialist is interested in sex. Thus in plain language it is advised that an exalted saintly person avoid the association of those who are materially inclined. Śrīla Narottama dasa Ṭhākura also recommends that one engage in the service of the *ācāryas,* and if one wants to live in association, he must live in the association of devotees (*tāṅdera caraṇa sevi bhakta-sane vāsa*). The Kṛṣṇa consciousness movement is creating many centers just to create devotees so that by associating with the members of such a center people will automatically become uninterested in material affairs. Although this is an ambitious proposal, this association is proving effective by the mercy of Śrī Caitanya Mahāprabhu. By gradually associating with the members of the Kṛṣṇa consciousness movement, simply by taking *prasāda* and taking part in chanting of the Hare Kṛṣṇa mantra, ordinary persons are being considerably elevated. Saubhari Muni regrets that he had bad association even in the deepest part of the water. Because of the bad association of the sexually engaged fish, he fell down. A secluded place is also not secure unless there is good association. (9.6.51 Text and Purport)

Unless one is extremely advanced in spiritual consciousness, household life is nothing but a dark well in which one commits suicide. (9.19.12)

The attraction between male and female always exists everywhere, making everyone always fearful. Such feelings are present even among the controllers like Brahmā and Lord Śiva and is the cause of fear for them, what to speak of others who are attached to household life in this material world.

As long as men feel attracted to women in this material world and women feel attracted to men, the bondage of repeated birth and death will continue. (9.11.17 Text and Purport)

Cāṇakya Paṇḍita has advised, *viśvāso naiva kartavyaḥ strīṣu rāja-kuleṣu ca:* "Never place your faith in a woman or a politician." Unless elevated to spiritual consciousness, everyone is conditioned and fallen, what to speak of women, who are less intelligent than men. Women have been compared to *śūdras* and *vaiśyas* (*striyo vaiśyās tathā śūdrāḥ*). On the spiritual platform, however, when one is elevated to the platform of Kṛṣṇa consciousness, whether one is a man, woman, *śūdra* or whatever, everyone is equal. Otherwise, Urvaśī, who was a woman herself and who knew the nature of women, said that a woman's heart is like that of a sly fox. If a man cannot control his senses, he becomes a victim of such sly foxes. But if one can control the senses, there is no chance of his being victimized by sly, foxlike women. (9.14.36)

During youth the material desire to enjoy the material senses is certainly present, and unless one fully satisfies these lusty desires in youth, there is a chance of one's being disturbed in rendering service to the Lord. We have actually seen that many *sannyāsīs* who accept *sannyāsa* prematurely, not having satisfied their material desires, fall down because they are disturbed. Therefore the general process is to go through *gṛhastha* life and *vānaprastha* life and finally come to *sannyāsa* and devote oneself completely to the service of the Lord. (9.18.40)

Attraction for woman is the impetus for economic development, housing and many other things meant for living comfortably in this material world. The union between male and female provides the impetus for gaining a nice apartment, a good income, children and friends. Thus one becomes entangled in this material world. (9.19.4)

Although one becomes a *gṛhastha,* or householder, to enjoy sex life to his heart's content, one is never satisfied. Like an unfortunate person who acts madly, haunted by ghosts, a materialist haunted by the ghost of lust forgets his real business so that he can enjoy so-called happiness in the bodily concept of life. (9.19.5-6)

A person who is lusty cannot satisfy his mind even if he has enough of everything in this world, including rice, barley and other food grains, gold, animals and women. Nothing can satisfy him.

To have a satisfied mind, one must give up his heart disease of lusty desires. This can only be done when one is Kṛṣṇa conscious. If one becomes Kṛṣṇa conscious, then he can give up this heart disease; otherwise this disease of lusty desires will continue, and one cannot have peace in his mind. (9.19.13 Text and Purport)

mātrā svasrā duhitrā vā
nāviviktāsano bhavet
balavān indriya-grāmo
vidvāṁsam api karṣati

One should not allow oneself to sit on the same seat even with one's own mother, sister or daughter, for the senses are so strong that even though one is very advanced in knowledge, he may be attracted by sex.

Learning the etiquette of how to deal with women does not free one from sexual attraction. As specifically mentioned herewith, such attraction is possible even with one's mother, sister or daughter. Generally, of course, one is not sexually attracted to his mother, sister or daughter, but if one allows himself to sit very close to such a woman, one may be attracted. This is a psychological fact. It may be said that one is liable to be attracted if one is not very advanced in civilized life; however, as specifically mentioned here, *vidvāṁsam api karṣati:* even if one is highly advanced, materially or spiritually, he may be attracted by lusty desires. The object of attraction may even be one's mother, sister or daughter. Therefore, one should be extremely careful in dealings with women. Śrī Caitanya Mahāprabhu was most strict in such dealings, especially after He accepted the *sannyāsa* order. Indeed, no woman could come near Him to offer Him respect. Again, one is warned herewith that one should be extremely careful in dealings with women. (9.19.17 Text and Purport)

One who has not understood that he is not the material body but an eternal spiritual soul, part and parcel of Kṛṣṇa, will invariably be unable to control the urges of the material senses. Therefore, if such a materially inclined person neglects the Vedic injunctions that administer regulated sense gratification, he will surely fall down into unregulated sense gratification in *pāpa,* or sinful life. For example, those who are affected by sexual desire are ordered to accept the *vivāha-yajña,* or religious marriage ceremony. We often see that because of false pride a so-called *brahmacārī,* or celibate student of Vedic knowledge, rejects the marriage ceremony as *māyā,* or material illusion. But if such a celibate student is unable to control his senses he will undoubtedly degrade himself by actually engaging in illicit sex. (11.3.45)

One who has failed to control his senses immediately feels attraction upon seeing a woman's form, which is created by the illusory energy of the Supreme Lord. Indeed, when the woman speaks with enticing words, smiles coquettishly and moves her body sensuously, his mind is immediately captured, and thus he falls blindly into the darkness of material existence, just as the moth maddened by the fire rushes blindly into its flames. A foolish person with no intelligent discrimination is immediately aroused at the sight of a lusty woman beautifully decorated with golden ornaments, fine clothing and other cosmetic features. Being eager for sense gratification, such a fool loses all intelligence and is destroyed just like the moth who rushes into the blazing fire. (11.8.7-8 Text)

A saintly person should never touch a young girl. In fact, he should not even let his foot touch a wooden doll in the shape of a woman. By bodily contact with a woman he will surely be captured by illusion, just as the elephant is captured by the she-elephant due to his desire to touch her body. A man possessing intelligent discrimination should not under any circumstances try to exploit the beautiful form of a woman for his sense gratification. Just as an elephant trying to enjoy a she-elephant is killed by other bull elephants also enjoying her company, one trying to enjoy a lady's company can at any moment be killed by her other lovers who are stronger than he. (11.8.13-14 Text)

Somehow or other one should avoid being cheated by allurement to the sensuous form of woman. One should not allow one's mind to be lost in lusty dreams of sex pleasure. There are various types of sense gratification to be enjoyed between men and women, including speaking, contemplating, touching, sexual intercourse, etc., and all of these constitute the network of illusion by which one is helplessly bound like an animal. Somehow or other one should remain aloof from sense gratification in the form of sex pleasure; otherwise, there is no possibility of understanding the spiritual world. (11.8.13)

One who is too affectionate to his own body will inevitably be seized by sex desire. (11.21.29)

QUOTES FROM OTHER BOOKS BY ŚRĪLA PRABHUPĀDA

The cult of *bhakti-yoga* is so powerful that one automatically loses sexual attraction, being engaged in the superior service of the Lord. (*Bg.* 6.13-14)

A *brahmacārī* hears only words concerning Kṛṣṇa consciousness; hearing is the basic principle for understanding, and therefore a pure *brahmacārī* engages fully in *harer nāmānukīrtanam*—chanting and hearing the glories of the Lord. He restrains himself from the vibrations of other sounds, and his hearing is engaged in the transcendental sound of Hare Kṛṣṇa, Hare Kṛṣṇa. (*Bg.* 4.26)

That happiness which is derived from contact of the senses with their objects and which appears like nectár at first but poison at the end is said to be of the nature of passion.

A young man and a young woman meet, and the senses drive the young man to see her, to touch her and to have sexual intercourse. In the beginning this may be very pleasing to the senses, but at the end, or after some time, it becomes just like poison. They are separated or there is divorce, there is lamentation, there is sorrow, etc. Such happiness is always in the mode of passion. Happiness derived from a combination of the senses and the sense objects is always a cause of distress and should be avoided by all means. (*Bg.* 18.38 Text and Purport)

Lust and love have different characteristics, just as iron and gold have different natures.

One should try to discriminate between sexual love and pure love, for they belong to different categories, with a gulf of difference between them. They are as different from one another as iron is from gold. (*Cc. Ādi* 4.164 Text and Purport)

The desire to gratify one's own senses is *kāma* (lust), but the desire to please the senses of Lord Kṛṣṇa is *prema* (love).

The author of *Śrī Caitanya-caritāmṛta* asserts with authority that sexual love is a matter of personal sense enjoyment. All the regulative principles in the Vedas pertaining to desires for popularity, fatherhood, wealth and so on are different phases of sense gratification. Acts of sense gratification may be performed under the cover of public welfare, nationalism, religion, altruism, ethical codes, Biblical codes, health directives, fruitive action, bashfulness, tolerance, personal comfort, liberation from material bondage, progress, family affection or fear of social ostracism or legal punishment, but all these categories are different subdivisions of one substance—sense gratification. All such good acts are performed basically for one's own sense gratification, for no one can sacrifice his personal interest while discharging these much-advertised moral and religious principles. But above all this is a transcendental stage in which one feels himself to be only an eternal servitor of Kṛṣṇa, the absolute Personality of Godhead. All acts performed in this sense of servitude are called pure love of God because they are performed for the absolute sense gratification of Śrī Kṛṣṇa. However, any act performed for the purpose of enjoying its fruits or results is an act of sense gratification. Such actions are visible sometimes in gross and sometimes in subtle forms. (*Cc. Ādi* 4.165 Text and Purport)

Sometimes jealous persons criticize the Kṛṣṇa consciousness movement because it engages equally both boys and girls in distributing love of Godhead. Not knowing that boys and girls in countries like Europe mix very freely, these fools and rascals criticize the boys and girls in Kṛṣṇa consciousness for intermingling. But these rascals should consider that one cannot suddenly change a community's social customs. However, since both the boys and girls are being trained to become preachers, those girls are not ordinary girls, but are as good as their brothers who are preaching Kṛṣṇa consciousness. (*Cc. Ādi.* 7.31-32)

Since the European and American boys and girls in our Kṛṣṇa consciousness movement preach together, less intelligent men criticize that they are mingling without restriction. In Europe and America boys and girls mingle unrestrictedly and have equal rights; therefore it is not possible to completely separate the men from the women. However, we are thoroughly instructing both men and women how to preach, and actually they are preaching wonderfully. Of course, we very strictly prohibit illicit sex. Boys and girls who are not married are not allowed to sleep together or live together, and there are separate arrangements for boys and girls in every temple. *Gṛhasthas* live outside the temple, for in the temple we do not allow even husband and wife to live together. The results of this are wonderful. Both men and women are preaching the gospel of Lord Caitanya Mahāprabhu and Lord Kṛṣṇa with redoubled strength. (*Cc. Ādi.* 7.38)

A devotee's most formidable enemy is association with women in an enjoying spirit. *(Cc. Madhya* 22, Introduction)

Marriage is a concession for people who are unable to control their senses. Generally a person cannot make much advancement in spiritual consciousness if he is married. He becomes attached to his family and is prone to sense gratification. Thus his spiritual advancement is very slow or almost nil. (*Cc. Antya* 13.112)

It is a fact that we are constantly being kicked by *māyā,* just as the male-ass is kicked in the face by the she-ass when he comes for sex. Similarly, cats and dogs are always fighting and whining when they have sex. These are the tricks of nature. Even an elephant in the jungle is caught by the use of a trained she-elephant who leads him into a pit. *Māyā* has many activities, and in the material world her strongest shackle is the female. Of course in actuality we are neither male nor female—for these designations refer only to the outer dress, the body. We are actually Kṛṣṇa's servants. In conditioned life, however, we are shackled by the iron chains which take the form of beautiful women. Thus every male is bound by sex life, and therefore when one attempts to gain liberation from the material clutches, he must first learn to control the sex urge. (*Teachings of Lord Caitanya*, Introduction)

The demands of the body can be divided into three categories—the demands of the tongue, the belly and the genitals. One may observe that these three senses are physically situated in a straight line, as far as the body is concerned, and that the bodily demands begin with the tongue. If one can restrain the demands of the tongue by limiting its activities to the eating of *prasāda*, the urges of the belly and the genitals can automatically be controlled. (NOI, Text 1, Purport)

As far as the urges of the genitals are concerned, there are two—proper and improper, or legal and illicit sex. When a man is properly mature, he can marry according to the rules and regulations of the *śāstras* and use his genitals for begetting nice children. That is legal and religious. Otherwise, he may adopt many artificial means to satisfy the demands of the genitals, and he may not use any restraint. When one indulges in illicit sex life, as defined by the *śāstras,* either by thinking, planning, talking about or actually having sexual intercourse, or by satisfying the genitals by artificial means, he is caught in the clutches of *māyā.* These instructions apply not only to householders but also to *tyāgīs,* or those who are in the renounced order of life. In his book *Prema-vivarta,* Chapter Seven, Śrī Jagadānanda Paṇḍita says:

vairāgī bhāi grāmya-kathā nā śunibe kāne
grāmya-vārtā nā kahibe yabe milibe āne

svapane o nā kara bhāi strī-sambhāṣaṇa
gṛhe strī chāḍiyā bhāi āsiyācha vana

yadi cāha praṇaya rākhite gaurāṅgera sane
choṭa haridāsera kathā thāke yena mane

bhāla nā khāibe āra bhāla nā paribe
hṛdayete rādhā-kṛṣṇa sarvadā sevibe

"My dear brother, you are in the renounced order of life and should not listen or talk about ordinary worldly things, nor should you talk about worldly things when you meet with others. Do not think of women even in dreams. You have accepted the renounced order of life with a vow that forbids you to associate with women. If you wish to associate with Caitanya Mahāprabhu, you must always remember the incident of Choṭa Haridāsa and how he was rejected by the Lord. Do not eat luxurious dishes or dress in fine garments, but always remain humble and serve Their Lordships Śrī Śrī Rādhā-Kṛṣṇa in your heart of hearts." (NOI, Text 1, Purport)

If there is some disease in the body which is neglected, it becomes incurable. Similarly, when one is not careful about restraining the senses and lets them loose, it is very difficult to control them at all. (*Kṛṣṇa*, Ch. 4)

The perfection of human life is based on knowledge and renunciation, but it is very difficult to attempt to reach the stage of knowledge and renunciation while in family life. (*Kṛṣṇa,* Ch. 87)

There are four types of *brahmacārīs.* The first is called *sāvitra,* which refers to a *brahmacārī* who after initiation and the sacred thread ceremony must observe at least three days of celibacy. The next is called *prājāpatya,* which refers to a *brahmacārī* who strictly observes celibacy for at least one year after initiation. The next is called *brāhma-brahmacārī,* which refers to a *brahmacārī* who observes celibacy from the time of initiation up to the time of the completion of his study of Vedic literature. The next stage is called *naiṣṭhika,* which refers to a *brahmacārī* who is celibate throughout his whole life. Out of these, the first three are *upakurvāṇa,* which means that the *brahmacārī* can marry later, after the *brahmacārī* period is over. The *naiṣṭhika-brahmacārī,* however, is completely reluctant to have any sex life; therefore the Kumāras and Nārada are known as *naiṣṭhika-brahmacārīs.* Such *brahmacārīs* are called *vīra-vrata* because their vow of celibacy is as heroic as the vows of the *kṣatriyas.* The *brahmacārī* system of life is especially advantageous in that it increases the power of memory and determination. It is specifically mentioned in this connection that because Nārada was a *naiṣṭhika-brahmacārī* he could remember whatever he heard from his spiritual master and would never forget it. One who can remember everything perpetually is called *śruti-dhara.* A *śruti-dhara brahmacārī* can repeat verbatim all that he has heard, without notes and without reference to books. The great sage Nārada has this qualification, and therefore, having taken instructions from Nārāyaṇa Ṛṣi, he is engaged in propagating the philosophy of devotional service all over the world. (*Kṛṣṇa,* Ch. 87)

In the rainy season, when the rivers swell and rush to the ocean, and as the wind blows the waves about, the ocean appears to be agitated. Similarly, if a person engaged in the mystic yoga process is not very advanced in spiritual life, he can be affected by the modes of nature and thus will be agitated by the sex impulse.

A person fixed in spiritual knowledge will not be attracted by the allurement of material nature in the form of beautiful women and the sex pleasure enjoyed in their association. One however, who is still immature in the cultivation of spiritual knowledge may be attracted at any moment by the illusion of temporary happiness, just as the ocean is agitated by the rushing rivers and blowing wind which occur during the rainy season. It is therefore very important to fix oneself at the lotus feet of a bona fide spiritual master who is a representative of God so that one will not be carried away by sex agitation. (LOB 17 Text and Purport)

The dark well of householder life kills the soul. (LOB, Text 17, Purport)

A student's education should begin with *brahmacarya*, which means freedom from sexual attachment. If he can, he should try to avoid all this nonsense. If not, he can marry. (*Teachings of Queen Kuntī*)

First of all, one must be trained in the *brahmacārī* system and learn how to deny the senses. A *brahmacārī* should be trained in *tapasya*, not in enjoyment. Formerly, *brahmacārīs* would have to go from door to door to beg alms for the *āśrama*, and they were trained from the very beginning to address every woman as mother. (*Teachings of Lord Kapila*, p. 131)

Refraining from sex enables one to be very determined and powerful. It is not necessary to do anything else. This is a secret people are not aware of. If you want to do something with determination, you have to refrain from sex. Regardless of the process—be it *haṭha-yoga, bhakti-yoga, jñāna-yoga,* or whatever—sex indulgence is not allowed. Sex is allowed only for householders who want to beget good children and raise them in Kṛṣṇa consciousness. By taking advantage and indulging in sex life, we are simply wasting our time. (*The Path of Perfection*)

As stated before, this determination can be attired only by one who does not indulge in sex. Celibacy makes one's determination strong; therefore, from the very beginning Kṛṣṇa states that the yogi does not engage in sex. If one indulges in sex, one's determination will be flickering. Therefore sex life should be controlled according to the rules and regulations governing the *gṛhastha-āśrama*, or sex should be given up altogether. Actually, it should be given up altogether, but if this is not possible, it should be controlled. Then determination will come because, after all, determination is a bodily affair. Determination means continuing to practice Kṛṣṇa consciousness with patience and perseverance. If one does not immediately attain the desired results, one should not think, "Oh, what is this Kṛṣṇa consciousness? I will give it up." No, we must have determination and faith in Kṛṣṇa's words. (*The Path of Perfection*)

"How can a person take pleasure in the enjoyment of sex life in this body, which is a bag of skin and bones, filled with blood and covered by skin and flesh, and which produces mucus and evil smells?" This perception is possible only for one who is awakened to Kṛṣṇa consciousness and who has become fully cognizant of the abominable nature of the material body. (*The Nectar of Devotion*, Ch. 48)

In Vedic civilization, boys were trained from the very beginning of life as first-class *brahmacārīs*. They went to the *gurukula,* the school of the spiritual master, and learned self-control, cleanliness, truthfulness, and many other saintly qualities. The best of them were later fit to rule the country. (*The Science of Self-Realization* p. 187)

To properly execute celibacy, one should not even think or even talk of sex life. Reading modern literature and newspapers which are filled with sexual material is also against the principles of *brahmacarya.* Similarly, indulging in sex in any way, looking at and whispering with girls, and determining or endeavoring to engage in sex life are all against the principles of *brahmacarya*. One executes real *brahmacarya* when all these activities come to a halt. *(Kṛṣṇa Consciousness, The Matchless Gift* Ch. 4)

In the darkness of this material world, the only happiness is in sleep and sex. (DS)

Śrīla Prabhupāda: Sex is animalistic. It is not love but lust. Sex means the mutual satisfaction of senses, and that is lust. All this lust is taking place under the name of love, and out of illusion, people mistake this lust for love. Real love says, "People are suffering from a lack of Kṛṣṇa consciousness. Let us do something for them so that they can understand the value of life." (DS)

Ordinary men take sex to be the highest pleasure. The entire material world is existing because of sex, but how long does this sex pleasure last? A few minutes only. A man who is wise does not want pleasure that lasts only a few minutes but pleasure that continues perpetually. *Nitya* means "eternal," and *ānanda* means "bliss." The Vedas state that those who are intelligent are not interested in transient pleasure but in eternal pleasure. They know their constitutional position; they know they are not the body. The pleasures of the body are transient and are sought by rascals. (DS)

Repression is always there. If we are diseased, and the doctor advises us not to take solid food, we have to repress our appetite. In the system of *brahmacarya*, the *brahmacārī* represses his desire for sex. This is called *tapasya,* voluntary repression. Of course, this is very difficult without some better engagement. Therefore, as I said, we have to replace an inferior engagement with a superior one. When you are captivated by seeing the beautiful form of Kṛṣṇa, you naturally no longer desire to see the beautiful form of a young woman. (DS, p, 494)

Śrīla Prabhupāda: We must understand why this sex problem is there. If we tolerate a little itching sensation, we will be spared much pain. *Yan maithunādi-gṛhamedhi-sukhaṁ hi tuccham kanduyanena karayor iva duhkha-duhkham*. "Sex life is compared to the rubbing of two hands to relieve an itch. *Gṛhamedhīs,* householders without spiritual knowledge, think that this itching is the greatest platform of happiness, although it is actually a source of distress." (*S.B.* 7.9.45) When ordinary men are overly attached to materialistic life, their only happiness is sexual intercourse. The *śāstra*s say that happiness derived from sexual intercourse is very, very insignificant. Indeed, it is not even happiness. At best, it may be considered a tenth-class happiness. Because people have no idea of the happiness of Kṛṣṇa consciousness, they think that sex is the highest happiness. But if we analyze it, what kind of happiness is it? When we have an itch, we scratch it and feel some pleasure, but after the pleasure passes, the effects are abominable. The itch becomes worse. The *śāstras* tell us that if we just try to tolerate the itching sensation, we will be spared a great deal of pain. This is possible if we practice this Kṛṣṇa consciousness.

Śyāmasundara dāsa: Freud believed that neuroses, disorders, anxieties, and frustrations have their origin in repression.

Śrīla Prabhupāda: And I am telling you that all these are due to sex. But we are not advocating repression. We give facility in the form of a wife. The sex impulse is to be directed to the wife.

Śyāmasundara dāsa: But Freud insisted that the sex impulse is present at the very beginning of life.

Śrīla Prabhupāda: We also admit that. We say that as soon as the living being is embodied, he experiences hunger and sex. Why is that? *Āhāra-nidra-bhaya-maithuna.* We find these impulses even in animals. These drives are already there. What is the use in philosophizing about them?

Śyāmasundara dāsa: Through psychoanalysis, pent-up emotions can be released; and the original shock mitigated by remembering and confessing.

Śrīla Prabhupāda: But what guarantee is there that we will not receive another shock? The living entity is receiving shock after shock. You try to cure him of one, and another comes. It is a fact that material life is painful. As soon as you receive this material body, you must suffer the threefold miseries. Everyone is seeking happiness, but unless materialistic life is stopped, unless we put an end to birth, old age, disease, and death, there is no question of happiness. Materialistic life is a disease, and Vedic civilization attempts to cure this disease. Our program is total cure. No more shock. (DS)

Śrīla Prabhupāda: Human life is meant for *tapasya,* for putting an end to sex. This is the process of *brahmacarya*. The only happiness in this material world is considered to be sexual. *Yan maithunādi.* (*S.B.* 7.9.45). The word *ādi* means the basic principle, which, in the material world, is sex. What is materialistic happiness? It is enjoying this life with one's friends and family. But what kind of pleasure is this? It is compared to a drop of water in the desert. Actually, we are seeking unlimited pleasure. *Ānanda-mayo 'bhyāsāt.* How can this drop of water in the desert, which is materialistic pleasure, ever satisfy us? No one is satisfied, although people are having sex in so many different ways. And now young girls are almost going naked, and the female population is increasing everywhere. As soon as there is an increase in the female population, the women say, "Where are the men?" Then there must be disaster because every woman is trying to attract a man, and men will take advantage of this situation. When milk is available in the market, what is the use in keeping a cow?" The more men become attached to women, the more the female population will increase. When you have more sex, your power to beget a male child is diminished. When the male is less potent, a girl is born, and when a man is more potent, a boy is born. If a man's discharge is larger, there will be a male child. If the women's discharge is larger, there will be a female child. When women are easily available, men become weak, and they beget female children because they lose their power from overindulgence. Sometimes they even become impotent. If you don't restrict your sex life, there will be so many disasters. Yāmunācārya says:

yad-avadhi mama cetaḥ kṛṣṇa-pādāravinde
nava-nava-rasa-dhāmany udyataṁ rantum āsīt
tad-avadhi bata nārī-saṅgame smaryamāne
bhavati mukha-vikāraḥ suṣṭhu niṣṭhīvanaṁ ca

"Since I have been engaged in the transcendental loving service of Kṛṣṇa, realizing ever-new pleasure in Him, whenever I think of sex pleasure, I spit at the thought, and my lips curl with distaste."

Śyāmasundara dāsa: Freud would consider this a form of repression.

Śrīla Prabhupāda: His idea of repression is different from ours. Our repression means rising early in the morning, attending *maṅgala-ārati,* chanting the Hare Kṛṣṇa *mahā-mantra,* and engaging in devotional service. In this way, we repress material propensities.

Śyāmasundara dāsa: In other words, it's repression with awareness and knowledge.

Śrīla Prabhupāda: Actual knowledge will come later. In the beginning, there is obedience to the spiritual master. In this way, we will not become habituated to undesirable activity. (DS)

QUOTES FROM BIOGRAPHICAL WORKS ON ŚRĪLA PRABHUPĀDA

To speak ill of sexual pleasure was certainly not a strategic move for one who wanted to create followers among the Lower East Side hippies. But Prabhupāda never considered changing his message. In fact, when Umāpati had mentioned that Americans didn't like to hear that sex was only for conceiving children, Prabhupāda had replied, "I cannot change the philosophy to please the Americans."

"What about sex?" asked the ISKCON attorney, Steve Goldsmith, one evening, speaking out from the rear of the crowded temple. "Sex should only be with one's wife," Prabhupāda said, "and that is also restricted. Sex is for the propagation of Kṛṣṇa conscious children. My spiritual master used to say that to beget Kṛṣṇa conscious children he was prepared to have sex a hundred times. Of course, that is most difficult in this age. Therefore, he remained a *brahmacārī.*"

"But sex is a very strong force," Mr. Goldsmith challenged. "What a man feels for a woman is undeniable."

"Therefore in every culture there is the institution of marriage," Prabhupāda replied. "You can get yourself married and live peacefully with one woman, but the wife should not be used as a machine for sense gratification. Sex should be restricted to once a month and only for the propagation of children."

Hayagrīva, who was seated just to Swamījī's left, beside the large, dangling cymbal, spoke out suddenly. "Only once a month?" And with a touch of facetious humor he added loudly, "Better to forget the whole thing!"

"Yes! That's it! Very good boy." Swamījī laughed, and others joined him. "It's best not to think of it. Best just to chant Hare Kṛṣṇa." And he held up his hands as if he were chanting on a strand of beads. "That way we will be saved from such botheration. Sex is like the itching sensation, that's all. And as we scratch, it gets worse, so we must tolerate the itching and ask Kṛṣṇa to help us. It is not easy. Sex is the highest pleasure in the material world, and it is also the greatest bondage." But Steve Goldsmith was shaking his head. Prabhupāda looked at him, smiling: "There is still a problem?"

"It's just that, well, it's been proved dangerous to repress the sex drive. There's a theory that, we have wars because –"

"People are eating meat," Prabhupāda interrupted. "As long as people eat meat, there will be war. And if a man eats meat, he will be sure to have illicit sex also."

Steve Goldsmith was an influential friend and supporter of ISKCON. But Prabhupāda would not change the philosophy of Kṛṣṇa consciousness "to please the Americans." (SPL Ch. 21)

Śrīla Prabhupāda objected to being called conservative. He was indignant: "Conservative? How is that?"

"In respect to sex and drugs," Mukunda suggested.

"Of course, we are conservative in that sense," Prabhupāda said. "That simply means we are following *śāstra.* We cannot depart from *Bhagavad-gītā.* But conservative we are not. Caitanya Mahāprabhu was so strict that He would not even look on a woman, but we are accepting everyone into this movement, regardless of sex, caste, position, or whatever. Everyone is invited to come chant Hare Kṛṣṇa. This is Caitanya Mahāprabhu's munificence, His liberality. (SPL Ch. 22)

Upendra was still bothered by sexual desires. He thought that maybe he should get married. But he was confused about what a Kṛṣṇa conscious marriage was supposed to be. How could you be married, he puzzled, if you don't love the girl you want to marry? And how could you love her without having sex with her? He wanted to ask Swamījī about this, but he kept it to himself, waiting for an opportunity and for the courage. Then one day he entered Prabhupāda's room as Prabhupāda paced back and forth from one end of the room, with its three large bay windows overlooking Frederick Street, to the other end, where his rocking chair sat. Now, Upendra decided, he could ask his question. "Swamījī," he began, "may I ask a question?" "Yes," Śrīla Prabhupāda replied, stopping his pacing. "If a boy is separate from a girl, then how can he learn to love her?" Prabhupāda began to walk back and forth again, chanting on his beads. After a moment he turned and said softly, "Love? Love is for Kṛṣṇa." And he walked toward the window and looked down at the street below. "You want a girl? Pick one." He pointed toward some women passing on the street. "There is no love in this material world," he said. "Love is for Kṛṣṇa." (SPL Ch. 24)

Śrīla Prabhupāda: Women and men can live separately. That is also essential. Butter and fire must be kept apart. Otherwise the butter will melt. You cannot stop it. (SPL Ch. 46)

"This is not the business of the guru," said Prabhupāda, "how to increase sex life and family life. They are not happy, these Western men and women. They become married, but they are not happy. Therefore I recommend *brahmacarya* and *sannyāsa* life." (SPL Ch. 49)

Control of the senses means that I can be in the midst of beautiful women, but I will feel no desire for sex. I have got sufficient strength, but I have no desire for this. That is real control of the senses. (*Prabhupāda-līlā*)

Yoga Student: What about sex desire? I want the spiritual, but I have such a strong desire for sex.

Prabhupāda: *Haṭha-yoga* is also for controlling sex desire. If you have such desire, you are making no progress.

Yoga Student: How does a devotee of Kṛṣṇa control sexual desire?

Prabhupāda: Automatically. Kṛṣṇa is beautiful. We are accustomed to this habit for a very long time. Become sincere, and Kṛṣṇa will protect you.

Yoga Student: Sometimes I have a sex urge. . .

Prabhupāda: What? You? Everybody! In birds, beasts, demigods, the binding force is sex. The material life means sex desire. If you have a strong sex desire, pray to Kṛṣṇa. Know that this is the attack of *māyā.* Pray, and *māyā* will go away. You cannot fight with *māyā* by your own energy. *Māyā is* presenting herself more beautiful than Kṛṣṇa. But Kṛṣṇa is more beautiful. (*Prabhupāda-līlā*)

Marriage means 75% chance you will not go back to Godhead. (Śrīla Prabhupāda, quoted in *Servant of the Servant*)

Then Prabhupāda proceeded to give a very powerful lecture about remaining *brahmacārī,* telling the men, "Why bother to get married? When you get married, your wife will immediately say, 'Where is the house? Where are the children? Where is the clothing? Where is the food?' In this way there will be so many problems." He said it was better to stay simple and remain *brahmacārī* and preach Lord Caitanya's mission. (*Servant of the Servant*)

Prabhupāda lectured on the advantages of remaining a *brahmacārī* throughout one's life. If one could do this, it would make going back to Godhead very simple. A *brahmacārī* need not worry where to sleep or how much to eat. He can sleep underneath a tree or even in the snow. His only concern is how to serve Kṛṣṇa more and more. He does so much service that at night, when it is time for him to take rest, he falls asleep immediately, because he is free of any anxieties.

Gṛhastha life, however, is fraught with problems. As soon as one is married there are so many responsibilities which unnecessarily increase life's problems. The wife will make demands: Where is our house? When will we have children? Where are my clothes? Food? In this way there will be so much disturbance, to no advantage. Instead one should be intelligent and avoid this botheration altogether. Simply spend your time distributing books, then there will be no time left for *māyā* lure you.

The *brahmacārīs* enjoyed hearing Śrīla Prabhupāda glorify a life of celibacy dedicated to preaching. They were already experiencing a carefree existence by avoiding the entanglement of the opposite sex. To have their spiritual master confirm their position strengthened their resolve to remain fixed in their vow. But it was not always easy. When Śrīla Prabhupāda called for questions, one devotee asked, "Śrīla Prabhupāda, we have to approach so many women while distributing books in the parking lots. Yet we have just come from material life and are still feeling attraction. So what is the best way to preach without becoming affected?"

Prabhupāda immediately replied, "Sex life is an itch. It has to be tolerated. If you become tolerant, then the itching sensation will go away. Just learn to tolerate it and concentrate more on your service." (*Servant of the Servant*)

QUOTES FROM ŚRĪLA PRABHUPĀDA'S LETTERS

A *brahmacārī* should not see any kind of naked picture. That is violation of *brahmacārī* law. (28/02/67) (Śrīla Prabhupāda specifies in this letter that this includes pictures of Kṛṣṇa and the *gopīs*.)

Kṛṣṇa consciousness means to increase the number of persons in Kṛṣṇa consciousness. Therefore it is the duty of a *brahmacārī* to go door to door as a beggar and enlighten people in Kṛṣṇa consciousness. Whenever you go to some person he will hear something from the devotee about Kṛṣṇa consciousness and that will be very much beneficial for both the devotee and the person who hears the devotee. In India the *brahmacārīs* are meant for begging from door to door for the spiritual master. But in your country this activity is not allowed, therefore some devices like selling the publications, recruiting members, inviting them to our meetings and likewise activities must be taken by the *brahmacārīs* and that will be nice. (13/04/67)

You have written to say that your wife and you have a problem on which you require my help. The whole world, beginning with the highest planet to the lowest in the material world, is facing this problem. Combination of husband and wife is a necessary satisfaction of the sex urge. The foolish people see every day this problematic situation, still they are not intelligent enough to avoid it. Training of *brahmacārī* life is especially meant for this purpose, and a student is advised not to indulge in sex life, just to avoid these problems. It is very difficult to satisfy a woman by a person who has no good income, neither very good health. The woman as a class wants sufficient means to eat and decorate and at the same time full satisfaction of sex. Any husband who cannot satisfy his wife by these three items, namely sufficient food, sufficient dress and ornament and sufficient satisfaction of sex, must meet all these problems. And as soon as one becomes engaged in solving these problems it is very difficult to make any progress in Kṛṣṇa consciousness. If one is serious to make any success in the matter of Kṛṣṇa consciousness, one should avoid the association of woman as far as possible. Married life is a sort of license to the incapable man who cannot avoid sex life. (13/11/67)

I thank you very much for your appreciation of my disciples in New York and you will be glad to know all my disciples in different centers are being so trained. The four principles of restriction, namely no illicit sex relations; no animal food; no intoxication and no gambling, are acting on their character. Character building is the groundwork for reaching Kṛṣṇa consciousness, and the Vedic injunction is that one can advance in spiritual life by following the rules of austerity and celibacy. (18/01/68)

Kṛṣṇa consciousness movement is actually declaration of war against *māyā.* The conditioned souls who wanted to enjoy this material world are captivated by the sex desires. If one wants to get out of material existence, he must control sex desires. The whole scheme of Vedic civilization is based on this principle of controlling sex desires. There are four orders of life: *brahmacārī, gṛhastha, vānaprastha,* and *sannyāsa.* The majority of the orders, namely *brahmacārī, vānaprastha* and *sannyāsa,* are forbidden sex life. Only the householders are allowed sex life. That is also restricted. That means sex life is condemned throughout because that is the cause of material bondage. Feeling of sex life in young boys and girls is quite natural, but one has to check such sex life by reason, argument and knowledge. The married boys and girls are there—in our society, sex life is not forbidden. If Jagatananda is feeling sex urge so urgently even at the age of 16 or 17, he must be prepared to take the responsibility of married life. I cannot allow in our society any nonsense like illicit sex life at any circumstance. Jagatananda must subdue his sex desire by chanting Hare Kṛṣṇa, and praying to Kṛṣṇa to help him. If not he must be prepared to marry and take the responsibility fully. Actually the association of young boys and girls is very much disruptive for *brahmacārī* life, but in your country it is impossible to stop free mixing of young boys and girls. So voluntarily they have to check these sex desires until they are married. If they are strong enough in Kṛṣṇa consciousness any amount of sex urge will not disturb them. Even if it disturbs, it will come and go. Kṛṣṇa is Madana Mohana, or the Enchanter of Cupid. And Cupid is the god of sex desire. So if anyone wants to enchant Cupid, instead of being enchanted by Cupid, he must take shelter of the Enchanter of Cupid, Śrī Kṛṣṇa. (21/01/68)

I understand that you sometimes feel sex urges and frustration. In the material world sex urge is the binding force for material existence. A determined person tolerates such sex urges as one tolerates the itching sensation of eczema. If not one can satisfy the sex urge by legitimate marriage. Immoral sex life and spiritual advancement are incompatible propositions. Your full engagement in Kṛṣṇa consciousness and constant chanting will save you from all inconveniences. (22/01/68)

If you want sex life, you are at liberty to get yourself married, But don't have illicit sex with some *māyā's* representative. That won't help you in your spiritual advancement. We don't forbid sex life, but we cannot allow illicit sex. For a young man it is very difficult to check sex desire, therefore best thing is for him to get himself married, and live like a responsible gentleman. Irresponsible man cannot make progress materially or spiritually. You are intelligent young man, you can understand things as we say, and you follow and you will be benefited. Mistakes we may commit because it is not out of human activity, but at the same time, you must use your good consciousness how to achieve the goal of your life, Kṛṣṇa. Please stick to this chanting process, sincerely, without offense, and everything will be all right with you. (12/02/68)

If we can make sex life nil we are 50% liberated. (15/02/68)

It does not matter whether one is a *brahmacārī* or householder; the real test is how he is executing Kṛṣṇa consciousness. (04/07/68)

Regarding your enemy, Mr. Lust, we should always remember that Kṛṣṇa is stronger than any demon, and Mr. Lust, or his father or grandfather. Nobody can do anything provided we take shelter of Kṛṣṇa tightly. But the proposal that marriage will solve the problem of lust is not practical. Neither wife should be accepted as a machine for satisfying our lust. The marriage tie should be taken as sacred. One who marries for subduing lust is mistaken. Because lust cannot be satisfied simply by engaging in sense gratification. It is compared with extinguishing fire with a large amount of petrol. For the time being, the fire may appear to be extinguished by pouring a large quantity of petrol, but the petrol itself is so dangerous that at any time, it can be in flame. So to subdue lust is a difficult process. Then you have to take to Deity worship. So apart from the marriage proposal, you may immediately take to Deity worship. I am sure this process, helped by your regular chanting, will kill Mr. Lust, rest assured. (07/10/68)

Unless our *brahmacārīs* are very adamant (to remain) as *brahmacārī,* I shall recommend everyone to marry. But if one can live as *brahmacārī,* that is better. (16/10/68)

The Deity worship must be continued by everyone. Another way of success is that when one is very much sexually disturbed he should think of Lord Kṛṣṇa's pastimes with the *gopīs* and he will forget his sex urge. To think of Kṛṣṇa's pastimes with the *gopīs*, but not to try to imitate. (08/11/68)

You write to say that you are having trouble with sex agitation. Why you do not marry then? Either you become *gṛhastha* or what choice is there? Either you train yourself and pray to Kṛṣṇa, begging that you remain *brahmacārī* or else get yourself married. (02/12/68)

I always recommend that one should remain *brahmacārī* if possible. (24/01/69)

I am pleased by your wish to remain as a *brahmacārī,* and if you stick to your decision you will be able to go Back to Godhead, back to home, in this very life without waiting for another birth. Please try in every way to stick to this principle, and simply engage yourself in Kṛṣṇa's service. That will protect you from any attack of *māyā. Māyā* can take Kṛṣṇa's place in our heart as soon as there is a slackness on our part. Otherwise, if Kṛṣṇa is seated always, *māyā* has no opportunity to occupy the seat. Try to follow this method and you will surely be successful. (01/02/69)

As far as your occasional agitation from *māyā,* the answer is very simple that one must either strictly control his senses, or else he must get himself married. If one is strong enough in Kṛṣṇa consciousness, then there is no reason to become *gṛhastha,* but if one is still disturbed by sex desire, then marriage is the only other possibility. But if one is still *brahmacārī,* then he must be sure to follow all the rules and regulations very strictly. There is no place in spiritual life for cheating in this matter. Caitanya Mahāprabhu has never criticized a householder for having sex life for the purpose of bearing children. But when it came to Junior Haridāsa, who was posing as a *sannyāsī* but was still engaging in lustful thoughts, Lord Caitanya would not tolerate, and Junior Haridāsa was banished from the association of the Lord. So this is very important that we remain very firm in our vow of *brahmacārī,* or if this is very difficult, then householder life is the next satisfactory solution. (08/02/69)

It is very nice that you are wishing to remain as a *brahmacārī.* Actually it doesn't matter if one is a householder or *brahmacārī.* Sincerity of purpose is the only qualification of Kṛṣṇa consciousness. Śrī Narottama dāsa Ṭhākura says that he hankers after the company of any person, never mind whether he is in the renounced order of life or in householder life, just as long as he is merged into the ocean of Kṛṣṇa consciousness. That is the one qualification. (13/02/69)

To become agitated is not very unusual thing, but to control it that is the real thing. Sex life is not sense gratification; unlawful sex life is sense gratification. (23/03/69)

As far as your decision to remain a *brahmacārī,* it is very good and if you follow the rules and regulations and chant regularly and pray to Lord Balarāma and Caitanya, surely He will give you the necessary strength and if you can continue as *brahmacārī* then you avoid so much botherations of worldly life. (21/05/69)

A *brahmacārī* has nothing to do except serve his spiritual master. That is the injunction of the *Bhagavat.* A *brahmacārī* is supposed to work as a menial servant of the spiritual master, and whatever collection he gets, it becomes the spiritual master's property, not the *brahmacārī's.* That is real *brahmacārī* life. If a *brahmacārī* earns money for his sense gratification, that is not *brahmacārī* life. Better one should become a householder and live peacefully. (29/06/69)

Regarding the question about marriage, the thing is that as I am a *sannyāsī,* I am not concerned with family life, but because I want to see all my disciples happy in Kṛṣṇa consciousness, therefore those who are feeling some sexual disturbance are requested by me to get themselves married. Another principle is that those who are *brahmacārīs,* they should sacrifice all of their income and collection for the Kṛṣṇa consciousness movement, whereas those who are married should work, earning money as much as possible, and at least 50% should be spent for the Kṛṣṇa consciousness movement. So we have no objection for allowing you to get married, but it is up to you to consider if you will work hard and earn money both for Kṛṣṇa and your family. You cannot get married and at the same time not earn money. Of course, by preaching *saṅkīrtana* movement, if you are satisfied with a small income, that is also nice. (05/07/69)

We shall always pray to Kṛṣṇa that we are weak and Māyā is very strong. So seek for His protection in every step so Māyā may not inflict upon us her trident injuries. Perhaps you have seen the picture of Durga carrying the trident in her hand, which is a symbol of the threefold miseries of material existence. Māyā's most attractive feature is women and money. We Kṛṣṇa conscious men have to deal with women and money in the course of preaching work, and the only prophylactic measure to save us is not to accept them for our sense gratification. Then we shall remain strong enough. Materialistic people take everything for sense gratification and Kṛṣṇa conscious people take everything for Kṛṣṇa's satisfaction. There is no fault in the thing as it is—namely women and money—but it becomes faulty by improper use. The improper use is to accept them for sense gratification. As it is stated in *Bhagavad-gita*, we can remain very strong from this by taking a firm shelter under the Lotus Feet of Kṛṣṇa, by chanting His Holy Name incessantly, and praying always for being engaged in His service. In this way He will protect us from our weakness. (18/10/69)

Kṛṣṇa consciousness is not limited within any circle. *Brahmacārī, gṛhastha,* or *sannyāsī,* everyone is eligible for cultivating Kṛṣṇa consciousness. These are the stages for gradual development of control of the strong senses in the material environment. But any order of life suitable for a particular person in which he can most favorably execute his Kṛṣṇa consciousness is the best position to take up. Generally, if one can remain a *brahmacārī,* it is very convenient, and from *brahmacārī* one can take *sannyāsa.* But in this age of Kali, Bhaktivinoda Ṭhākura recommends that it is better to cultivate Kṛṣṇa consciousness as a householder. (02/11/69)

Kṛṣṇa is very merciful to His sincere devotees, but also we have to remember that *māyā* is very strong. Therefore we always have to be engaged in serving Kṛṣṇa. At every moment we should be doing this or that service for Kṛṣṇa's transcendental pleasure. If we do not remember this, then *māyā* is right there to grab us. It all depends on our leaning toward Kṛṣṇa or toward *māyā.* If you lean toward Kṛṣṇa, you will be in Kṛṣṇa consciousness; and if you lean toward *māyā,* then you will be captivated by material nature. Kṛṣṇa and *māyā* are just like light and shadow which are directly next to one another. If you move a little this way, you are in light and there is no question of shadow. But if you move a little the other way, you are in darkness. So if we remember to always be engaged in Kṛṣṇa's service, then there will be no *māyā* and everything will be all right. Please always remember this great secret of advancement in Kṛṣṇa consciousness. (20/11/69)

(It) is my open opinion that if anyone can remain a *brahmacārī* all the time, without being disturbed by sex urge or who can tolerate such urges, there is not any need for him to marry and take some extra responsibilities. But one who is disturbed in mind, he must get himself married. Therefore, it has to be decided by oneself if he should marry or not marry. It is a fact however, that if one is thoroughly engaged in Kṛṣṇa's service, this sex urge does not have much disturbance. But you have got to work outside with *karmīs* and different types of people. Under the circumstances, if you have a good wife to help you, that will be very nice. Another difficulty is that in the modern civilization everyone is independent spirited. The girls are no longer very much humble and submissive to their husbands. So you must be prepared to tolerate such whims of your future wife. According to our Vedic civilization, disagreements between husband and wife are not taken very seriously. But the modern age allows divorce even, either by the husband or the wife. These things are not good. But after marrying, certainly there will be some disagreements or misunderstandings between husband and wife. So consider all these points, and you can decide yourself. But if you marry, I have no objection. (26/11/69)

Because he is a family man, he should have some special consideration. A *brahmacārī* can tolerate any inconvenience, but women and children cannot. (15/12/69)

My open advice is that if anyone can remain a *brahmacārī,* it is very nice, but there is no need of artificial *brahmacārīs.* In *Bhagavad-gītā* it is stated that one who exhibits himself outwardly as self restrained, but inwardly he thinks of sense gratification, he is condemned as *mithyācāra,* which means false pretender. We do not want any false pretenders in numbers, but we want a sincere soul. There is no harm in accepting a wife and living without any disturbance of the mind and thus sincerely advancing in Kṛṣṇa consciousness. (02/02/70)

So far as controlling *kāma,* or lust, the best thing is don't eat any highly spiced foodstuffs and always think of Kṛṣṇa. Chant regularly and get yourself married as soon as possible, and live a peaceful householder's life in Kṛṣṇa consciousness. (27/05/71)

Rejection of illicit sex life is our first motto. (14/10/71)

Brahmacārī life or celibacy is better, because if the semen is saved it fertilizes the brain for sharpening the memory, and if there is good memory, our Kṛṣṇa consciousness becomes perfect:

hearing, chanting, remembering—that is the process. (20/01/72)

Our thoughts are always changing—that is the nature of the mind—so you cannot expect that even the great saintly persons are free from thoughts coming and going. But after thinking there is feeling and willing—willing being the stage of putting the thoughts into action. So if we are able to employ our intelligence, then we kill the thoughts before they become manifest in activity, but because we are so much inclined to enjoy something intelligently, we have to therefore daily sharpen our intelligence faculty by reading and discussing, and preaching to others. In this way we are able very easily to defeat all challengers to our philosophy, and everything becomes very clear as it is revealed from different angles of vision. (28/02/72)

This *brahmacārī* system is there, but if one is not so strong, then he is allowed to marry, but he must expect that the after effects will always be troublesome. Everywhere I see people, man and wife with family, and all of them suffer, but still they go on producing more. Sex means trouble. Therefore one should become *dhira* and not be attracted by this sex life. Henceforward, anyone proposing to marry must produce some outside income and live outside the temple; they must know this in advance and be prepared to carry such burden. Let them be married, but at their own risk. I cannot sanction anymore. My Guru Mahārāja never allowed, but when I came to your country it was a special circumstance so I gave concession. But I am not so much inclined anymore, so I shall not sanction. But they may marry on their own risk of knowing that such arrangements are always troublesome. (28/02/72)

Regarding your question about thinking about sex: is that also one form of illicit sex or against our four principles? Yes, even thinking sex is the same as illicit sex, but one who is not advanced cannot avoid it. But that does not disturb our regular procedure. We should strongly follow all the regulations and principles and chant and these thoughts will come and go away. Thinking will come; even saintly persons like Lord Siva are not free of thoughts that come, so what to speak of you. So we must say that such thinking is no offense because you are accustomed to this habit. But beyond thinking are feeling and willing. So even thoughts of sex connection may come—that is difficult even for saintly persons to avoid—still, in the further stages of feeling and willing we can easily conquer over this sex urge. Willing should be avoided and acting stopped, or else there is the offense of breaking this basic prohibition of illicit sex life. "Because thinking comes I shall give it practical shape": that is nonsense, but because it is an old habit we are unable to check it unless we can understand the nature of feeling, willing and then action, and how by proper use of intelligence we can prevent thoughts which must come from maturing into actions. That is the practical application of Kṛṣṇa conscious regulative principles. Even Lord Caitanya Himself said that sometimes when I see a wooden form of a woman, my mind becomes agitated. But that does not mean that we should give it practical shape; that is intelligence. One must be convinced that sex life without exception means trouble; therefore he is able to stop it at the thinking stage by not allowing it to be felt, much less willed and acted. I am so much disgusted by this troublesome business of marriage, because nearly every day I receive some complaint from husband and wife, and practically this is not my business as *sannyāsī* to be a marriage counselor. So henceforward I am not sanctioning any more marriages, and those who want to marry must know in advance and be prepared to make outside income to support wife and home separately from the temple. And in the temple husband and wife shall live separately. That must be, or what is the meaning of spiritual society like ours? I made a concession, but how can I encourage something which has proven to be so much trouble? (28/02/72)

Your question is how much or how little *brahmacārīs* should associate with the unmarried *brahmacārīnis* in the temple. As a *brahmacārī* you should not mix at all with *brahmacārīnis.* Actually they should not at all see the face, but that is not possible in your country. But as far as possible remain separate and talk almost nil. A *brahmacārī* is advised not to go near a young woman anywhere. A *brahmacārī* should always address every woman as mother. In your country it is a little difficult, but the principle is to avoid. To talk secretly or privately is strictly prohibited. If you want to discuss philosophy and other matters you can discuss publicly in a meeting, but not privately. A *brahmacārī* and unmarried woman in the same room together alone is strictly forbidden. (30/09/72)

Outside of loving God there is no possibility of loving. Rather there is lusty desire only. Within this atmosphere of matter, the entire range of human activities—and not only every activity of human beings but of all living entities—is based upon, given impetus and thus polluted by sex desire, the attraction between male and female. For that sex life, the whole universe is spinning around—and suffering! That is the harsh truth. So-called love here means that "you gratify my senses, I'll gratify your senses," and as soon as that gratification stops, immediately there is divorce, separation, quarrel, and hatred. So many things are going on under this false conception of love. Actual love means love of God, Kṛṣṇa. (Letter to Lynne Ludwig, 27/11/73, published in *The Science of Self-Realization*)

You leaders see that the Kṛṣṇa conscious standards in regard to initiation, cleanliness, dress and activities of the devotees, the restriction of association between men and women, all be strictly followed. Devotional service cannot be done whimsically. (01/01/74)

Human life is meant for *tapasya,* and *tapasya* must begin with *brahmacārī* life at *gurukula.* The boy is supposed to sleep on the floor. During the day he should collect alms for the spiritual master. He does not try very hard to make a comfortable material arrangement. The result of our *gurukula* training is that, although everyone in this age is born a *śūdra,* we are producing first-class *brāhmaṇas* who can actually do good for their fellow man. (11/04/74)

Kṛṣṇa is always strong. If you are fully engaged in Kṛṣṇa's service, attraction of woman will be a myth only. It is only Kṛṣṇa's grace. Of course we are old men now, but even old men are attracted still by women. So even old man or young man, if one's mind is fixed up in Kṛṣṇa's lotus feet, there will be no such mundane attraction. (01/09/74)

If you can remain a *brahmacārī* that is the best way of life. (07/09/74)

The more you become Kṛṣṇa conscious the more you will forget sex life. Sex life is the original root cause of material bondage. When one takes to Kṛṣṇa consciousness gradually sex becomes at last abominable; then he is fit to enter back home back to Godhead. (07/09/74)

If there is agitation in the mind then there is no fault. Actually this is only natural in the material world, unless the mind is fully purified in Kṛṣṇa consciousness. But by engaging in devotional service gradually the mind will become purified and the agitation will vanish. So if there is simply agitation in the mind there is no fault. But if there is indulgence in sex, then there is big fault. If one engages in illicit sex life he has broken the promise to the spiritual master and that is a great offense. (28/12/74)

A *brahmacārī's* business is to study and then to go to make some collection on behalf of the guru. Woman is good and man is good, but if you combine them, both become bad, unless there is regulation. In India private talks with women are immediately condemned. (14/07/75)

In Delhi there is a certain kind of *laddu* which has such a taste, that anyone who has tasted it once, he laments, oh how I would like to taste again. And anyone who has never tasted, and one who has tasted, both are lamenting. Wife is like that. Sex life is nasty, but out of illusion we think it is nice. (01/09/75)

There are two things: Kṛṣṇa and sex life. So if you want to have Kṛṣṇa, one must be above illicit sex life. That requires some strength. So you have to impress upon them that following these rules and regulations, especially by chanting Hare Kṛṣṇa, one will become strong. Unfortunately, we have no taste for this chanting. This is our misfortune. (18/11/75)

Marriage is not recommended. Are you prepared to get a job, live outside the temple in an apartment, provide the wife with bangles, saris and sex? Better you concentrate on this chanting and hearing process, teach others and give them *prasāda*. (06/12/75)

Regarding your getting married, I have no objection. However as a *brahmacārī* you are not obligated to marry; what is the advantage to your getting married? That should be considered. If one can remain *brahmacārī* that is best. Finish this life and go back to Godhead; that is the basic idea of Kṛṣṇa consciousness movement. So you decide. (31/12/75)

The *brahmacārī* lives at the place of and works for the benefit of the spiritual master by begging for his maintenance, by cleaning, by learning the principles of Kṛṣṇa consciousness, and by engaging in the process of *bhagavata-dharma.* Thus, due to strong training in the beginning, his life has a firm, sane foundation with which he can overcome the forces of *māyā.* (20/01/76)

The only way that we can overcome *māyā* is to sincerely and seriously take shelter of Kṛṣṇa. So chant very sincerely and follow the four required principles strictly, and very soon you will be able to find shelter from the miseries of material attachment. (08/07/76)

By controlling sex desire one becomes the most perfect sober person. (07/09/76)

If you feel *māyā* attractive, then live an honest life as a householder and contribute to our movement… My request is that you don't become an ordinary foolish man. Keep Kṛṣṇa consciousness in any condition of life. That is success. (29/10/76)

If one is fully engaged in preaching, his mind will be subdued. That is the only way. (20/12/76)

Sex indulgence is not good; it is grossly material and we have to surpass it. But when one has staunch faith in Kṛṣṇa, he'll be able to transcend the urge. Now you will be able to chastise your sex dictations. You are determined, so Kṛṣṇa will help you. (19/01/77)

QUOTES FROM ŚRĪLA PRABHUPĀDA'S LECTURES

Atyāhāra means to eat more than what you need or to accumulate more than what you need. *Āhāra* means eating, and *āhāra* means accumulation. So, of course, any householder, he requires some deposit in the bank for emergency. That is, of course, allowed for householders. But just for us, we are *sannyāsī*;

we are renounced order of. . . We haven't got to accumulate any money. You see? That is the system of Indian philosophy. But those who are householder, family men, they may have some deposit for emergency. Otherwise, those who are renounced order, those who are *brahmacārī*, for them to keep money separately for his maintenance or for accumulating bank balance is not allowed. (28/03/66)

If my mind is concentrated on the beauty of Kṛṣṇa I can see these beautiful girls as Kṛṣṇa's *gopīs*. (01/09/66)

Simply by desiring to go back to home, back to Godhead one is supposed to follow the vow of *brahmacārī*. *Brahmacārī*, to live the life of celibacy, this is called *brahmacārī*. So it has got so nice effect that if anyone from the birth to the death simply observe this life of celibacy he is sure to go back to home. Simply by observing one rule: *yad icchanto brahmacaryaṁ caranti*. It is so nice, *brahmacārya*. (01/09/66)

And *brahmacāri-vrate sthitaḥ*. *Brahmacāri-vrata* means celibacy, no sex life at all. Completely prohibited. *Brahmacārī*. *Brahmacāri-vrate*. *Vrata* means with a vow that "I'll have no sex life," with a vow. Such person can execute yoga system.

One who has his relationship with wife under rules and regulation and does not know any other woman, he is also *brahmacārī*. That is also called *brahmacārī-vrata*. And one who lives complete celibacy life, that he is also *brahmacārī*. So that *brahmacārī-vrata* is essential for yogi. (07/09/66)

When a man or woman comes to sixteen years, that is the beginning of youthful life. So 16 to 20 years, this is very nice. In full energy. And that is the time for growth, intelligence. Unfortunately, we spoil this period. So we become less intelligent, life becomes shorter. If we spoil this period, then our life will be shortened. And if we keep this period complete celibacy, *brahmacārī*, then you can live up to hundred years. (19/07/71)

Those who are too much lusty, lover of the vagina, they may worship Indra. If you want vagina instead of Kṛṣṇa, all right, do it. You have it. So unfortunately, if our student falls a victim of vagina instead of Kṛṣṇa, that is very regrettable. Then better he worship Indra instead of Kṛṣṇa. (22/05/72)

There may be thousands of beautiful women before a devotee, but that does not disturb his mind. He sees they are all energies of Kṛṣṇa. "They are *gopīs* of Kṛṣṇa. They are enjoyable by Kṛṣṇa. I have to serve them. They're *gopīs*. Because I am servant of the servant." *Gopī-bhartuḥ pada-kamalayoḥ dāsa-dāsa-dāsānudāsaḥ*. So a devotee should try to engage all beautiful women in the service of Kṛṣṇa. That is his duty—not to enjoy them. That is sense gratification. This is the position of a devotee. He's not pierced by the arrows of Cupid, but he sees everything in relationship with Kṛṣṇa. (11/11/72)

So this materialistic life means sex life. Very, very abominable, *tuccham*. If anyone has understood this, then he's liberated. But if, when one is still attracted, then it is to be understood that there is still delay in liberation. And one who has understood and has left it, even in this body he's liberated. He's called *jīvan-muktaḥ sa ucyate. īhā yasya harer dāsye karmaṇā manasā girā nikhilāsv apy avasthāsu jīvan-muktaḥ sa ucyate.* So how we can become free from this desire? *Īhā yasya harer dāsye*, If you simply desire to serve Kṛṣṇa, then you can get out. Otherwise, not. That is not possible. If you desire anything else except the service of the Lord, then *māyā* will give you inducement, "Why not enjoy this?" (26/08/73)

A *brahmacārī*, from the very beginning of his life, he is trained to act only for guru. That is *brahmacārī*. It is enjoined that a *brahmacārī* live at the shelter, at the care of guru just like a menial servant. Kṛṣṇa also, although He is the Supreme Personality of Godhead, when He was living as *brahmacārī* at His guru's house, Sāndīpani Muni, he was collecting wood, fuel, from the jungle. He was going daily. It is not that because He was Personality of Godhead, therefore He should not go.

A *brahmacārī* is trained up from the very beginning how to become a *sannyāsī* at the end of life. How he is trained up? He is trained up to collect for guru alms. He is trained up in that way that although he has collected everything, but he does not claim anything. He does not keep anything with him. Even though he has to eat in the *āśrama*, but that he will eat upon the calling by the guru, "My dear such and such, please come and take your *prasāda.*" It is said, if the guru forgets to call him one day, he will not take his food. This is called *brahmacārī*, means strictly following. And they used to call every woman from the beginning of life, "Mother." This is training. *mātṛvat para-dāreṣu*. From the very beginning of life, all women they are treated as mother. (05/04/74)

This is *brahmacārī* life, voluntarily accepting hardship for making life successful. (12/06/74)

Sometimes we enjoy subtle pleasure, thinking of sex life. That is called *nārī-saṅgame. Nārī* means woman, and *saṅga* means union. So those who are practiced, so when there is actually no union, they think of union. So Yāmunācārya said that "Not actually union with woman, but if I think of union," *tad-avadhi bata nārī-saṅgame smaryamāne, smaryamāne*, "Simply by thinking," *bhavati mukha-vikāraḥ*, "Oh, immediately I become disgusted: 'Ah, what is this nasty thing?'" *Suṣṭhu niṣṭhī*. . . (spits) This is perfect. (chuckles) This is perfection. Yes. So long we'll think of, that is called subtle sex, thinking. They read the sex literature. That is subtle sex. Gross sex and subtle sex. So one has to become completely free from these lusty desires, not to become implicated which will never be satisfied, unsatiated, *duṣpūram*. (06/02/75)

The material world means there is a heart disease, which is called *kāma. Hṛd-roga-kāma.* If I see one engaged in lusty or sex affairs naturally my sex desire also becomes awakened, even though I am trying to control it. In the neophyte stage, still if I see in front of me some lusty affairs naturally I will be inclined.

(Ajāmila) was a *brahmacārī* practicing *sama, dama,* but he could not control. All of a sudden he became very much attracted. This is the social condition. If in society we have no restriction then naturally those young boys and girls will be inclined. And as soon as one is sexually inclined he forgets all other culture and gradually becomes downfallen, as we will see from the life of Ajāmila, although he was trained up. Similarly, this is a warning to our students that they are learning how to become Kṛṣṇa conscious. It is a very difficult job to become Kṛṣṇa conscious; it is not an easy thing. But by the grace of Caitanya Mahāprabhu we are trying to teach and it is becoming effective, otherwise how you all Europeans and Americans can give up these four sinful activities? So try to preserve. It can be preserved only by remaining in devotional service, the *śuddha-sattva, vasudeva,* platform. These rules and regulations, restrictions, means to keep one on the *vasudeva* platform. Rising early in the morning, offering *maṅgala-ārati,* then gradually one after another, attending class, *guru-pūjā,* and so on. Up till you go to bed you should always be engaged. Then you will be above these three *guṇas.* And if we keep on the *vasudeva* platform these things will not entice us; otherwise we shall be enticed and fall down.

Sometimes we go to hear or see *rāsa-līlā,* but unless we are advanced in spiritual consciousness, this hearing or seeing of *rāsa-līlā* brings us down. If one is actually seeing *rāsa-līlā,* heard from a realized person, one who is actually advanced in spiritual consciousness, the result will be that our natural lusty desires will disappear. But instead of disappearing our lusty desires, if we increase our lusty desires, that means we are spoiling our life. Therefore it is forbidden for neophyte students to indulge in these affairs of *rāsa-līlā.* You should be very careful. People are very much accustomed to see *rāsa-līlā* in Vṛndāvana. Maybe they are advanced, but the test is that he has given up his lusty desires. If he has given them up, after seeing *rāsa-līlā* he should not have returned home. My Guru Mahārāja used to say, "Do not go to Vṛndāvana with a return ticket." It is very confidential.

Brahmacārī, there are so many restrictions. There are eight kinds of subtle sex. But in the Kali-yuga it is very difficult to follow the rules and regulations. One is not trained up. Even up to ripe old age one becomes attracted by beautiful women, especially in the Western countries.

When you are no longer attracted by this sex desire then you should understand that, "I am now making progress in Kṛṣṇa consciousness." This is the test. We should be very careful, but simply becoming careful is not enough; we must advance in Kṛṣṇa consciousness. That is very easily done by chanting the Hare Kṛṣṇa mantra. If you keep yourself always engaged in Hare Kṛṣṇa, Hare Kṛṣṇa, Kṛṣṇa Kṛṣṇa, Hare Hare/ Hare Rāma, Hare Rāma, Rāma Rāma, Hare Hare. . . simply by chanting if you follow the rules and regulations, then you will not be victimized. You will progress without any fear. (28/08/75)

(Ajāmila saw in front of him a young man and woman embracing and kissing. In such a situation) it is very difficult to restrain. Unless one is very advanced it is not possible. Unless one is very strong in Kṛṣṇa consciousness it is very difficult to restrain the mind and senses. Cupid is always disturbing. This whole material world means Madana, Cupid. People work very hard in cities like hogs and dogs. They say we are hungry, we must work very hard. But that is not the fact.

The real fact is that we want to enjoy sex. As far as hunger is concerned, you can control, but sex desire is very difficult to control. *Yan maithunādi.* Sexual intercourse is the beginning of material life. You know how strong sexual desires are in the Western countries. Even an old man, going to die, he has also. Although he cannot enjoy sex, still he's trying his best by medicine, by intoxication, by stimulants. That is the only happiness of this material world.

Human civilization means to create a population of *dhīra.* Not to be disturbed by the sex impulse. Not that so many so-called *sādhus* now preaching openly yoga by sex.

This mental agitation will go on as long as we are not attracted by Madana-mohana. So long as we are not attracted by Madana-mohana we must be attracted by Madana. Unless you can control your mind not to be disturbed by Madana, there is no question of liberation or devotional service.

Just like a thief is going to steal. He also tries to control it. "I'm going to steal, the after effect will be that I'll be arrested and I'll have to go to jail. And it is forbidden by *śāstra* and state laws also. I'm going to steal but there is risk." The consciousness beats him but he cannot control. This is the position. He knows everything but still he steals. The same thing happened here. Ajāmila was a learned *brāhmaṇa.* He knew that "I am being agitated by the sex desire, it is not good." He had sufficient education in Vedic knowledge. He tried to control the mind as far as the intelligence concerned, but he could not control. Why? The mind was too much agitated by lusty desires. This is the point. Lusty desires are very strong.

Therefore *śāstra* says "Don't be alone even with your mother, daughter or sister." Even a *vidvān* (like Ajāmila) can be disturbed. Don't talk in a solitary place with a woman even if she happens to be your mother, daughter or sister. The mind is so susceptible, but the mind can be controlled only by Kṛṣṇa consciousness. Ambarīṣa Mahārāja showed us the example. Simply engage your mind in thinking of Kṛṣṇa and talk of Kṛṣṇa, then this agitation will not disturb you. (29/08/75)

Material life means sex. *Yan maithunādi-gṛhamedhi-sukhaṁ hi tuccham.* In the material world, not only in the human society but also in the birds, beasts, animals and insects—everywhere—the sex impulse is very strong. And if you indulge in sex life then you'll be implicated more and more in this material body. This is the law of nature. Therefore the whole Vedic civilization is meant for curtailing sex life. First of all *brahmacārī.* No sex life. First training is *brahmacārī*—how to train him to remain without sex, that is *brahmacārī. Tapasā brahmacaryena. Tapasya* means to remain *brahmacārī.* This is *tapasya.* Very, very difficult, therefore it is called *tapasya.* Because the whole world is attracted by sex life, *puṁsaḥ striyā mithunī-bhāvam.* The whole world, not only in this planet but in every planet, even in the demigods' planet. So this Kṛṣṇa consciousness movement means not bodily conscious. The material world means bodily conscious, how to keep the body comfortable. But that is not possible. Body means misery. You cannot keep it with comfort. That is *māyā.* It will never be comfortable but they are all trying to make it comfortable. This is called *māyā. Kleśada āsa deha.* So long you have a material body, you'll have to suffer.

So this Kṛṣṇa consciousness movement is not on the bodily platform. It is on the spiritual platform. To come to the spiritual platform it is necessary that you reduce or make nil sex life. So if one remains *brahmacārī* throughout the whole life it becomes very easy for him to go back to home, back to Godhead. This is a secret. Therefore the whole Vedic civilization is based on, first of all, *brahmacārī*—no sex life. *Gṛhastha,* that is also very regulated. Only for begetting a child can one have sex life. Father, mother, men and women. *Dharmāviruddha kāmo 'smi.* In the *Bhagavad-gītā* Kṛṣṇa says sex life which is prescribed by the religious system is Me. Otherwise it is illicit sex. So for illicit sex there is punishment.

So *tapasya* means *tapasā brahmacaryeṇa śamena ca damena ca.* We have to control. The more one controls he becomes advanced in spiritual culture. The yoga system means *yoga indriya-saṁyama.* Yoga means how to control the senses. Therefore Kṛṣṇa says *mayy āsakta-manāḥ pārtha.* So sex indulgence is against spiritual advancement of life. Therefore we have seen that for the *brahmacārī* it is very easy to enter into the spiritual kingdom. So that you can do here also. If you increase your attraction for Kṛṣṇa then naturally you'll lose the attraction for sex. That is Kṛṣṇa consciousness. Therefore Kṛṣṇa's name is Madana Mohana. Madana means sex life. You can enchant him, Madana. So these are things which the devotee will learn by studying the literature. But even without studying if you sincerely chant the Hare Kṛṣṇa *mantra* under regulation, everything, all good qualifications will come. (27/10/75)

There is a very instructive story, and it is a historical fact. The Muslim emperor Akhbar once inquired from his minister, "How long does one remain in lusty desires?" The minister replied, "Up to the last point of death." Akhbar did not believe it, and he said, "No, no, how can you say that?" "All right," said the minister, "I shall reply in time." So one day, all of a sudden, the minister approached the emperor and said, "You be immediately ready to come with me with your young daughter." Akhbar knew that his minister was very intelligent, and there must be some purpose. He went with him, and the minister took him to a person who was going to die. The minister then asked Akhbar, "Kindly study the man who is about to die, on his face." So Akhbar noticed that as he and his young daughter were entering, the dying man was looking to the face of the young girl. In this way, Akhbar understood, "Yes, what he said is true. Up to the last point of death the desire is there to see the face of a young girl." "This is called *duṣpūreṇa*—it is never fulfilled. This attraction of man and woman and family life continues." (10/12/75)

Brahmacarya means restraining sex life. Celibacy. When one is serious about advancement of spiritual consciousness, he must live under the control of the guru, to learn how to become a *brahmacārī*. A devotee doesn't need to practice *brahmacarya* separately—he is not attracted to sex (because he has a higher taste).

In our society, compulsorily, we have to mix with women—not only women—very beautiful young girls. But if one is not agitated, even in this association of beautiful women and girls, then he is to be considered a *paramahaṁsa,* very advanced. So we cannot avoid in Kṛṣṇa consciousness movement. That was the problem from the beginning. In India there is restriction between man and women freely intermingling, but in your country there is no such restriction. Therefore I got my disciples married. They criticized me that I have become a marriage maker. Anyway I wanted at least to regulate. That is required. *Dharmāviruddho bhūteṣu kāmo 'smi.*

Kṛṣṇa also says. A married man can also be a *brahmacārī.* If a married man sticks to one wife and if before sex he takes permission from his spiritual master then he is a *brahmacārī.* Not whimsically. When the spiritual master orders him that now you can beget a child, then he's *brahmacārī.*

Śrīla Vīrarāghavācārya has described in his commentary that there are two kinds of *brahmacārī.* One kind is *naiṣṭhika-brahmacārī;* he doesn't marry. And another kind, although he marries, he's fully under the control of the spiritual master even for sex. He is also a *brahmacārī.*

Why so much restriction on sex life? People do not understand throughout the whole world. They are captivated by sex life, especially in the Western countries. Material existence means desire for sex life, both man and woman. We are already bewildered, attached to the material world, but when we are united, man and woman together, our attachment for this material world increases.

This human form of life is meant for *tapasya*, to learn how to become detached from this material world. And the beginning is this *brahmacārī* life. *Brahmacārī gurukule vasan dāntaḥ. Dānta* means self-controlled. That is real teaching. According to Vedic civilization, there is no sex life except for begetting a nice child, and that also with *garbhādhāna-saṁskāra.* In other words, whimsical sex life is completely stopped in Vedic civilization. There everything is under regulation. Therefore *brahmacārī* means how to control the senses, to keep under his own control, not that, "I am now sexually inclined. I must immediately have sex." We should always remember that this human life is meant for controlling the senses. *Athāto brahma jijñāsā.* It is simply meant for inquiring about spiritual life. That is perfect civilization.

Therefore *brahmacārī* means living under the direction of the guru. *Guror hitam* means how he can simply be thinking of benefiting the spiritual master. Unless that position comes nobody can serve guru. It is not an artificial thing. The *brahmacārī*, disciple must have genuine love for guru, then he can be under his control. Otherwise why should one be under the control of another person? Therefore it is said, *ācaran dāsavat. Dāsa* means menial servant. A disciple is expected to live in *gurukula*. *Gurukula* means at the shelter of guru, *nīcavat,* as a menial servant. This can be possible when one is very thickly related with the guru. Otherwise an ordinary relationship will not do. (12/04/76)

A machine works systematically. Everyone has seen that the machine of the watch is working very systematically, correctly. Similarly, every student, every disciple, must work very correctly like a machine. There is no question, why you did not attend the school or the class. You cannot say that you did this and this, no. As a machine works, so everyone should attend the class, rise early in the morning, attend *maṅgala-ārati.* No discrepancy. That is wanted.

Then, in the beginning the student should come and offer obeisances to the lotus feet of the guru. This is the beginning. *Ādau gurvāśrayam. Yasya prasādad bhagavata prasādah.* This is the principle. If you offer your respectful obeisances to the guru he becomes pleased. Anyone, even if one is an offender, if he comes and offers obeisances to the superior, guru, then even if there was an offense, he forgets. That should be done regularly. Just like a machine. As soon as one sees guru, immediately he must offer obeisances. Beginning and end. When he comes to see guru, he must offer obeisances, and when he leaves that place, he must offer obeisances. In between coming and going he should learn from the guru Vedic understanding. This is the principle of living in *gurukula*

Our students are very obedient. If they see the guru a hundred times, he practices this process of offering obeisances while meeting and while going away. These things are to be practiced then *dānta, brahmācāri gurukule vasan dānto.* Then he'll be self controlled. Obedience is the first way of discipline. If there is no obedience there cannot be any discipline, and if there is no discipline you cannot manage anything. That is not possible Therefore, this is very essential that the students should be very disciplined. Disciple means one who follows discipline. The Sanskrit word *śiṣya,* comes from the verb *śās, śāsana,* ruling. So *śiṣya* means one who voluntarily accepts the ruling of the spiritual master. (14/04/76)

The recommendation is there. *Tapasā brahmacaryena* Celibacy. No sex life. That is the beginning of *tapasya.* Meditation means *tapasya. Tapasā brahmacaryeṇa śamena. Śama,* to control the senses. To keep so the senses may not be agitated. *Damena* Even if it is agitated, by my knowledge I have to cut down. Just like if I become agitated by seeing a beautiful woman, a beautiful boy—that is natural. Young boy, young girl, they're naturally attracted. There is nothing surprising. But *tapasya* means "I have taken a vow—no illicit sex." That is knowledge. "Even if I am attracted I shall not do." This is *tapasya.* "Because I am attracted now we shall enjoy"—that is not *tapasya. Tapasya* means even if one is attracted he should not act. That is *tapasya.* There may be some difficulty to control but that should be practiced. It can be practiced. It is not very difficult but one has to practice with determination. Now I have taken a vow before the Deity. Because at the time of initiation it is promised before the Deity, before the fire, before the spiritual master, and before the Vaiṣṇavas that I will not have illicit sex. That is promised. How can I break it?

I have taken a vow before the Deity, before the fire, before my spiritual master, before the Vaiṣṇavas: "No illicit sex, no meat eating, no drinking or intoxication, no gambling." I have promised it. If I am a gentleman, how can I break my promise? This is called *jñāna.* With knowledge one has to practice. That is called *tapasya.* Otherwise to become attracted is not unnatural.

Caitanya Mahāprabhu, He was a *sannyāsī,* He used to say that even if I see a doll made of wood like a beautiful woman My mind becomes agitated. So what to speak of us. This is the example. Caitanya Mahāprabhu is giving an example. To be agitated in the mind, that is not unnatural, but if you practice you will not be agitated any more—if you practice by your knowledge. That is called *dhīra. Dhīras tatra na muhyati.* We have to become *dhīra. Dhīra* and *adhīra,* there are two classes of men. One is sober. Even if there is cause of agitation, still he remains firm. He is called *dhīra.* And *adhīra* means, as soon as there is a cause of agitation, he becomes a victim. That is called *adhīra.* So we have to become *dhīra.* We have been *adhīra* in so many different forms of life because I am coming to this human form of life after evolution of 8,400,000 forms of body. Why not practice a little *tapasya* in this life? If by practicing *tapasya,* restraint, I can get relief from this repetition of birth and death, why should I not do it? This is knowledge. And if I again become victimized, the law of nature is there. If you want you can enjoy. Nature will give you. All right, you want so much sex. Alright, come on. Become a hog, yes. Nature is ready; it is not very difficult.

Therefore *śāstra* says, no, no, this life is not meant for becoming a hog or a dog. *Nāyaṁ deho deha-bhājāṁ nṛ-loke kaṣṭān kāmān arhate viḍ-bhujāṁ ye.* The whole world is working so hard. They are going to the office to earn a livelihood, but what is the pleasure? The pleasure is sex, that's all. Their ultimate goal is sex, that's all. *Yan maithunādi-gṛhamedhi-sukhaṁ hi tuccham.* So one should consider, the sex indulgence is given to the hogs and dogs, and for the same enjoyment I'll have to work so hard. This is knowledge. I have got this human form of life for understanding Kṛṣṇa, for understanding God, my position, what I am.

Our main problem is sex life, because sex life is the basic principle of material life. Either you are a human being or you are a demigod or you are a bird or you are a beast or you are a fly or you are a fish or you are a tree, plants, everything. The basic principle of material life is sex. *Puṁsaḥ striyā mithunī-bhāvam etat tayor mitho hṛdaya-granthim āhuḥ.*

Everything is there. You have got books; study and follow the practice. Be a little sober, then you'll be able. It's not that you'll not be able. You'll be able. And Kṛṣṇa will help. As soon as we are very eager then Kṛṣṇa will help. Therefore the Deity worship is there. Along with the Deity worship we should always pray "Kṛṣṇa, kindly save me from the pitfalls of *māyā.*" He'll do it.

But if you want to cheat Kṛṣṇa and cheat the guru then you'll be cheated. That's all. The guru is neither cheated, nor Kṛṣṇa will be cheated. You will be cheated. That's all. If you want to be cheated then do whatever you like, and prolong this term of repetition of birth and death. And if you want to stop then here: *tapasā brahmacaryeṇa ṣamena ca damena ca tyāgena. Tyāgena.* This is also one of *tapasya.* Don't keep with you anything. Then you'll make plans. Let me have illicit sex. Let me have intoxication. As soon as you have got money. Best thing is as soon as you get money immediately spend it for Kṛṣṇa. *Tyāgena.* Charity. *Tyāgena.* means charity. Not that you starve. You keep yourself fit to execute Kṛṣṇa consciousness, but don't keep much money. Immediately give in charity to Kṛṣṇa. (14/05/76)

A *brahmacārī* is trained to refrain from sex life. That is *brahmacārī.* Celibacy. But if he's still not able then he's allowed to accept *gṛhastha* life. There is no cheating, hypocrisy, that I proclaim myself as *brahmacārī* or *sannyāsī* and I secretly do all nonsense. This is hypocrisy. The hypocrisy life will not make one advanced in spiritual life. There is the example given by Śrī Caitanya Mahāprabhu.

(Then Śrīla Prabhupāda related how Lord Caitanya rejected Choṭa Haridāsa, a renunciate who looked lustfully at a young woman, but when He saw that Śivānanda Sena's wife was pregnant He gave a name to the unborn child.)

One man, simply he saw with lusty desires a young woman, he was rejected. And one man had his wife pregnant—He approved it, "That's alright."

So sex life is not forbidden in this movement, but hypocrisy is forbidden. If you become a hypocrite then there is no way. That is Caitanya Mahāprabhu's teaching. Choṭa Haridāsa presented himself as a *brahmacārī* and he was looking at a young woman. Then He understood: he was a hypocrite, reject him. And Śivānanda Sena, he was a *gṛhastha. Gṛhastha* must have children—what is wrong with that? He said yes, My remnants of foodstuffs should be given.

So our request is, don't be a hypocrite. There are four *āśramas: brahmacārī, gṛhastha, vānaprastha,* and *sannyāsa.* Whichever *āśrama is* suitable for you, you accept—but sincerely—don't be a hypocrite. If you think that you want sex, all right, you marry and remain like a gentleman. Don't be a hypocrite. This is Caitanya Mahāprabhu's movement. He didn't like hypocrisy. Nobody likes hypocrisy.

But for a person who is seriously engaged in Kṛṣṇa consciousness, sex life and material opulence are not very good. Therefore Caitanya Mahāprabhu voluntarily accepted *sannyāsa.* He was very nicely situated in His family life. When He was a family man He married twice. One wife died, He married again. But when He took *sannyāsa* He was very, very strict. No woman could come very near to Him. This is Caitanya Mahāprabhu's teaching. So we have to follow strictly the rules and regulations, if we are serious. (23/05/76)

So we have to give up. So there is therefore regulative principle. At least, no illicit sex. Get yourself married, live like a gentleman, take responsibility, then gradually you'll be able to give up this sex desire. Unless we give up this sex desire, completely unagitated, there is no possibility of stopping this repetition of material birth—birth, death, old age and disease. That is not possible. (01/07/76)

To see a woman is not dangerous, but to think of enjoying, that is dangerous. You cannot avoid that. You are on the street here. But to see with the spirit of enjoyment, that is dangerous. So we should be very careful. That requires very strong training in Kṛṣṇa consciousness. Unless one is strongly in Kṛṣṇa consciousness, that habit of enjoying spirit cannot be given up. (10/09/76)

Not that a *brahmacārī* has to become a very learned scholar in grammar. . . These are secondary things. First thing, he has to learn how to control the senses, *dānta*, how to control the mind. *Śamo damaḥ*. This is the beginning of brahminical life. If you cannot control your mind, if you cannot control your senses, there is no question of becoming *brahmacārī*. (25/11/76)

QUOTES FROM ŚRĪLA PRABHUPĀDA'S CONVERSATIONS

Why should one hate women so much? You should be trained up so that in spite of women, you'll not be agitated. That training is required. That training is there. We are training in that way. I am always surrounded by young girls. In European countries, if you restrict in that way, that will be fanaticism. Why Europe? Nowadays here (India) also. It is simply utopian. That is the training of Cāṇakya Paṇḍita. *Mātṛvat para-dāreṣu.* There may be thousands of women, but you see them as mother. If you become agitated even by seeing mother, then what can be done? Then you are a *go-khara* (animal). This (strict injunction for separation of men and women) cannot be carried. Do you mean to say that by avoiding sex life one becomes *siddha* (perfect)? Then impotents are all *siddhas. Siddha* means that in spite of agitation, he's not agitated. This is *siddha.* (27/03/74)

Unless we are very sincere, we cannot cope with *māyā.* That is not possible. If you remain a servant of *māyā,* you cannot conquer over *māyā.* You must be a very sincere servant of Kṛṣṇa. Then you can conquer. *Mām eva ye prapadyante māyām etāṁ taranti te.*

Otherwise you are subjected to the tricks of *māyā.* (13/07/74)

From five years to twenty-five years, the *brahmacārī* has nothing to learn except about God. He is simply interested in Brahman. That is called *brahmacārī.* He has no material interest. That is the foundation of spiritual life. (01/03/75)

Everyone wants to fulfill lusty desires. So unless one is in the mode of goodness or is transcendental, everyone will like. That is the material world, *rajas-tamaḥ. Rajas-tamo-bhāvāḥ kāma-lobhādayaś ca ye.* It is all discussed in the *śāstra.* Just like, I am a hungry man. There is foodstuff. I want to eat it. So if I take by force, that is illegal, and if I pay for it, then it is legal. But I am a hungry man, I want it. This is going on. Everyone is lusty. Therefore they say "legalized prostitution." They want it. So marriage is sometimes legalized that's all. The passion and desire is the same, either married or not married. So the Vedic law says, "Better married. Then you will be controlled." He will not be so lusty as without married life. So the *gṛhastha* life is a concession—the same lusty desire under rules and regulations. Without married life he will commit rapes in so many ways, so better let them be satisfied with one (partner), both the man and woman, and make progress in spiritual life. That is the concession. Everyone in this material world has come with these lusty desires and greediness. Even demigods like Lord Śiva and Lord Brahmā. Lord Brahmā became lusty after his own daughter. And Lord Śiva became so mad after Mohinī-mūrti. So what to speak of us insignificant creatures. So lusty desire is there. That is the material world. Unless one is fully Kṛṣṇa conscious, this lusty desire cannot be checked. It is not possible.

The first *tapasya* is *brahmacarya,* how to restrain this sex desire. Where is their *tapasya?* "It is very difficult to do this *tapasya.*" Therefore Caitanya Mahāprabhu has given *harer nāma.* If you chant the Hare Kṛṣṇa *mantra* regularly, you'll be cured. Otherwise, regular *tapasya* is almost impossible nowadays. (11/05/75)

Don't go alone to preach. There should be at least two devotees together, or if possible, more. (12/05/75)

Brahmacārī guru-kule vasan dānto guror hitam/ ācaran dāsavan nīco gurau sudṛḍha-sauhṛdaḥ. The *brahmacārī* should live at *gurukula,* controlling his senses and acting for the benefit of his guru, not for his personal benefit. He should act just like a servant. The master orders and the servant carries out the order. Although he may come from a very aristocratic or *brāhmaṇa* family, still he should be humble, ready to do whatever the spiritual master or teacher asks. The student should not challenge.

Why should he be submissive? He is not getting any money. These things are accepted out of love for the spiritual master. You are not working. I am not paying you, but why are you working? Out of love for me. This is the basic principle. One should be convinced, "My spiritual master is my best friend; therefore I must render service to him." The service which you are rendering is not possible to be done even if I pay somebody one thousand dollars per month. It is not possible. Because it is done out of love. This is the basic principle. *Yasya deve parā bhaktir yathā deve tathā gurau.* When one is fixed up in devotion to Kṛṣṇa and His representative guru, everything becomes revealed automatically. *Tasyaite kathitā hy arthāḥ prakāśante.* These are all revealed experiences. *Brahmacārīs* especially are under the protection of the guru. There is no question in the beginning of how much one has learned ABC. The first thing is that one should live in the *gurukula* and practice sense control. The basic principle should be that one is living for the benefit of the guru, not for one's own benefit. Whatever he orders, one must execute. (Śrīla Prabhupāda speaking to *gurukula* teachers in Dallas, July 1975)

That is one of the defects in our society, that women are there and one falls victim of these women. And it is not possible to keep the society strictly for men. That is also not possible. But actually no women should live in the temple.

Devotee: Śrīla Prabhupāda, the Christians have one place for the women and another place for the men. But we find the women can't organize themselves very well. So it is difficult to do something like that also.

Śrīla Prabhupāda: Therefore, if we do not give up these lusty desires, either we keep separately or together they fall down. In Kali-yuga the sex impulse is so strong, but it is utilized in so many ways. The yogis, swamis, schools, college, philosophy—at the end, sex, that's all. That example, dog's tail. (Referring to the example of the dog's tail, which, despite all endeavors, cannot be straightened.) (14/07/75)

Tapasya means *brahmacarya*. *Brahmacarya* means complete cessation from sex life. This is *brahmacarya*. *Tapasya* means *austerities*. That is the greatest austerity, to cease sex. *Tapasā brahmacaryena*. Our Vedic civilization, the boys are trained to be *brahmacārī* from the very beginning of life. Our existence should be purified. How? *Tapo*, by *tapasya*. But we are enjoying life, why should we undergo *tapasya*? You are not enjoying, you are suffering. Even if you think you are enjoying, there are so many sufferings. That the foolish do not know.

(The main forms of suffering in the material world are birth, death, old age and disease.) Apart from this, there are so many other sufferings. But he thinks he will be happy. And that happiness is centered around sex, that's all. *Yan maithunādi-gṛhamedhi-sukhaṁ hi tuccham.* Their only happiness is sex. Therefore in the Western countries they're simply trying for sex enjoyment, that's all. The whole civilization is based on how to enjoy sex very nicely. This is their basic principle of civilization.

Devotee: On the best selling charts of the books there's always some book about how to enjoy sex.

Śrīla Prabhupāda: Yes. You see. There are books here also, *kāma-śāstra.* So sex enjoyment also we cannot enjoy unlimitedly; then we'll become impotent. This homosex is another side of impotency. That is natural. If you enjoy too much then you become impotent.

Devotee: They're trying to make that more and more accepted in America, homosex.

Śrīla Prabhupāda: Yes, the churches accept. It is already law. The whole world is on the verge of ruination. Kali-yuga. (06/09/75)

Without sex life one cannot be materially enthusiastic. And if you stop sex life, then you become spiritually advanced. This is the secret. If you stop sex life, then you become spiritually advanced, and if you indulge in sex life, then you will be materially enthusiastic. And for *jñānīs*, yogis, *bhaktas,* sex life prohibited. (18/10/75)

Devotee: Śrīla Prabhupāda, should we call all the women "mother"?

Śrīla Prabhupāda: Yes. And treat them like mother. Not only call, but treat them like mother.

Harikeśa: Actually we have not even any idea how to treat a mother.

Śrīla Prabhupāda: Learn it. At least mother should not be proposed for sex. (25/10/75)

Devotee: (One *brahmacārī*) does not want to chant with women in the temple room. He says, "I do not want to chant in a room with women. I would rather be away from the women."

Śrīla Prabhupāda: That means he has got distinction between men and women. He is not yet a *paṇḍita. Paṇḍitaḥ sama-darśinaḥ.* He is a fool. (02/11/75)

Devotee: If a person loses semen or if they masturbate or if they unnecessarily use their sexual energy, they'll go insane. Their brains will become very weak, and physically they'll become very weak.

Śrīla Prabhupāda: Yes. That is a fact. (15/03/76)

After remaining *brahmacārī,* if he is inclined, he may marry. Otherwise, immediately *sannyāsa. Gṛhastha* is not necessary. But if one feels that he cannot remain celibate, he is allowed to marry. That is also restricted. Of course, material life is based on sex. As long as there is sex desire, one is not liberated. Our process is to become free from sex life. The main point is freedom from sex desire. This is the best thing. Despite provocation, when one is steady, he is called *dhīra. Dhīras tatra na muhyati.* So if our boys become *dhīra,* just like our Guru Mahārāja, that is a very good thing. (Śrīla Prabhupāda speaking to *gurukula* teachers in Vṛndāvana, April 1976)

Rūpānuga: A *brahmacārī* used to complain to you about how sick he was all the time, and you said, "Are you not a *brahmacārī?* Are you not following the *brahmacārī* principles?" Did you imply that if he were doing it sincerely he would not be so sick all the time?

Śrīla Prabhupāda: Yes, that's a fact. (09/07/76)

Sex impulse ruins the whole character. (31/07/76)

Our life is simple. We don't want luxury. Life should be very simple. To increase unnecessary things unnecessarily, that is material life. We don't require much. We just want to subsist. We hate the idea of luxury, unnecessary. (31/07/76)

If you want to avoid trouble, then don't marry, remain *brahmacārī*. If you cannot, then, all right, have a legal wife, get children and raise them very nicely, make them Vaiṣṇavas, take the responsibility. So we are organizing this society, we welcome. Some way or other we shall arrange for shelter. But to take care of the children, to educate them, that will depend on their parents. (03/08/76)

If one wants to keep oneself pure, he can keep pure in any circumstances. (22/08/76)

Sex life in this material world is so strong, even in the heavenly planets. Big, big ṛṣis. Sex life with animals also there is... Sex life is so strong... Man cohabiting with animal. It makes one blind. Sex affairs, just see, in the highest circle. Bṛhaspati, the spiritual master of the *devatās*, he became so much mad for his brother's wife who was pregnant, and forcibly they had sex. Just see. These are examples. Brahmā became attracted with his daughter. Lord Śiva became attracted with the beauty of Mohinī-mūrti, even in the presence of his wife. So this sex life can be controlled only by becoming Kṛṣṇa conscious. Otherwise there is no... The *Bhāgavata* has discussed all this because in this material world there is no escape unless we become Kṛṣṇa conscious, from the sex impulse. It is not possible. *Yad-avadhi mama cetaḥ kṛṣṇa*... When one is fully Kṛṣṇa conscious, then he'll reject all this nonsense: "What is this?" *Bhavati mukha-vikāraḥ suṣṭhu*. He'll spite (spit): "Eh! Get out. Is that enjoyment?" It is possible for a Kṛṣṇa conscious... No other can do it. And that is the bondage. He'll have to work hard for maintaining sex issues. And so long you are bound up by the karmas, you have to accept another body and then continue. Who knows this, how we are bound up and conditioned? If you talk in the modern society they will laugh: "What nonsense this man is... 'By sex life one becomes conditioned.'" They cannot understand. (07/01/77)

What we have renounced? We are using the motorcar, we are using this machine, we are eating, we are sleeping in nice room—what is the renouncement? The only renouncement is no connection with woman. That is the real platform of renouncement. If one can renounce woman's connection, then he's a liberated man. That is very, very difficult. (31/01/77)

Not only a trained-up child, even a grown-up person, if he takes Kṛṣṇa consciousness seriously, he also forgets sex life. (From a discussion on Sigmund Freud)

So long one has the sex inclination, he will have to accept a material body. (From a discussion on Sigmund Freud)

EXTRACTS FROM OTHER SOURCES

NOTES ON TRADITIONAL BRAHMACĀRĪ LIFE

(Compiled from various sources by Bhānu Swami)

(1) Types of brahmacārī:

(a) *Gāyatrī:* One who learns the *gāyatrī* mantra, abstains from salt and spices for three days, and then takes up family life.

(b) *Brahman:* one who learns the *gāyatrī* mantra and then stays in the *gurukula* for the full period of 12-20 years, studying, begging, practicing rituals, and then, upon graduation, takes up married life.

(c) *Prajāpati:* one who learns the *gāyatrī* mantra and stays three years maximum in the *gurukula*, then marries.

(d) *Naiṣṭhika:* one who learns the *gāyatrī* mantra, then lives and studies in the *gurukula* and dwells in the teacher's *āśrama* (i.e., upholds his *brahmacārī* vows) until death. He remains chaste, pure, unmarried, wearing reddish cloth, having *śikhā, upavīta* and *daṇḍa,* eating unsalted and unspiced food, and lives on alms given to his teacher.

(2) Activities of the brahmacārī:

He should engage in cultivating good character, controlling the senses, controlling speech, treating others properly, study, performing sacrifices, and begging.

(a) Cultivating character and sense control:

He should give up lying, lust, anger, greed, infatuation, pride, envy, violence, fear and lamentation.

He should give up all forms of sex life.

He should not lose semen by any means.

He should not look at, touch, or talk to women.

He should not sleep in the daytime.

He should not sleep on a bed.

He should not apply oil to his body.

He should not take a hot water bath.

He should give up cosmetics and perfumes, flower decorations, shoes and umbrellas.

He should give up hearing and singing popular songs.

He should give up excessive bathing, eating, sleeping, wakefulness and criticizing.

He should rise in the *brahma-muhūrta* and then brush his teeth, bathe, chant the *gāyatrī* mantra, and worship the Lord.

"At both junctions of day and night, namely in the early morning and in the evening, he should be fully absorbed in thoughts of the spiritual master, fire, the sun god and Lord Viṣṇu and by chanting the *gāyatrī* mantra he should worship them." (*S.B.*. 7.12.2)

(b) Speech:

He should speak what is pleasing and truthful, expressing his true feelings, without hatred in his words.

He should not criticize, speak unpleasant or untrue words, even if his mind is in distress.

(c) Respect for the Ācārya:

He will obey the orders of the *ācārya* as long as they are in accordance with dharma.

He should study the Vedas under the teacher.

He should perform what is pleasing to the *ācārya*.

He should offer his respects to the *ācārya* in the morning and evening saying, *aham. . . bho abhivādaye:* "Sir, I, . . ., offer greetings to you."

The teacher will answer, *saumya, āyuṣman bhava:* "May you live long, O gentle one."

The student should then touch his ears, cross his hands and touch the teacher's feet.

He should address the *ācārya* and elders by formal name.

If the teacher rises the student should rise; if the teacher is standing, the student should remain standing; if the teacher walks the student should follow; if the teacher sits down or lies down, the student should take permission and sit on a lower seat.

(d) Study:

He should not act without the permission of the teacher except in matters of study and worship, which he should perform without being told.

He should not study with legs outstretched, in a tree, on a boat, in a vehicle, on a bed, at a crematorium, during the *sandhyā*, during a thunderstorm, earthquake, eclipse, catastrophe, or meteor shower, after eating forbidden food, after vomiting, at the time of death of a student, teacher, or teacher's son or wife, or in the presence of a corpse.

(e) Eating:

He should eat with the permission of his teacher.

He should eat twice a day, having taken bath, having chanted the *gāyatrī* mantra, after washing feet, hands and mouth, wearing lower and upper cloth, from an unbroken plate, which does not touch his lap or the *āsana*.

He should not take food remnants (except that of his guru) or food touched by a woman in her period, or by a person who has had a birth or death in his family.

He may take raw food from a *śūdra* who is living by legitimate means.

He should avoid excessively hot, sour, astringent, bitter, salty or purgative foods.

He should not take meat, intoxication or any forbidden food.

(f) Sacrifice:

The *brahmacārī* should perform a fire sacrifice in the morning and evening every day.

(3) Graduation:

When the student's studies are complete and if he plans to return home and take up household life, he should undergo the *saṁskāra* called *samāvartana* and take up wearing two sets of sacred threads.

SEX IS DEATH

From the very beginning of Kṛṣṇa consciousness one gains the positive taste for spiritual existence, and so the addictions of the senses become relatively easy to give up. The four greatest impediments to spiritual life—illicit sex, intoxication, meat-eating, and gambling—can be abandoned with surprising ease. When one has the real thing, a real life of unceasing bliss and knowledge, there is no difficulty in putting aside the counterfeits.

Unconditional love for Kṛṣṇa is manifest in unconditional engagement in the service of Kṛṣṇa, in service that has no desire for reward and no interruption. This is the characteristic that distinguishes love from its perverted material transformation, lust, in which personal gain is the motive. Even the sexual union of a man and a woman can be used in the service of Kṛṣṇa. It is extremely good fortune for a child to be born from parents engaged in self-realization, for from his earliest moments he lives in an atmosphere uncontaminated by lust and greed, and he takes in the principles of spiritual life with his mother's milk. Such children can be conceived only when the parents unite specifically for that purpose and insure the good qualities of their offspring through their own purification of consciousness. The first duty of parents is to be able to deliver their children from death, and family life dedicated to that purpose is conducive to self-realization, and as such need not be artificially renounced.

But sex for any other purpose—sex to exploit the body for enjoyment, to fuel the delusions of the ego—is the cause of death. Sex more than anything else fixes our false identification of ourselves with the body, rivets us into the flesh, and addicts us to material aggrandizement. Sexual desire can never be satisfied, for it grows by what it feeds on. This permanently frustrated desire causes a deep and abiding rage, which deepens our illusion. The twin delusions of desire and hate drive us on through interminable bodily incarcerations, hurtling us over and over into forms that fill us with fear, suffer the ceaseless onslaught of injury and disease, disintegrate while we still occupy them, and are destroyed. In reality none of this happens to us, but we have erroneously identified ourselves with the body and have thereby taken these torments upon us. Death is an illusion we have imposed upon ourselves by our desire to enjoy this world. Sex is the essence of that desire. Sex, therefore, is death.

It is only right that we struggle against the sentence of death. It is only proper that we seek a life of uninterrupted and unending pleasure uncompromised by shame or fear. It is only natural that we want to be whole and at one with ourselves, uncompromised by duality. The most deadly delusion is that sex is a way to these goals, for in fact it is the greatest single impediment. It is the cause of our disease, which we embrace as the cure.

The restrictions upon sexual activity enjoined by religions were originally meant to assist in overcoming this greatest block to human happiness. Unfortunately, now only the restrictions and negations survive, while the real reason for them has been forgotten.

But the viable path of self-realization is once again open. It may seem to you that, whatever good intentions you may have, the sexual drive is too powerful for you to overcome. It is true that it is too strong for artificial suppression. But I know from experience that if you simply begin by taking up the positive practices of *bhakti-yoga*, especially the reciting of the name of Kṛṣṇa in the form of the Hare Kṛṣṇa mantra, you will find that what seemed so formidable a barrier becomes easy to cross and that your authentic life, beyond the world of birth and death, is at hand. (From *Endless Love* by Ravindra Svarūpa dāsa)

ENDLESS LOVE

Our propensity to love tends naturally to expand without limit, yet in this world it meets with repeated impediments. The baffling of our urge to love becomes one of the most tragic features of life. The crux of the problem is that although we want to love, we are never more vulnerable than when we do. As soon as we love someone, we open ourselves to rejection, betrayal, separation, loss, and all the attending anguish and pain. Experience of these things has filled the world with bitter and disappointed people, cynics and misanthropes.

But even before we have suffered the pains of thwarted love, we aren't able to love fully and unconditionally. There is an essential incompatibility between what we are and what we can love in this world, and in our hearts we know it. Our desire to love without limit and without end is a clear indication that we are ourselves eternal, spiritual beings. At the same time, whatever we can love in this world is temporary and material. Consequently, we cannot love without fear, and, consciously or unconsciously, from the outset we cannot help but withhold the full investment of our love.

A frequent theme in literature concerns a hero or heroine who loves recklessly and without restraint, inevitably undergoes the most intense sort of suffering, and finally meets with a tragic or pitiful death. We may take these stories as cautionary tales. Yet we really don't need them to remind us of the constant frustration of our being. There is no adequate object for our love in this world.

Therefore, out of boundless compassion for us, Kṛṣṇa reveals His kingdom of transcendental, unrestricted love, in which He is eternally manifest as the ultimate object of affection—the most perfect hero, master, friend, child, and lover. His beauty is unrivaled, and His personality, expressed in infinitely varied exchanges of love, is ceaselessly fascinating. When we turn to Kṛṣṇa, our loving propensity breaks loose at last from the tight confines of matter and opens up into an ever-expanding flow that never meets any resistance. That is why Kṛṣṇa is perpetually inviting us to come to Him and His eternal abode and enjoy with Him forever the delights of an endless love. (From *Endless Love* by Ravindra Svarūpa dāsa)

INSTRUCTIVE WORDS

An extract from the Śrī Vaiṣṇava text, *Vārtā-mālā* ("A Garland of Instructive Words").

If a Vaiṣṇava engages in improper relationships with women (or women with men), he has to accept the following types of *anarthas* or results.

1) By this, his/her body is affected badly and so it is an *anartha* or unwanted thing.

2) Seeing him, others may also follow suit. So it is an *anartha* not only for the Vaiṣṇava who falls, but also for those who follow his bad example, and to the woman who is spoiled by him. (The above two results can be seen in this birth itself.)

3) By indulging so one disrespects the *śāstric* injunction that "one should not engage in an illicit relationship with a woman, for by doing so surely the path to hell is opened."

4) He will also incur the wrath of the Lord, because the Lord has told, "Those who violate *śāstric* laws are my enemies."

5) By such illicit actions he will incur the wrath of the Vaiṣṇavas.

6) By the same said reasons he will incur the wrath of his spiritual master also.

7) It will increase opportunities to associate with sinful persons. (As stated in *Tiru-mālai:* "When I associate with persons

who are interested in sense enjoyment, I also fall into the illusory traps of the dangerous eyes of women.")

8) Such engagement is contradictory to his eternal nature as that of being enjoyed by the Lord, because the thought that "sense enjoyment is nice" is an obstacle to realize his eternal nature as a servant.

9) Because one has to make so much endeavor to enjoy sex pleasure it is a great stumbling block to the thought that "the Lord is my only means and He is my maintainer."

10) Because one may no longer be able to think that "service to my Lord is sweet," it is an *anartha*.

11) As stated elsewhere in Śrī Vaiṣṇava literature, if one engages in sex enjoyment then he will not go to the supreme destination. If one worships demigods, he may in some lifetime become a Vaiṣṇava. But one who engages his mind in sex enjoyment always attains hellish planets, because once he is captivated by such thoughts, his involvement in it will keep on growing. A Vaiṣṇava who engages in illicit sex is caught like the prey of a crocodile, who, once catching the legs, will never let it go but will completely swallow it up to the head. Similarly, sense enjoyment completely devours the nature of a devotee.

Once a prostitute came to the guru of the author of *Vārtā-mālā*. She asked him, "If at noon a Vaiṣṇava comes to me and says that he is hungry then I will certainly give him food to relieve his hunger. Similarly, if a Vaiṣṇava comes to me in the night and says that bodily hunger or want of union with me is troubling him, then what is wrong in relieving him of his bodily hunger by offering him my body ?"

The *ācārya* replied, "A lady gets a child after many years of penance. If that child asks his mother, 'Please give me a rope to hang myself, or a knife to cut my throat,' then will she give him what he wants? Similarly, if a Vaiṣṇava comes to you maddened by lust, you should not agree. By agreeing to his proposal you destroy his eternal nature and the thoughts that are conducive to realize his nature."

THE STORY OF ṚṢYAŚṚṄGA

The instructive story of Ṛṣyaśṛṅga is found in the *Rāmāyaṇa* and *Mahābhārata.* Ṛṣyaśṛṅga was the son of a sage who was determined that his son be brought up as a spotless *brahmacārī.* Accordingly, from his very birth the child was brought up in a forest atmosphere far away from women or even talk of women. He was trained in meditation, scriptural study and brahminical rituals. Thus, on reaching youth, he had no idea of even the existence of the opposite sex.

Meanwhile, in the neighboring state, a severe drought ensued. The worried king called his court astrologers, who by their mystic insight were able to ascertain the only method by which good fortune could return to the land: the boy-sage Ṛṣyaśṛṅga, a resident of the nearby jungle, must come to reside in the kingdom. The court astrologers also told how the boy could be brought: he must be enticed by beautiful women.

A few days later, when Ṛṣyaśṛṅga was alone at his father's *āśrama,* he was shocked out of meditation by the sound of laughter and giggling. Opening his eyes, he was amazed to behold a group of young boys playing with a gay frolic and abandon he had never known before. How charming these boys were! Ṛṣyaśṛṅga's mind became captivated by the beautiful features of their faces and bodies, their attractive smiles and glances, the tinkle of their voices, and their exulting mood of enjoyment. "Who are you?" he asked.

"We are *muni-putras* (sons of forest sages)," they replied—for indeed, these young girls from the city were dressed as *brahmacārīs.* "Come play with us," they invited. How could Ṛṣyaśṛṅga refuse? In the course of play, his body touched the bodies of the girls, and again his senses were attracted. Next, the *muni-putras* shared their deliciously prepared food with Ṛṣyaśṛṅga. The boy, who had been brought up on forest roots and fruits, was now completely captivated. But all too soon his new-found friends went away.

When Ṛṣyaśṛṅga's father returned, he immediately noticed his son's disturbance of mind. Intuitively understanding that that which he had feared all his life had now come to pass, he demanded that his son relate all that had happened in his absence. On hearing the description of the *muni-putras,* he strictly forbade Ṛṣyaśṛṅga to talk with or even look at those boys again, and under no circumstances to go anywhere with them.

But the damage was done. Ṛṣyaśṛṅga could no longer concentrate on his meditation, for his mind was yearning after his friends. When his father went away again the next day, the *muni-putras* had little difficulty in enticing the boy-sage to come with them. A boat waiting on the nearby river took them swiftly to the city. Before his father could arrive to protest, the king married Ṛṣyaśṛṅga to his daughter.

Some of the morals of this story are: 1) Association with women awakens and aggravates sexual desire; 2) even though one may be a *brahmacārī*, he should never consider himself beyond the fascinating power of a woman's charms; 3) mere avoidance of women is not enough to overcome sexual desire; the negative process must be supplemented by the only positive process sufficient to conquer *māyā,* namely Kṛṣṇa consciousness; 4) sexual desire is very deep-rooted and strong.

TULASĪ-DEVĪ ON DEGRADED MEN AND WOMEN

(Spoken to Śaṅkhacūḍa, recorded in the *Brahmā-vaivarta Purāṇa*. Tulasī-devī's strong assertions expose the exploitive mentality of men and women who desire to enjoy each other.)

Who are you? And why are you talking to me? If a noble man sees a virtuous woman alone, he doesn't talk to her. So go away. The *śāstras* say that only a degraded man desires a woman. At first a woman is sweet to a man but later proves fatal. Through her mouth rains honey, but her heart is like a jar of poison. She uses sweet words, but her heart is sharp like a razor. To achieve her own selfish ends, she is submissive to her husband; otherwise she is unsubmissive. While her face looks cheerful, her heart is dirty. A wise man never trusts a base woman. She has no friend or enemy, for all she wants are new lovers. When a woman sees a well dressed man, she inwardly desires him, but outwardly she appears chaste and modest. Being naturally passionate, she attracts a man's mind. A woman likes a good lover more than sweet foods or refreshing drinks, and even more than her own son. But if that lover becomes impotent or aged, she regards him as an enemy. Quarrels and anger ensue, then she devours him as a snake eats a rat. She is rashness personified and a mine of vices.

A woman is hypocritical, obstinate and unfaithful. Even Lord Brahmā and other gods are deluded by her. She is a hindrance on the path of austerity, an obstacle to liberation, an impediment to developing faith in Lord Hari, a refuge of all delusion and a living chain that binds man to this world.

She is like bucket of stool and is as false as dreams. She appears to be very beautiful, but she is a bucket of blood, urine and stool. When God created her, He arranged that she should become the spirit of delusion to the deluded and poison to those who desire liberation. Thus, on no account should a woman be desired, and by all means she should be avoided.

A man who is conquered by a woman is very impure and condemned by people in general. The forefathers and the demigods regard men who are conquered by women as low and contemptible. Even their fathers and mothers mentally despise them. The Vedas say that when a child is born or a relative dies, the *brāhmaṇas* are purified in ten days, the *kṣatriyas* in twelve days, the *vaiśyas* in fifteen days and the *śūdras* and other low classes in twenty-one days. But a man conquered by a woman always remains impure. Only when the body is burned to ashes does he becomes purified. Neither the ancestors, nor the demigods accept from him cakes, flowers or any other offerings.

Men whose hearts are totally conquered by women acquire no fruits from their knowledge, austerities, *japa*, fire sacrifices, worship, learning or fame.

THE VALUE OF SEMEN

Semen is found in a subtle state in all the cells of the body. Just as sugar is all-pervading in sugar-cane, and butter in milk, so also, semen pervades the whole body. Just as milk becomes thin after the butter is removed, so also, semen is thinned by its wastage. The more the wastage of semen, the more the body becomes weak. The *yoga-śāstras* state, *maraṇaṁ bindu pātena jīvanaṁ bindu rakṣanāt:* "falling of semen brings death; preservation of semen gives life." Semen is the real vitality and hidden treasure in man. It imparts spiritual luster *(brahma-tejas)* to the face, and strength to the intellect.

The influence of semen in the body can be understood from comparison with a tree, that draws the essence or *rasa* from the earth. This essence is circulated throughout the twigs, branches, leaves, flowers and fruits. The shining colors and life in the leaves, flowers and fruits are due to this *rasa.* Similarly, the *vīrya* (semen) that is manufactured from blood by the cells of the testes gives color and vitality to the human body and its different organs.

According to Āyurveda, semen is the last *dhātu* (substance) that is formed out of food. Out of food is manufactured chyle. Out of chyle comes blood. Out of blood comes flesh. Out of flesh comes fat. Out of fat comes bone. Out of bone comes marrow. Out of marrow comes semen. These are the seven *dhātus* that support this life and body. Semen is the last essence. It is the essence of essences.

Semen is the quintessence of food or blood. According to modern medical science, one drop of semen is manufactured out of forty drops of blood. According to Āyurveda, it is developed from eighty drops of blood. Just as bees collect honey drop by drop in the honeycomb, so also, the cells of the testes collect semen drop by drop from the blood. Then this fluid is taken by the two ducts to the *vesiculae seminalis.* When a man is sexually excited, the semen is discharged by the ejaculatory ducts into the urethra where it is mixed with the prostatic juice.

Semen nourishes the physical body, the heart and the intellect. Only that man who uses the physical body, the heart and the intellect can have perfect *brahmacarya.* A wrestler who uses his physical body only, but keeps the intellect and the heart undeveloped, cannot have full *brahmacarya.* He can have *brahmacarya* of the body only, but not of the mind and the heart. The semen that belongs to the heart and the mind will certainly flow out. If an aspirant does only *japa* and meditation, but does not develop the heart or practice physical exercise, will have only mental *brahmacarya.* The portion of the semen which goes to nourish the heart and the body will flow out. But an advanced yogi who dives deep into meditation will have full *brahmacarya* even if he does not physically exercise.

Mind, *prāṇa* (essential energy) and *vīrya* are three links of one chain. By controlling the mind, the *prāṇa* and semen can be controlled. By controlling *prāṇa,* the mind and semen can be controlled. And if the *vīrya* is controlled, and if it is made to flow upwards into the brain by pure thoughts, the mind and the *prāṇa* are automatically controlled.

The mind is set in motion or rendered active by two things: the vibration of *prāṇa* and by subtle desires. Mind and *prāṇa* are intimate companions, like a man and his shadow. If the mind and the *prāṇa* are not restrained, all the organs of sensation and action keep actively engaged in their respective functions. When a man is excited by passion, the *prāṇa* is set in motion. Then the whole body obeys the dictate of the mind, just as a soldier obeys the command of his commander. The vital air or *prāṇa* moves the internal sap or semen. The semen is put into motion. It falls downwards, just as the clouds burst into rain water, just as the fruits, flowers and leaves of the trees drop down by the force of the blowing winds.

(The above is adapted from the writings of Swami Śivananda. Although not a Vaiṣṇava, Swami Śivananda was a serious spiritual practioner of the modern age.)

MEDITATION ON THE LORD

(A devotee from South India describes what he does when some non-*brahmacarya* thought tries to creep into his consciousness.)

Whenever some unnecessary thoughts come, I meditate that I am standing in queue for having *darśana* of the Lord. There are so many devotees, pilgrims from all over India who are all lined up in great expectation of having the beautiful *darśana* of the Lord's lotus feet. Everyone around is very anxious, 'Our queue is moving slowly but steadily. Soon we will be near the Lord and can have the *darśana* of His lotus feet'.

All these devotees are so pure, they have so much attraction for the Lord. I am so fallen that even though I stand in their midst, but still I don't have this eagerness. Anyway, the Lord is so merciful that somehow or other He is going to let me have the *darśana* of His Holy Feet. I am so fortunate. Oh… How beautiful the radiant face of the Lord must be. Oh… How sweet that smile is. Oh… How beautiful those lotus eyes are. Oh… how wonderful the Lord's associates are. Oh my dear Lord, why is this queue (line) not moving fast? I want to have your *darśana*, which is most pleasing to the mind and the senses.

Thinking like this, in my mind, I open my eyes and I see those most softest of the lotus feet of the Supreme Personality of Godhead, and after worshipping them, slowly I take *darśana* of His most beautiful form and the charming smile. Then I honor *caraṇāmṛta* and thus I overcome all my disturbances and am properly situated.

MISCELLANEOUS

Once a devotee asked Śrīla Prabhupāda, "We have the perfec philosophy, Kṛṣṇa consciousness, and we have the perfect spiritua master, Your Divine Grace. Everything about Kṛṣṇa consciousnes is perfect, yet we always seem to have so many problems. Why?"

Śrīla Prabhupāda replied, "Because the *brahmacārīs* anc *sannyāsīs* associate too much with women." (Told by Girirāj Swami)

There is a story of two holy men who were walking on a road They came to a chest deep river, which had no bridge. As the were about to wade through, a woman came up and asked them t help her over. One of the monks let her climb on his shoulder forded the river, then put her down. The two *sādhus* continued o their way in silence. After an hour or two, the monk who had no carried the woman blurted out "Brother, how is it that you allowe yourself to be touched by a woman?" Surprised, his companio turned to him and replied, "I only carried her across the river, bu you have carried her all the way here in your mind."

nārī-stana-bhara-nābhī-deśaṁ
dṛṣṭvā mā gā mohā-veśam
etan māṁsa-vasādi-vikāraṁ
manasi vicintaya vāraṁ vāram

Having seen the supposed beauty of a woman's heavy breast and her thin waist, do not become agitated and illusioned, fo these attractive features are simply transformations of fat, fles and various other disgusting ingredients. You should consider thi in your mind again and again. (Śaṅkarācārya)

kāśāyan na ca bhojanādi-niyammān no vā vane vāsato
vyākhyānād athavā muni-vrata-bharāc cittodbhavaḥ kṣīyate
kintu sphīta-kalinda-śaila-tanayā-tīreṣu vikrīḍato
govindasya padāravinda-bhajanārambhasya leśād api

Not by wearing saffron cloth, not by restricting food and other sense activities, not by living in the forest, not by discussing philosophy, and not by observing a vow of silence, but only by even the slightest beginning of devotional service to the lotus feet of Lord Govinda, who enjoys pastimes on the Yamunā's wide banks, is Kāmadeva stopped. (Śrī Rūpa Gosvāmī's *Padyāvalī)*

The *brahmacārī* should completely renounce the following eight things—his lust, anger, greed, desire for sweets, sense of decorating the body, excessive curiosity (interest in mundane things), excessive sleep, and excessive endeavor for bodily maintenance. (*Nīti-śāstra* 11.10)

One single object (a woman) appears in three different ways: to the man who practices austerity it appears as a corpse, to the sensual it appears as a woman, and to the dogs as a lump of flesh. (*Nīti-śāstra* 14.15)

Women completely destroy spiritual life. (Śrīla Prabhodānanda Sarasvatī)

Quod omne animal post coitum triste est.
Every animal is sad after sex. (Aristoteles)

Love, in the form in which it exists in society, is nothing but the exchange of two fantasies and the superficial contact of two bodies.
Sebastien-Roch Nicolas de Chamfort (1741-1794)

The generative energy, which, when we are loose, dissipates and makes us unclean, when we are continent invigorates and inspires us. Chastity is the flowering of man; and what are called Genius, Heroism, Holiness, and the like, are but various fruits which succeed it.

Henry David Thoreau (1817–62), U.S. philosopher, author, naturalist. *Walden,* "Higher Laws" (1854).

If you want your heart to be always absorbed in drinking the ambrosial mellows of the lotus feet of Lord Hari, then give up household life, which is full of quarrels and strife, and just worship Lord Gaura, the moon of Godruma's forest bowers.

Material riches, youth, long duration of life, and royal happiness—none of these are eternal. At any moment they may be destroyed. Give up all useless topics of mundane conversation and just worship Lord Gaura, the moon of Godruma's forest bowers.

O friend, ultimately the pleasure to be had in the company of beautiful young women turns to fearfulness and distracts one from the real goal of life. Just worship Lord Gaura, the moon of Godruma's forest bowers, with your mind intoxicated by the nectarean mellows of the holy name. (From *Śrī Godruma-candra Bhajanopadeśa* by Śrīla Bhaktivinoda Ṭhākura)

On being firmly established in sexual continence vigor *(vīrya)* is attained. (Patañjali Yoga-sūtra 2.38)

ENDNOTES

1 *S.B.* 1.1.10
2 *Cc.* Antya 2.172
3 See *S.B.* 1.18.7
4 *Yājñavalkya-smṛti*, as quoted in *Bg.* 6.13-14
5 See *S.B.* 6.1.13 Purport
6 *S.B.* 3.22.19
7 See *S.B.* 7.12.1
8 See *S.B.* 7.12.7
9 *S.B.* 3.24.20
10 *S.B.* 6.17.8
11 *S.B.* 4.28.3
12 Cited from *Practice of Brahmacharya* by Shivananda Swami; original source unknown.
13 Lecture, 4/4/75
14 Airport Reception, 18/09/69
15 *Cc. Madhya* 13.80
16 *S.B.* 5.12.12
17 See Cc. *Ādi* Chapter 7 and *Madhya* Chapter 25
18 *Cc. Madhya* 20.108
19 See *Cc. Antya* 4.66-67
20 NOI, Text 1
21 *S.B.* 5.25.5
22 *S.B.* 5.5.4
23 *S.B.* 11.14.30
24 *Endless Love,* Ravindra Svarūpa dāsa
25 *S.B.* 3.20.23
26 *Endless Love,* Ravindra Svarūpa dāsa
27 *Bg.* 2.60
28 *S.B.* 4.25.20
29 *Bg.* 18.38
30 *S.B.* 4.28.12
31 NOI, Text 1
32 *Bg.* 17.16
33 *S.B.* 4.22.30
34 *S.B.* 2.9.23
35 *Bg.* 5.23
36 Lecture, 06/02/75
37 *S.B.* 7.12.10, text
38 See Conversation, 31/07/76
39 *S.B.* 7.15.36
40 See *S.B.* 3.24.20
41 See Lecture After Play, 06/04/75
42 *S.B.* 6.18.41
43 Lecture, 16/08/73
44 See *S.B.* 9.19.17
45 *S.B.* 7.12.8
46 Purport to the song *Parama-karuṇā*
47 See *S.B.* 1.2.6
48 *S.B.* 1.9.12
49 Lecture, 17/01/71
50 SPL Ch. 19
51 *Cc. Madhya* 24.171
52 *S.B.* 2.9.24
53 Conversation, 20/04/75
54 *S.B.* 2.9.40
55 Conversation, 10/01/74
56 *S.B.* 7.12.1
57 Lecture, 12/09/69
58 *S.B.* 5.5.1
59 NOD, Ch. 18
60 *S.B.* 6.4.46
61 *S.B.* 6.4.50
62 *S.B.* 3.12.4
63 *S.B.* 6.1.13-14
64 *S.B.* 1.2.7
65 *S.B.* 2.9.9
66 See *S.B.* 9.4.26
67 *S.B.* 1.2.8
68 Lecture, 25/11/73
69 *Path of Perfection,* Chapter 4

70 Letter, 15/02/68
71 *S.B. 5.6.4*
72 *Cc. Madhya* 17.14
73 *Vedānta-sūtra* 1.1.12
74 *Kaṭha Upaniṣad* 1.3.14
75 *S.B.* 3.25.25
76 *S.B.* 3.31.34 Text and Purport
77 *S.B.* 7.6.20-23
78 *S.B.* 4.9.11
79 Conversation, 31/07/76
80 *Cc. Antya* 2.117
81 *S.B.* 7.15.21
82 *S.B.* 10.8.4
83 Quoted by Dhanurdhara Svāmī
84 *Bg.* 12.9
85 From *ISKCON in the 70's* by Satsvarūpa dāsa Gosvāmī; Vol.1, p. 40
86 See *Bg.* 9.3
87 *Bg.* 4.42
88 *S.B.* 10.1.4
89 *Cc. Madhya* 25.278
90 *Cc. Madhya* 22.113
91 Lecture, 05/04/74
92 Letter, 05/06/74
93 Letter, 12/01/74
94 *S.B.* 7.9.46
95 *S.B.* 4.7.44
96 Conversation, 12/12/73
97 Conversation, 09/06/69
98 Conversation, 15/08/71
99 *S.B.* 7.6.5
100 Letter, 17/02/69
101 *Kṛṣṇa,* Ch. 87
102 *Teachings of Lord Caitanya,* Ch. 1
103 *Bg.* 6.16-17
104 *S.B.* 1.9.27
105 *S.B.* 6.1.13-14
106 *S.B.* 4.18.10
107 Conversation, 14/07/74
108 Conversation, 30/04/73
109 *S.B.* 8.6.12
110 Lecture, 15/01/74
111 Conversation, 14/07/74
112 Letter, 20/11/69
113 Letter, 09/01/75
114 See NOI, Text 2
115 Told by Basu Ghosh dāsa
116 *Bg.* 6.16
117 *Bg.* 6.17
118 *S.B.* 1.9.27
119 Told by Jayādvaita Svāmī
120 See *S.B.* 4.28.36
121 Told by Śatadhanya dāsa
122 Letter, 28/02/72
123 *S.B.* 12.3.33
124 *S.B.* 3.12.4
125 *S.B.* 4.28.1
126 *S.B.* 7.12, Introduction
127 *S.B.* 3.4.57
128 *S.B.* 7.11.8-12
129 Quoted by Bhūrijana dāsa
130 *Bg.* 6.20-23
131 *S.B.* 7.12.4
132 Conversation, 05/05/72
133 See NOI, Text 2
134 *S.B.* 3.21.47
135 See *S.B.* 9.14.22-3
136 Spoken to Upendra dāsa, 1976
137 *S.B.* 7.12.1
138 *S.B.* 6.1.17
139 *S.B.* 4.11.34
140 *S.B.* 7.12.1
141 *S.B.* 9.9.42
142 Conversation, 09/07/73
143 *S.B.* 7.14.8
144 *S.B.* 7.12.6
145 Told by Prabhaviṣṇu Svāmī
146 Told by Ānandamaya dāsa
147 Lecture, 01/11/72

148 *S.B.* 11.8.12
149 SPL Ch. 33
150 Letter, 01/10/69
151 *S.B.* 3.16.5
152 Told by Dānavīra Gosvāmī
153 Letter, 29/09/75
154 Letter, 03/12/72
155 Told by Jadurāṇī-devī dāsī
156 Told by Jadurāṇī-devī dāsī
157 *S.B.* 3.31.40
158 Told by Girirāja Svāmī
159 Letter, 06/10/68
160 Told by Śrutakīrti dāsa
161 *S.B.* 6.1.65
162 SPL Ch. 22
163 Letter, 29/03/68
164 *S.B.* 11.2.46
165 *S.B.* 6.1.67
166 Conversation, 29/05/77
167 *Cc. Antya* 6.220
168 *Bhakti-rasāmṛta-sindhu* 1.2.255-6
169 *Bg.* 16.21
170 See *S.B.* 6.1.56-63
171 *Bg.* 3.39-41
172 *S.B.* 7.9.45
173 Conversation, 30/08/73
174 *Caitanya-bhāgavata Madhya* 23.78
175 Conversation, 11/05/75
176 *S.B.* 5.6.3
177 *S.B.* 10.33.39
178 Lecture, 30/03/75
179 *S.B.* 11.28.40
180 *S.B.* 3.28.32
181 See *S.B.* 11.22.56
182 See *S.B.* 9.6.39-53
183 *Bg.* 2.70
184 *S.B.* 1.9.27
185 *S.B.* 9.4.18
186 *Cc. Ādi* 2.117
187 *S.B.* 6.8.17
188 *Śīkṣāṣṭakam* 5
189 Lecture, 08/04/75
190 Conversation, 14/06/74
191 *S.B.* 6.1.15
192 Conversation, 28/05/74
193 The devotee who asked was Dīna Bandhu dāsa.
194 *S.B.* 3.12.32
195 See *S.B.* 4.29.69
196 *Cc. Madhya* 25.279
197 Letter to San Francisco devotees, 30/03/67
198 Letter, 09/01/73
199 See *Bg.* 3.36
200 *Bg.* 7.14
201 Conversation, 27/06/75
202 Letter, 09/12/68
203 *S.B.* 3.20.26
204 Told by Satsvarūpa dāsa Gosvāmī
205 See *Bg.* 6.14 purport
206 1957, Health Research Labs, Mokelumne Hill, California
207 See *S.B.* Canto 6, Chapter 5
208 Told by Praghoṣa dāsa
209 Conversation, 11/08/76
210 *Mahābhārata, Ādi-parva*
211 See *S.B.* 11.17.36
212 Letter, 02/02/70
213 Lecture, 05/04/74
214 Letter, 31/12/68
215 Lecture, 03/05/73
216 See Letter, 05/06/74
217 See *S.B.* 3.14.20
218 *S.B.* Canto 5, Chapters 13 and 14
219 Letter, 08/11/68

Collected Lectures on Brahmacarya by Bhakti Vikāsa Swami

(The DVD with lectures is included inside the back cover)

No.	Title	Duration	CODE
	ENGLISH		
	Attitudes of a Brahmacārī		
01	SB 1.11.24, Proper Relationships with Women, 06-06-1996 (Ireland)	23:12	417
02	SB 2.2.5, Dependence on Kṛṣṇa, 21-05-2006, Udupi, Karnataka (India)	59:05	575
03	BG 5.1, Spiritual Life doesn't Mean to Do Nothing, 02-09-2004, Los Angeles (USA)	36:01	649
04	SB 1.4.10, Parīkṣit Mahārāja's Model Renunciation, 05-08-2008, Rijeka (Croatia)	34:43	811
05	SB 3.26.31, Prestige Means Sex Life, 01-01-2006, Hyderabad (India)	01:03:42	836
06	BG 6.10, Don't be a Miser or an Irresponsible Prince, 13-11-2008, Vellore, Tamil Nadu (India)	26:27	897
07	BG 18.41–46, Hanumān's Fame is for Fighting not Bhajana, 19-01-2004, Salem (India)	44:25	1115
08	SB 5.1.11, Institutional and Individual Needs, 04-09-2008, Toronto (Canada)	36:25	1139
09	Iṣṭagoṣṭhī, Purifying an Atmosphere of Faultfinding, 29-11-2007, Salem (India)	33:15	1140
10	Living Without Electricity, 26-11-2007, Salem (India)	52:08	1168
11	Sacrifice in Brahmacārī Life, 21-08-2008, London (UK)	26:50	1218
12	SB 5.18.4, The Power of Māyā is Magnificent, Let's be More Precautious, Salem (India)	01:11:31	2097

13	Two Foundation Stones of Brahmacārī Life, Kaunas (Lithuania)	34:08	2228
14	BG 2.58, Two Excuses For Avoiding Rules, 19-05-2011 (Kanhaiyadesh)	51:26	8005
15	The Necessity of Discipline, 12-06-2011, San Diego (USA)	44:58	8023
16	SB 4.10.1, Rare Renunciation, 15-08-2011, Ljubljana (Slovenia)	38:26	8074
17	Cc 2.23.18 , Detachment and Absence of False Prestige, 13-01-2011, Dwarka, Gujarat (India)	51:57	8219
18	The Brahmacārī Principle of Selflessness, 26-02-2011, Valsad, Gujarat (India)	01:02:13	8263
19	Eternal Idealism, 01-02-2012, Valsad, Gujarat (India)	35:23	10103
20	SB 2.3.17, Don't Waste Time, 29-12-2012, Vellore, Tamil Nadu (India)	01:03:44	10282
21	BG 2.47, Enjoyment, Renunciation, Service, 05-01-2013, Singapore (Singapore)	55:38	10286
22	BG 3.27, The Myth of Freedom, 06-01-2013, Singapore (Singapore)	01:24:19	10287
23	SB 3.13.10, Strained Guru-disciple Relationships, 26-10-2013, Bhopal (India)	01:10:16	10679
24	BG 6.10, Yukta-vairāgya is not an Excuse, 01-02-2014, Rajapur, West Bengal (India)	01:03:04	10793
25	Perspectives on Renunciation, 02-02-2014, Rajapur, West Bengal (India)	29:32	10796
26	Why Bābājīs are Important, 02-03-2014, Secunderabad, Andhra Pradesh (India)	01:14:56	10829
27	BG 1.43, Why Authorities are Needed and Distrusted, 09-05-2014 (Kanhaiyadesh)	01:23:30	10857
28	To be a Sincere Follower of Śrīla Prabhupāda, Part 1, 29-04-2014, Rishikesh (India)	50:38	10875a
29	To be a Sincere Follower of Śrīla Prabhupāda, Part 2, 29-04-2014, Rishikesh (India)	01:10:15	10875b
30	To be a Sincere Follower of Śrīla Prabhupāda, Part 3, 30-04-2014, Rishikesh (India)	01:05:08	10875c

31	Cc 1.1.35, Guru Qualifications and Disciple Duties, Part 1, 17-08-2014, Govindadvipa (Ireland)	01:06:35	10956a
32	Cc 1.1.35, Guru Qualifications and Disciple Duties, Part 2, 17-08-2014, Govindadvipa (Ireland)	47:27	10956b
33	BG 9.3, Not Falling Down and Not Going Up, 01-09-2014, Munich (Germany)	01:12:38	10974
34	BG 6.17, Smartphones for Brahmacārīs, 05-10-2014, Gauragrama, Telangana (India)	51:15	11008
35	Eternal Idealism, 01-02-2012, Valsad, Gujarat (India)	35:15	20040
36	Gaura-kiśora Bābājī Mahārāja's Vairāgya, 06-11-2011, Bhimavaram, Andhra Pradesh (India)	15:59	20043
Dedicating One's Life to Kṛṣṇa			
01	SB 3.24.41, Prabhupāda Insists, Leave Home, 27-04-2006, Mumbai (India)	01:01:45	133
02	Youth, A Golden Opportunity, 16-02-2005, Belgaum, Karnataka (India)	01:07:15	137
03	SB 3.26.19, School Means Contamination, Manipulation, not Education, 20-07-2006, Mumbai (India)	52:12	236
04	Prospects and Perks of a Career in Kṛṣṇa Consciousness, 15-09-2005, Chicago (USA)	01:09:53	297
05	BG 4.11, Difficulties of Preaching, 09-12-2007, Salem (India)	30:06	624
06	SB 3.30.14, Material Life is a Disastrous Waste of Time, 17-09-2004, Los Angeles (USA)	41:01	762
07	Youth is the Time for Life Decisions, 25-04-2008 (Damodaradesh)	57:10	1240
08	Come and Join Full-time, 22-07-2007, Delhi (India)	55:49	1776
09	Urinal-smelling Civilization—A Talk to Brahmacārīs, 20-10-2008, Chowpatty, Mumbai (India)	45:01	2037
10	Utopia—Perfectly Possible, 23-05-2009, Bangalore (India)	01:04:04	5004

11	The Vision of Eternity, 30-05-2011, Bhaktivedanta Manor, London (UK)	42:36	8010
12	The Most Important Project, 22-09-2013, Almviks Gard (Sweden)	51:55	10641
13	ASK BVKS, Leaving Home in Pursuit of Self-realization, 09-01-2014, Salem (India)	48:49	10832
14	IT Donkeys, 12-10-2014, Miyapur, Hyderabad (India)	01:11:43	11018
15	SB 1.2.20, Be Enlivened, Be a Brahmacārī, 13-11-2014, Vellore, Tamil Nadu (India)	56:37	11059
16	SB 1.3.44, Brahmacarya and Strictness Required to Go Back to Godhead, 18-08-2012, Silicon Valley, California (USA)	01:10:15	20090
	Mind Control and Difficult Times		
01	Remaining Steady in Kṛṣṇa Consciousness (Russia)	35:54	19
02	The Power of Habits, 12-02-2005, Bangalore (India)	59:45	241
03	SB 1.2.20, Knowledge and Intelligence Help to Overcome Lust, 24-08-1999	41:14	302
04	BG 14.7, Māyā Doesn't Take a Holiday, 29-08-2001, Ljubljana (Slovenia)	53:43	552
05	BG 4.42, We Are Our Own Worst Enemy, 18-05-2005, Vellore, Tamil Nadu (India)	51:00	825
06	How to Make Advancement in Kṛṣṇa Consciousness, Part 1, 06-03-1998, Mayapur (India)	01:03:46	1254a
07	How to Make Advancement in Kṛṣṇa Consciousness, Part 2, 07-03-1998, Mayapur (India)	01:10:04	1254b
08	How to Make Advancement in Kṛṣṇa Consciousness, Part 3, 08-03-1998, Mayapur (India)	01:06:33	1254c
09	How to Make Advancement in Kṛṣṇa Consciousness, Part 4, 09-03-1998, Mayapur (India)	56:31	1254d
10	How to Make Advancement in Kṛṣṇa Consciousness, Part 5, 10-03-1998, Mayapur (India)	01:08:46	1254e

11	How to Make Advancement in Kṛṣṇa Consciousness, Part 6, 11-03-1998, Mayapur (India)	11:30	1254f
12	BG 2.54, Positive and Negative Methods of Sense Control, 09-04-1999, Salem (India)	31:15	1528
13	BG 14.26, Remaining Fixed Amidst Struggle, 28-06-2007, Portland (USA)	01:06:53	1610
14	BG 5.22, Rained-out Talks on Sense Control, 12-08-2006, Lika (Croatia)	16:38	1924f
15	SB 1.4.10, Don't be a Stool Pakora, Rijeka (Croatia)	34:23	2096
16	SB 9.6.41–42, The Downfall of Saubhari Muni, 20-06-1998, Baroda, Gujarat (India)	45:18	2109
17	SB 6.1.61, Overcoming or Overcome by Lust, 20-04-2007, Chennai (India)	48:18	2200
18	BG 7.14, How Māyā Mixes with Bhakti, 10-10-2010, Chennai (India)	53:55	7320
19	SB 11.21.19, Sensual Gratification Causes Misery, 12-06-2011, San Diego (USA)	58:06	8027
20	BG 7.14, Unreal Material Reality, 09-01-2011, Bangalore (India)	01:09:34	8217
21	Brahmacārīs Who Need to Marry, 21-03-2012, Salem (India)	54:05	10150
22	BG 3.35, Knowing What One is Fit For, 25-03-2013, Vellore, Tamil Nadu (India)	01:28:10	10443
23	ASK BVKS, Too Much of an Abnormality, 30-04-2013, Karumandurai, Tamil Nadu (India)	01:37	10494
24	SB 1.12.27, The Easy Difficult Path, 20-11-2013, Gauragrama, Telangana (India)	44:14	10695
25	BG 3.6, Dirty Things in the Mind, 05-08-2014, Lika (Croatia)	50:11	10944
26	SB 1.1.1, Why We Remain Attached to Māyā, 28-08-2012, San Diego (USA)	58:57	20084
27	SB 1.2.17, Warnings Regarding Women and Wealth, 27-09-2012, Charlotte (USA)	01:30:19	20197
28	BS 5.44, Talking About Māyā, Durgā-pūjā, Part 1, 01-10-2014, Gauragrama, Telangana (India)	31:02	11004

29	SB 2.5.13, Talking About Māyā, Durgā-pūjā, Part 2, 02-10-2014, Gauragrama, Telangana (India)	40:58	11005
30	SB 10.2.11–12, Talking About Māyā, Durgā-pūjā, Part 3, 03-10-2014, Gauragrama, Telangana	59:59	11006
	Sādhana-bhakti		
01	SB 3.4.11, How to Become a Pure Devotee, 21-04-2003, Salem (India)	43:55	814
02	BG 6.37, Falling Down and Getting Up, 23-09-2009, Baroda, Gujarat (India)	53:38	826
03	BG 6.16, Intelligent Balance in Bhakti, 11-06-2008, Vellore, Tamil Nadu (India)	41:12	909
04	Constantly Associating with Guru, 10-12-2011, Secunderabad (India)	48:56	10080
05	BG 18.38, Rajo-guṇa Impedes Bhakti, 11-03-2013, Vellore, Tamil Nadu (India)	01:03:07	10417
06	SB 5.8.8, Advanced Devotees also Follow Strictly, 12-01-2014, Salem (India)	01:19:05	10766
07	SB 5.8.11–12, Don't Neglect Rules and Regulations, 16-01-2014, Salem (India)	58:10	10780
08	ASK BVKS, Standard of Environment and Way of Chanting Japa for Temple Residents, 20-04-2014, Rishikesh (India)	04:34	10894
09	SB 1.2.6, Sevā and Siddhānta, 28-05-2014, Dallas (USA)	46:55	10909
10	BG 14.26, Going Beyond the Modes, 25-11-2014, Salem (India)	01:05:44	11072
	Sex Life		
01	Brahmacārīs Should Always Think of Women, 20-06-2006, Vellore, Tamil Nadu (India)	27:07	219
02	SB 1.16.10, Sex—Solution of All Problems or Cause of All Problems?	55:49	232
03	SB 1.4.25, Spiritual Family Planning, 29-03-2002 (Damodaradesh)	01:39:45	504a

04	SB 4.3.9, Lesbianism is Very Good, 07-06-2008, Salem (India)	01:10:49	1100
05	SB 4.8.1, On Not Discharging Semen, 24-04-2008, Mumbai (India)	54:46	1114a
06	Celibacy For All, 09-08-2008, Lika (Croatia)	52:22	1203e
07	Sex Life is Suffering, 21-11-1995, Baroda, Gujarat (India)	36:09	1844
08	Love is a Hoax, 23-11-2004, Hyderabad (India)	10:09	1869
09	Sex Beyond Pleasure	38:25	2010
10	SB 7.5.5, Black Hole Disaster, 10-05-2000 (Avataridesh)	01:14:17	2102
11	SB 3.9.6, Sex Life is Miserable, 26-08-1998, Belgrade (Serbia)	01:11:06	2347
12	Basic Points about Illicit Sex and Deity Worship, 26-07-2010, Kazan (Russia)	01:03:38	7103
13	Cc 2.22.87, Giving up Female Association, 07-06-2011, Dallas (USA)	01:22:35	8014
14	Love Kṛṣṇa or the Vagina, 27-09-2011, Valsad, Gujarat (India)	42:13	8101
15	SB 5.2.22, Sexual Attraction Blocks Kṛṣṇa's Attraction, 27-01-2012, Mumbai (India)	47:14	10124
16	BG 7.11, Sex and God, 17-01-2013, Chennai (India)	33:20	10288
17	Viṣṇu-sahasranāma 295, Kāmahā, 20-12-2013, Vellore, Tamil Nadu (India)	41:39	10746
18	Viṣṇu-sahasranāma 295–296, Kāmahā, Kāmakṛt, 22-12-2013, Vellore, Tamil Nadu (India)	49:42	10750
19	Viṣṇu-sahasranāma 298–300, Kāma, Kāma-prada, Prabhu, 26-12-2013, Vellore, Tamil Nadu (India)	40:48	10755
20	The Fourth Regulative Principle, 28-04-2012, Salem (India)	01:04:36	10911

21	SB 6.8.17, Saintly Discussion of Sex, 20-06-2014, Mumbai (India)	57:47	10930
Talks on Brahmacarya			
01	Talk on Brahmacarya, 19-10-2005, Mayapur (India)	18:00	68
02	Issues Facing Brahmacārīs Today, Part 1, 03-07-2009, Bhaktivedanta Manor, London (UK)	01:20:03	694a
03	Issues Facing Brahmacārīs Today, Part 2, 03-07-2009, Bhaktivedanta Manor, London (UK)	01:34:23	694b
04	BG 4.26, Gṛhastha-āśrama to be Trained from Brahamacārī-āśrama, 19-06-2005, Vellore, Tamil Nadu (India)	43:24	773
05	SB 6.16.9, Talking About Māyā, 22-11-2000	43:52	796
06	BG 7.3, Advice to New Brahmacārīs, 19-06-2006, Vellore, Tamil Nadu (India)	23:13	954
07	BG 7.30, Practical Points on How to Serve Kṛṣṇa, 20-01-2008, Vellore, Tamil Nadu (India)	01:02:56	968
08	Qualities Required For Brahmacārīs, 19-06-2008, Pune (India)	01:22:07	1194
09	A Talk To Brahmacārīs, 04-08-2008, Ljubljana (Slovenia)	23:06	1225
10	Questions and Answers with Temple Brahmacārīs, 09-04-2007, Pune (India)	59:18	1759
11	Issues Facing Brahmacārīs Today, 01-05-2007, Simhacalam (Germany)	01:44:15	1852
12	Negative and Positive Reasons to Remain Brahmacārī, 15-07-2006, Pune (India)	01:00:01	1883
13	A Talk to Aspiring Brahmacārīs, 31-05-2009, Belgaum, Karnataka (India)	29:09	5024
14	Brahmacārī Seminar, Day 2, 27-09-2008, San Diego (USA)	01:09:52	5048b
15	Brahmacārī Seminar, Day 3, 28-09-2008, San Diego (USA)	01:12:55	5048c

16	Rāsa-līlā, 08-10-2005	01:26:19	7090
17	Happy Brahmacārī Life, 09-07-2010, Mahuva, Gujarat (India)	42:47	7166
18	Advice to Brahmacārīs, 04-09-2010, Zurich (Switzerland)	34:47	7228
19	Ideal Brahmacārīs, 28-09-2011, Valsad, Gujarat (India)	01:06:52	8099
20	SB 4.28.13, Detachment in Indian Culture, 25-01-2011, Juhu, Mumbai (India)	56:37	8231
21	A Brahmacārī Training Centre, 08-11-2011, Bhimavaram, Andhra Pradesh (India)	17:02	10000
22	Viṣṇu-sahasranāma 190–192, Govidāṁ Pati, Marīci, Damana, 28-02-2013, Gauragrama, Telangana (India)	28:29	10428
23	Preparing for Sannyāsa, 29-10-2013, Bhopal (India)	01:11:43	10660
24	The Principle of Paramparā, 18-07-2014, Dobromysh, Tatarstan (Russia)	54:32	10934
25	BG 9.24, Don't Be Foolish, Part 1, 13-12-2014, Bangalore (India)	43:41	11099a
26	BG 9.24, Don't Be Foolish, Part 2, 14-12-2014, Bangalore (India)	39:18	11099b
27	BG 9.24, Don't Be Foolish, Part 3, 21-12-2014, Salem (India)	35:59	11099c
28	BG 9.24, Don't Be Foolish, Part 4, 28-12-2014, Salem (India)	35:50	11099d
29	Throw Away Your Stones, 09-11-2014, Chennai (India)	31:40	11055
	BENGALI		
01	ব্রহ্মচারির অপরিচ্ছন্নতা, 11-03-2011	35:27	8271
02	অর্ধ ব্রহ্মচর্য চলবে না, 29-01-2014, মায়াপুর, পাশ্চিম বঙ্গ (ভারত)	15:14	10799

HINDI

क्रम	शीर्षक	अवधि	कोड
01	श्री.भा. 2.7.32, 'एकनिष्ठ शरणागति' का मतलब, 02-04-2006, मंगलौर, कर्नाटक (भारत)	44:07	372
02	श्री.भा. 1.13.51, 'आश्रम' शब्द का अर्थ, 12-07-2003, नई दिल्ली (भारत)	47:17	574
03	सेवा और साधना, 25-06-2008, बड़ौदा, गुजरात (भारत)	46:57	614
04	भ.गी. 2.62, पतन कैसे होता है?, 19-02-2006, वल्लभ विद्यानगर, गुजरात (भारत)	50:51	715a
05	भ.गी. 6.1, क्या भक्ति कर्तव्यों से पलायन है?, 15-04-2003, हैदराबाद, तेलंगाना (भारत)	41:49	774
06	श्री.भा. 1.19.17, भक्ति में नियमों का पालन क्यों?, 03-02-2005, मंगलौर, कर्नाटक (भारत)	37:34	916
07	ब्रह्मचारी बन जाओ, 03-05-2009, नई दिल्ली (भारत)	01:27:40	5014
08	ब्रह्मचारियों का शत्रु, 31-05-2009, बेलगाम, कर्नाटक (भारत)	54:46	5027
09	भ.गी. 3.39, सब के चरम शत्रु, 12-02-2011, वल्लभ विद्यानगर, गुजरात (भारत)	51:47	8244
10	भ.गी. 3.40, इससे बड़ा पागलपन और क्या है?, 13-02-2011, वल्लभ विद्यानगर, गुजरात (भारत)	44:04	8247
11	प्रबल इन्द्रियों का दमन, 14-02-2011, वल्लभ विद्यानगर, गुजरात (भारत)	29:20	8249
12	नित्य अनित्य का स्मरण करना, 05-02-2012, अंकलेश्वर, गुजरात (भारत)	46:03	10130
13	BG 6.30, भौतिक रसों की तुच्छता, 29-02-2012, बड़ौदा, गुजरात (भारत)	35:54	10158
14	श्री.भा. 6.12.27–35, शत्रुओं पर विजयी होना, 20-02-2013, वल्लभ विद्यानगर, गुजरात (भारत)	35:33	10395
15	एक गृहस्थ के तैंतीस बच्चें, 12-05-2013, नासिक, महाराष्ट्र (भारत)	35:58	10469

Download or share these lectures using the CODE from the last column of the above list. E.g. www.bvks.com/10469

Printed in Great Britain
by Amazon

34858772R00155